TACKLING STRATEGI

TACKLING STRATEGIC PROBLEMS

The Role of
Group Decision Support

edited by

Colin Eden and Jim Radford

SAGE Publications
London · Newbury Park · New Delhi

First published 1990

SAGE Publications Ltd
28 Banner Street
London EC1Y 8QE

SAGE Publications Inc
2111 West Hillcrest Drive
Newbury Park, California 91320

SAGE Publications India Pvt Ltd
32, M-Block Market
Greater Kailash – I
New Delhi 110 048

British Library Cataloguing in Publication data
Eden, Colin
 Tackling strategic problems : the role of group decision support.
 1. Organisations. Management. Decision making. Support systems.
 I. Title   II. Radford, Jim
 658.403028

ISBN 0 – 8039 – 8259 – 3
ISBN 0 – 8039 – 8260 – 7 pbk

Library of Congress catalog card number 90 – 060585

Filmset by Mayhew Typesetting, Bristol, England
Printed in Great Britain by Dotesios Printers Ltd, Trowbridge, Wiltshire

Contents

Introduction

COLIN EDEN and JIM RADFORD

This book is about decision-making and problem-solving in groups. It discusses current developments in group decision support consultancy, where group decision support is defined broadly. In particular these developments are based, for the most part, on experience of working with teams on what they regard as strategic issues. The methods attempt to address themselves to issues that are complex because the possible actions imply worrying ramifications, they represent dilemmas where there is unlikely to be any portfolio of actions that will be correct. To make matters worse, the agreed actions are likely to be seen as practically irreversible and often involve a shift in culture. The issues which these methods address are of strategic significance because they have wide organizational and inter-organizational ramifications. More importantly they generally involve the non-routine development of commitment and ownership of key members of the organization, because the issue itself is non-routine and members of the decision-making group will have many complex views about the nature of the issue.

In recent years it has become accepted wisdom that strategic issues cannot be dealt with by some form of routine strategic analysis, but rather that they involve the design of a strategic thinking *process* (Foster, 1989; Porter, 1987; Bryson, 1988). Group decision support methods that deliberately pay attention to the complex process issues as well as the analysis of complex content are beginning to demonstrate success in this area. The problems of strategic solutions having any real impact on organizational decision-making has been acknowledged for many years (Ansoff, 1965; Denning, 1984). Group decision support systems are likely to be one way of addressing these problems simply because they seek to design non-prescriptive solutions that involve a consideration of the process by which decisions are reached by those who have the power to act and many of the methods discussed in this book address ways of analyzing the dynamics of the interactions generated by strategic action.

The terms *group decision support system* and *decision support* will be used extensively in this book. They are used in a common-or-garden coupling of ordinary words and are not taken to have any profound jargonistic implications, although it is important to recognize that there has been a burgeoning interest in group decision support systems (GDSS) in the 1980s. These systems have been developed mostly in the US and often represent the interests of computer scientists in providing computer-based support to groups. Indeed many of the developments have been sponsored by the computer industry. These systems involve participants in direct keyboard entry into structured problem-solving techniques, brainstorming, or word processing systems. The benefits of the systems to executive teams is a matter for debate (Ackermann and Eden, 1989) and their orientation is often to computer supported cooperative work (known as CSCW). They are not discussed in this book, which has been written by organizational and management scientists rather than computer scientists or information scientists.

Most of the authors are writing about their experiences as practitioners of particular methods for providing support to senior executive teams. Eden, Friend, Hickling, Mayon-White, and Radford have developed ways of working that are based on work with teams over the past ten to fifteen years. Their work has been within a wide range of organizations including extended work with government on issues relating to environmental policy, the development of coherent strategy for the provision of a prison service and within health service units; and work in the private sector including strategy development in publishing, oil, computers, confectionery, finance, and brewing for large national and multinational organizations.

Friend and Hickling practise their method as full-time consultants whereas others act as consultants from within an academic setting. Some of the methods have been written about in detail elsewhere and this book will not repeat the content of these publications (see Friend and Hickling, 1987; Rosenhead, 1989; Radford, 1990; and Bryant, 1989). The contents of this book are designed to go beyond the methods themselves and explore:

1 aspects of the nature of group processes both within and between organizations;
2 the reality of providing decision support to these groups by considering the interaction between method and consultant style;
3 developments that are leading to the thoughtful combination of some of these methods, including the addition of computer support to supplement methods;

and

4 some of the practical 'trivialities' of making a group decision support *system* and consultancy successful, including attention to the physical environment of decision-making teams.

Whilst the book is made up from chapters written by different authors, the content is taken from discussion at a focused workshop at which the authors built the content of the book as a linked story. Most of the authors have worked together on projects over a number of years and are able to share their experiences so that synergy is a practical outcome of such workshops.

The common feature of the approaches discussed in this book is a belief that models of complex situations that are amenable to analysis and elaboration can provide a basis for negotiation about action. At the same time, though, there is a belief that such models cannot contribute to the effectiveness of group decision-making without the modelling approach being embedded within the style and *personality of the consultant* and without designing *processes* that support work with models. The contents of the book represent the potential for bringing together the skills of the 'pure' facilitator with the skills of the 'backroom' model builder analyst. The book represents an arena of development appropriate to those working in the field of public sector and business strategy development, as well as those intending to help groups work on complex strategic issues.

Throughout the book, extensive reference is made to a number of well established methods that have been developed by the contributors. In particular SODA (strategic options development and analysis), strategic choice, metagame and hypergame analysis, and decision conferencing are taken as established methods. A recent textbook entitled *Rational Analysis for a Problematic World* (Rosenhead, 1989) presents a description of, and case study to illustrate, most of these methods. It is not necessary for readers of this book to have an understanding of these methods. Nevertheless, for completeness, a brief overview of the methods is contained in the appendix.

The Structure of the Book

The book is laid out in five sections, each section building from the previous sections. Readers will find that it is not essential to read the book in its entirety, or to read some chapters before others; it is possible to dip into sections or chapters. Nevertheless the book is designed to 'tell a story', that should make sense as a whole. Each section is introduced by a linking 'commentary' intended both to summarize the key elements that might be kept in mind as the reader reads that section, and to relate these to the other parts of the book.

The first section is concerned with setting a context to the provision of group decision support. The first two chapters by John Churchill and John Friend explore the organizational context for decision-making. Churchill writes his chapter after several years of observation of senior management team meetings that have not been facilitated by a group decision support consultant but more typically have been overseen by the chairman of the board. Our purpose in this chapter is to consider the 'natural' processes of decision-making within which a group decision support system might sit. Friend extends this context by considering how this setting changes when the decision-making group involves members from several organizations or agencies. Friend has spent much of his life working within this context and pulls together a number of significant issues that the consultant must face.

The next three chapters by Steve Cropper, Colin Eden, and John Rohrbaugh consider a decision support consultant in relation to method. Cropper has conducted research on the relationship between the style and personality of consultants and the way in which they use decision support methods. Chapter 3 explores what Cropper identifies as 'approaches to' in contrast to 'approaches in' decision support. The chapter introduces some of the different elements of the role of the consultant within a contingency framework for understanding this role. Each of these chapters exemplifies the significance of the *process* of both decision-making and decision support consultancy.

In the light of these contextual aspects of decision-making groups and consultancy Colin Eden and John Rohrbaugh use the next chapters of this section to explore a framework for evaluating the dimensions and inclinations of consultants and their method. In the final chapter, Eden attempts to tie together the two aspects of support – the management of process and the management of content – as necessarily intertwined aspects of successful decision support consultancy, and to suggest a broad definition of a *group decision support system*. Thus this first section sets the scene for the rest of the book but also stands alone as a statement about a context and role for group decision support.

The second section introduces, as background, one of the perspectives that arise in a number of the following chapters. A basis of much decision-making and strategy development lies in the ability of a group to understand the interactions between competing organizations, groups, or individuals. Game theory, metagame theory and hypergame theory have been attempts to prescribe the nature of these interactions and analyze them. The first chapter in the second section, by Ted Mitchell and others, sets out the practical elements of doing this. They have used specially developed computer software designed to be used in the practical decision-making world, and have studied the impact of this on the groups they have worked with. Most of the problems they identify from these 'real-world' experiments relate to the systemic solutions offered by the notion of a group decision support system. Thus, while it is not the purpose of this book to focus on game-theoretic based decision support, the research is alone in identifying relevant problems from an empirical study. The second chapter of the section introduces a 'base line' extension of game-like considerations into the business of providing a successful methodology for group decision support. Jim Radford discusses a perspective and method that has been applied in a wide variety of settings with senior management teams as the client. He turns away from an overly formal analysis for deciding how to act with respect to competitors and introduces a more contingent and flexible approach which will be reflected in the other approaches developed later in the book.

The final chapter of Part II, by Bill Mayon-White, broadens the concerns of methods to include issues of process. Thus Part II introduces three different characteristics of the methods that might appropriately serve the needs of a decision-making group. These are introduced through the elaboration of practitioners working in very different ways. Mitchell et al. are disposed to uncover the shortcomings of straight-forward analytical approaches, and so corroborate the observations encompassed in Part I. Radford begins to demonstrate how the pure analytic approach which addresses content without attention to process can be developed conceptually and practically. He shows that the content should not be taken for granted but derived through the design of group processes. Mayon-White shifts our attention further towards process by taking a view of decision support consultancy which is driven from the perspective of behavioural science. This then is the setting for exploring advances in decision support methods through the combination of approaches.

Part III concentrates on developments in mixed approaches. The authors describe and discuss developments that seek to combine the perspectives offered by considering a number of interacting actors, by examining more carefully and explicitly the network of actors, and by enabling choice to be influenced by considerations of overall strategy with respect to, for example, competitors. At the beginning of this part, Steve Cropper develops a critical analysis of these attempts to combine methods. He suggests a number of ways in which the approaches both address and ignore the elements identified in earlier parts, and yet at the same time suggests that they offer a way forward. Peter Bennett explores the links between cognitive mapping as a method of problem or strategy formulation, and 'hypergame' considerations for evaluating interactions between players within the strategic setting. As the 'inventor' of the hypergame formulation Bennett has considerable experience of analyzing conflict (both actual and potential) at the individual, intergroup, company, and international level. In this chapter he reflects on experience of enhancing these analyses through the process of qualitative modelling.

Part IV concentrates on exploring two methods that utilize computers to help provide decision support to groups. These approaches lie closer to the US view of group decision support, but differ because of their devotion to the provision of a professional facilitator rather than the process being computer driven. The first chapter, by Fran Ackermann, discusses the method known as SODA (strategic options development and analysis) where the computer is used in 'real-time' to capture and analyze discussion during a decision support workshop. The second chapter, by Larry Phillips, discusses an approach originally developed in the US which provides 'decision analysis' support to groups involved in strategic tasks such as resource allocation. The computer provides the analysis of the utility of a set of possible options and displays the results graphically. These methods have been used extensively in both the public and the private sector and represent methods that are under continual development.

Part V addresses what is probably the most important element in the success of group decision support, that of designing and creating an effective environment within which a group can work. The authors – Colin Eden and Allen Hickling – have devoted themselves to a practical study of these issues through their experience in the use of SODA and strategic choice respectively. The issues they raise are often seen as 'trivial' and yet professionals in the field are always engaged by the commentary offered on this subject. In the third chapter in this part Chris Huxham offers some explanation and comments about the importance and apparent triviality of the issues raised by Colin Eden and Allen Hickling.

An important chapter from Rolfe Tomlinson considers the general issues raised in the book. In particular he addresses the distinction we need to draw between theory, methods, techniques, and tools. In doing so he addresses the future directions for this type of decision support practice.

PART I
GROUPS AND ORGANIZATIONS: A CONTEXT FOR GROUP DECISION SUPPORT

Introduction

COLIN EDEN

Part I of this book sets out to explore the organizational setting for the application of group decision support. Later in the book attention will be focused on support systems themselves.

In chapter 1 John Churchill provides a broad commentary on the nature of group decision-making and seeks to identify a number of characteristics of groups that are likely to be significant in designing facilitated group decision support. He reminds us that real groups are often simply confused about the situation they face and that they don't necessarily want support to resolve the situation but rather to give clarity and focus to the issues they face. Thus a group can use its own internal resources at many points during the resolution of difficult situations but might seek support at the times when its own resources seem to fail. This suggests that a support system needs to be flexible, contingent, and very sensitive to the specific nature of the group and to the needs of the group at the time of the intervention. This is a point accepted by Friend (in chapter 2) when he acknowledges that 'experienced facilitators adapt their approach in various ways to deal more realistically with the organizational complexities they encounter in their work'. He identifies the need for an *organizing framework* rather than a tight method, where the facilitator responds as flexibly to group judgement as to direction.

Churchill emphasizes the nature of groups as 'interactions between different players, each with competing values, views, and objectives'. As we shall see later, a number of the support systems discussed in this book reflect this characteristic by considering the potential for negotiation between different players. However, Churchill is particularly interested in noting that the client group is itself made up of players with different interests. Rosenhead (1989) refers to the difference between some problem-structuring techniques that are designed to facilitate negotiation within a group and others that tend to focus on the group with respect to other players outside the organization. Similarly in this book, the support systems based on game theory tend to focus on an analysis of 'external' conflict and less on resolving internal conflict whereas others, such as SODA and decision conferencing, aim at helping negotiation within the group itself.

Churchill also argues that 'how the group reached decisions rather than their ability to reach the right decision' is a significant factor in the performance of a group. The group decision support systems discussed in this book will need to be evaluated with respect to this need, rather than focusing solely on their analytical prowess. His extensive research with senior management groups has highlighted this aspect, although it follows other research of a similar nature.

Alongside these points about negotiation, procedure, and the significance of the social interactions he indicates the importance of the nature of the 'decision forum or context' within which groups work. As well as the impact of 'style and culture within the organization' this also implies attention to the design of the forum itself in terms of elements such as the physical setting, a theme which is developed later in this book.

Churchill's assertion that 'as issues became clearer and more information was available' an 'unbundling or liberating of facts from personal values and personal perceptions' occurred, is an interesting observation of group progress, and one that might be used as an important goal for a group decision support system. It is an important practical aim for GDSSs, for it implies that the role of a GDSS might be to facilitate this process and thereby encourage personal commitment from group rather than personal problem ownership. This focus on process is a part of the reasoning behind Eden's wish (in chapter 5) to promote a '$P \times C$' model of a GDSS intervention.

This first part is also designed to signal other important elements in the context of providing group decision support. Friend provides an inter-organizational dimension and suggests that there are important distinctions to be made between working for a group where the members are from the same organization compared to the oft-occurring setting for public sector work where the group members are representatives of several organizations. To some extent these are two common extremes of a spectrum where the middle might be a group consisting of members of the same organization but each with strong loyalties and commitments to departments (indeed not unlike university work groups). The continuing emphasis within industry are profit centres encouraging some of the same tensions within corporate teams.

The theme that runs throughout Friend's chapter is that of the consultant managing organizational complexity. Indeed Friend introduces the need for consultants to develop a repertoire of 'approaches to' (and implicitly 'approaches in') complex organizational situations. But the thrust of his concerns is considering ways of tackling the complexities that derive from a group existing in a wider environment, for example complexities such as 'conflict between two or more policy guidelines emanating from different sources'. As is the case with most GDSSs, his aim is to gain a high level of commitment from group members. The notion of a commitment package which is introduced in strategic choice is not to be treated simplistically: he is careful to see this as a part of the need for 'milestones' in the process of deciding and yet not see it as something that closes off options without consideration of robustness (Rosenhead, 1989). It is an attention to incrementalism that is important in this idea. The organization change literature often argues for a recognition of incrementalism but this has rarely been discussed in relation to the *process* of making decisions in groups. (Radford discusses this issue in the second part of the book, in chapter 7.) It is an important distinction between the belief that a decision is a single agreement to the more realistic view of decision-*making* as *progress*. For Friend this is identified through the use of a more low key term such as 'progress package' rather than 'commitment package'.

Another significant distinction upon which Friend and Hickling (1987) have laid great emphasis is the difference between 'invisible' and 'visible' products from providing support to a group. The attention to process that is the major theme throughout the first part clearly implies that the outcome of a GDSS is likely to be invisible. Inevitably clients, as well as facilitators, are going to find these products more difficult to identify and reward. The *invisible products become those elements of professional support that are necessary but not sufficient conditions for the overall product*.

Friend amplifies some of the descriptive elements introduced by Churchill, by considering the politics of the relationship of the group to those outside it. His discussion of the difficulties of getting a group to be explicit within the group setting about such matters has particular relevance to game-theoretic perspectives where actors and their preferences have to be discussed. Bryant, later in the book (chapter 11) discusses a method of mapping these complexities of actor interaction. Such an approach can be used only if the facilitator remembers Friend's experience that it is easier to get a group to undertake the comparatively 'safe' activity of mapping relationships between decisions. The practical business of gradually enabling a group to discuss these issues by allowing it to unfold during the 'unofficial' time is a useful tip. It is one which supports the need to wrap methods within one another so that, for example, the analysis of interconnected decision areas that is a primary focus of strategic choice and SODA precedes the 'hypermapping' approach discussed by Bryant.

The third perspective offered by Cropper (chapter 3), addresses the significance of the personal style of the consultant for the successful practical application of any GDSS. To prove the point Rohrbaugh and Eden (chapter 4) use the critical values approach (CVA) in a new way to analyze the relationship between method and the personal style of Eden using SODA. As Cropper argues, 'there are significant differences in practice between consultants using ostensibly the same methods' and therefore 'method is not all' in understanding the nature of decision support of messy problems. His analysis importantly 'dispels any notion that techniques and their associated procedures are reliable in any scientific sense', an assertion that becomes clearer as Mitchell et al. discuss (in Part II, chapter 6) their experiences of applying the highly formalized method developed from metagame analysis. In order to understand the material in the rest of the book it is imperative that the reader accepts that the method-in-use is often guided by implicit and personal theories about the nature of organizational interventions – the 'methods-in-use are highly individual creations'. In the second part Mayon-White (chapter 8) expands this view by directly considering the role of a facilitator as a change agent, where the facilitator may act as 'parent', trainer, and timemanager to the group, roles which are independent of method.

1
Complexity and Strategic Decision-Making

JOHN CHURCHILL

The purpose of this chapter is to provide a basis for understanding the relationship between so-called strategic problems (the focus of interest of this book), complexity as a characteristic of these problems, and the problems that senior decision-makers spend their time addressing.

One possible model of decision-making which may be used to guide decision support methods in complex situations is the classical model provided by Herbert Simon (1960), but modified to include political and behavioural dimensions. The appeal of this model lies in its conciseness and apparent explanatory power. The important characteristics of the decision complexity are thus incomplete information; lack of definition of, or agreement over, quantitative parameters; conflicting multiple objectives; and conflicting participants. This view of senior-level decision-making is, however, restrictive and most decision scientists seem aware of its omission of other important complexities.

Yet such a model has been used by some authors, such as Radford in this text, as a retrospective device for analyzing a fairly complicated set of negotiations. A case described by Radford involved the bidding between two major parties for control of a Canadian retail organization (Radford and Fingerhut, 1980). Radford (1984) subsequently used the model as the basis for the development of a simulation exercise which, reportedly, has been of some help in preparing senior managers facing complex decision problems to negotiate and bargain their way towards resolutions. Decision-aiding methods following Simon assume certain 'givens' as to the nature of the decisions facing senior management and the manner and context in which these are resolved.

The Nature of Complexity

Although some decisions faced by senior management may be fully described by the type of complexity discussed above, not all are. Complexity beyond that of *intractability of analysis* and of an *overwhelming quantity of information* usually characterizes the decisions of senior management. Complex problems show a great deal of variation from a little to a lot in the amount of information available, the presence of agreed upon parameters and evaluative criteria, and conflict over objectives.

'Crucial' may better describe the nature of senior-level decisions. Not all issues are complex in the sense suggested earlier, nor surrounded by conflict, but at the senior level the outcome of most decisions is consequential for the future course of the organization. Thus operational and administrative decisions can be crucial, in the sense that they have significant consequences for the future of the organization and members of it, and therefore also strategic. This is so by nature of organization where routine, specified (Radford, 1975) decisions filter to the lower levels and these crucial decisions rise to the top. Crucial decisions are also those that rise to the top because they *grab the attention* of the senior management team. Selective perception is located around the extent to which the decisions are and are seen as, crucial.

Even with effective structures of delegation in place, senior management will consider operational as well as administrative and strategic issues (Ansoff, 1965) when they see that they have a critical or crucial aspect and when it is felt that 'ultimate' responsibility should be taken for them. In addition, senior-level decisions are self-selectingly crucial because of time constraints on senior executives who must decide on what issues to spend their limited energy. It is usually presumed that no organization will effectively survive and grow if its senior management languishes in a morass of minutiae. Thus it is not only because decisions are complicated that senior management may ask for assistance, but also because there is a felt need for the best decision possible when matters of importance and critical significance are being deliberated. We may have come to associate complex decisions with senior-level management decision-making because it is often left to senior management to deal with the issues which require an overview of the firm since they also have the authority to balance out competing objectives.

However, to return to the issue of complexity, the characteristics of complex decisions mentioned at the beginning of this chapter assume that the issue is clear and sides have been taken. A tenet of this book is that this context of conflict between parties with competing views and preferences needs to be broadened to include *confusion and lack of clarity* over what the issues are, and what objectives are appropriate and realistic. Decisions which are perceived as complex by senior management in this way are seen to be so because there is often a lack of formulation of the appropriate questions which need to be put and resolved. The decision-making group can be a *cauldron of competing values, views, and objectives*. The decision-makers realize that an optimal outcome is not possible since bringing improvement to one of the problem elements in the system will also result in intensifying difficulties in another part – *issues are recognized to be a system of interacting problems* (Ackoff, 1978; Eden et al., 1983).

One element of complexity that has been represented by the *game theory* perspective, and which was referred to earlier, focuses on the *interactions between different players in decision situations*. Game-theoretic formulations have been most applicable to two situations: those involving negotiations with unions, major suppliers and customers, or 'significant others' in the firm's environment; and with governmental organizations and agencies in the public sector where various factions lobby for their particular choices. In presenting the formulation, it is assumed that the decision process includes participants outside the organization and is suggested that these complex problems are considered and resolved in an atmosphere of contention where participants are seeking to maximize their own utility, and devise tactics to do so, until they come up against the harsh realization that they cannot have all that they want, therefore they must bargain and accept compromise.

For this type of decision situation the most important stage of the decision process is that labelled '*interaction*'. It is in this stage that *negotiation* and compromise are expected to occur and the eventual result is a decision outcome to which all participants agree. *There is complexity in the dynamics of reaching consensus.*

While not denying the political and conflictual dimensions of decision-making processes, it is also important to consider that senior management decision-making does not always take place in an atmosphere of conflict where compromise is the only means to an outcome. The major participants in complex decisions are often only from within the firm. There are often other attendant motives than self-interest. There can be superordinate goals which override individual, parochial preferences and which sustain the group as a 'team' seeking an overall good (Marschak, 1954). Compromise is not always the only outcome. Senior managers demand that *creativity* plays a role in devising options which satisfy competing objectives.

So far this chapter has not considered the role of leader or chairperson in the decision process. All participants in the management team have been assumed to act from a position of equal power. Banker and Gupta (1980) have proposed a method for decision resolution when there are multiple competing objectives but also a senior manager charged with making the final choice. The point, however, is that most organizational decision processes are not leaderless, rather there are *power differentials between members*. In this context, the *management of the process is particularly important*. Chamberlain (1950) makes the point that we need to recognize the difference between a decision and the decision *process*.

To this point, the purpose of this chapter has been to show that the issues relating to the decision process faced by senior managers are complex in a much broader sense than is suggested by either classical considerations of content or considerations of the complexity of process. The interface between managers and decision support facilitators go beyond those allowed for in traditional models of intervention or problem-solving.

In addition it has been argued that the notion of a *crucial decision* might often be a more helpful descriptor for those decisions that concern senior management teams. Following the traditional typology of decisions, these decisions are likely to involve operational, administrative as well as strategic issues.

So, given the nature of complexity presented and the argument about the extent to which a problem is crucial, it may be helpful to define a strategic problem as containing all the following characteristics: crucial, complex, and involving operational and administrative considerations.

A strategic problem is *crucial* because:

–   it is about choosing between portfolios of options that have significant ramifications for the future of the organization itself, for the future of members of the organization, and for the future of the relationship of the organization to other organizations with whom the organization importantly interacts.

It is *complex* because:

–   it is characterized by intractability of analysis because of *incomplete information, lack of definition of, or agreement over, quantitative parameters, conflicting multiple objectives*, and *conflicting participants.*
–   it is characterized by an *overwhelming quantity of both qualitative and quantitative information.*
–   it can be described by *confusion and lack of clarity* about the problem definition.
–   it involves members of a team who have *competing values, views, and objectives* with respect to the situation.
–   it reflects important *interactions between different players* outside of the management team.
–   solving it will involve complexity in the *interactions between team members* as they *negotiate* their way through the *dynamics of reaching consensus.*
–   the solving process will be significantly influenced by *power differentials between team members* and so the management of the problem-solving process will be particularly important.
–   solving it demands *creativity* in the discovery of portfolios of options.

If decision support facilitators and their methods are to be effective in senior management teams then they must address these characteristics. Similarly, the provision of decision support to senior management must account for the decisions for which support is required always being strategic.

The Forum for Decision-making

At the upper level of management, decisions are mostly made by groups, either by consultation or by meetings, and the eventual choice is often the function of the preference of the chief executive officer.

Consider two well-known companies the author has experienced. Each is controlled by the same investment group but has different decision forums. One has a chief executive officer who values participatory management and the involvement of his vice-presidents in all major decisions. He feels that all vice-presidents should be aware not only of the issues in the other functional areas but should have some part in the making of decisions relating to them. A belief structure constructed from tenets about good decisions being those in which people participate and for which they share responsibility, and the exponential creativity of additional people, feed his values and the way in which he constitutes the decision forum. The weekly, senior-level decision meetings often last six hours. The other chief executive rarely calls his senior executives together but consults with them individually about decisions in their particular areas. He tends to make unilateral decisions and asks others to do so under his supervision. His belief in his prerogative as chief operating officer to make decisions and feelings about the efficient use of time underlie his approach. In between the set styles of these two senior officers is the possibility of a contingency approach which adopts a style somewhere between autocratic and participatory based upon judgement about the nature of the issue (Vroom and Jago, 1984).

Thus the culture within which the decision is to be made and the style of management have a significant bearing on the sort of help that can be provided to a management group. *Culture and style within the organization* represent complexity that methods for decision support must address.

These differences in the nature of the organization are important for the decision support facilitator for it will influence how he or she approaches the decision event and will determine the skills he or she will need and the methods he or she will use. Beyond this, an additional characteristic may be the availability of a greater degree of financial and human resources which can be brought to the problem than at other organizational levels. This can give the decision facilitator more scope, access and initiative.

The nature of the forum for decision-making not only adds to the complexity of the issue, but also profoundly influences the outcome of the decision support consultant's relationship with the management team and the applicability of the method used. Chapters 3 and 4 in this part of the book go on to explore this dimension of complexity further.

Difficult Aspects of Decision-making for Senior Management

What aspects of decision-making do senior managers find difficult? The question is difficult to research. Our hunches are based largely upon the samples taken from our involvement in particular situations. The author has been involved with the senior management group of a large Canadian organization, for the purpose of gathering data for research about complex decision-making processes. The author was able to negotiate attendance at the weekly management meetings where the president and senior vice-presidents met to review significant weekly operating results, to initiate corrective action where it was felt necessary, and to develop strategy about future markets, products, and acquisitions. Access to this group was enabled because the president, also chairman of the committee, was interested in having an outside person give their assessment of the process of the group's decision-making. Any observations considered important and which might improve the decision-making ability of the group were to be fed back to the group.

The president had just assumed his position and was trying to 'turn around' this company which had incurred major financial losses for the previous two years. In contrast to the former president, he wanted the decision forum to be, not himself nor a subgroup of senior management, but this larger group representing the main functional areas. His first concern was to have an efficient and effective decision-making group process. Observations of members of the group, the researcher, and the views of the president himself suggest that this president worried more about *how the group reached decisions rather than its ability to reach the right decision* (inasmuch as these might ever be seen as unrelated).

The major portion of the issues considered by the group were crucial in nature and sometimes complex in structure. Complex issues (as defined earlier) were handled in an 'incremental' way over a period of weeks. Initial decisions were often made to get action initiated or 'up and running'. These decisions were usually later modified *as issues became clearer and more information was available* (as confusion and lack of clarity was resolved). The motive for approaching complex matters in this way seemed to be to prevent inactivity and any languishing in confusion – characteristics of the former decision process.

The processing of the content of decisions in the group seemed to *cycle* through definite stages, similar to those described by Mintzberg et al. (1976), Eden (1987) and in recent studies by Cray et al. (1984) and Nutt (1984). Most of the energy and time of the group was spent in getting the issues clear, understanding the background and causes of existing conditions, and envisaging the possible results of suggested alternatives. Major steps forward seem to come when the key questions to be resolved were able to be 'put' or formulated. Also important was the providing of 'frames' or perspectives conditioned by values which could be used as ways to view aspects of the problem so that members of the group could feel comfortable with it. Members of the team also saw as important a process, somewhat the reverse of the providing of frames, that of *'unbundling'* or *liberating facts from personal values and personal perceptions*.

The major contributor in making the decision process a good one (the company has gone on to record profits) was the skill of the president in managing the decision process. He delegated, reinforced accountability, was able to devise creative solutions for conflicting objectives, formulated the central questions, drew out the thinking and feeling of members of the group and drew in those most related to issues under discussion. Notwithstanding tensions between functional areas and personalities, the members of the group seemed committed to the overall good of the company. In the group, most of the frames and formulations were his. He also seemed responsible for the devising and initiating of many of the successful strategies and tactics.

The president's major concerns were how the group was progressing and the relative strengths and weaknesses of its individual members. He also realized that he was doing most of the work in the decision process and carrying most of the responsibility for it. The finding of a strategic resolution to the content of issues did not appear to be a problem. The president seemed to have a belief in the 'inherent wisdom' of the group.

Concluding Remarks

It has been the purpose of this chapter to explore the context of decision-making in senior management teams, by considering some of characteristics of the problems they address and by considering the forum within which they are addressed. By considering the nature of complexity from these two dimensions it becomes clear that the task of providing group decision support to such groups must also be a complex process. Ashby's Law of Requisite Variety argues that complexity must be matched with complexity.

This is a daunting task for both group decision support method and for the facilitator. The methods discussed in this book clearly go some way to working with such complexity, for they seem to have attracted success (albeit a restricted success that is largely but not exclusively related to the proponents of the methods). Nevertheless the subsequent chapters when combined with the parameters identified here might indicate an agenda for the future development of appropriate decision support for work on strategic issues with senior management teams.

2

Handling Organizational Complexity in Group Decision Support

JOHN FRIEND

The purpose of this chapter is to open up for discussion some of the more challenging issues that appear to arise in facilitating group decision processes in organizational environments of a complexity that cannot realistically be matched through the composition of the group alone.

This will be done by contrasting some familiar but simplified models of group accountability with some other ways of representing organizational complexity that stem from research in inter-organizational decision processes. Four aspects of the provision of decision support to groups will be considered in turn – products, process, organization, and technology. These four headings have been found useful in characterizing any particular approach to decision support, and comparing it to others.

The chapter will conclude by pulling together a few lessons for the future development of practice.

Some Simple Models of Group Accountability

In the first instance a few simplified models of accountability in decision-making groups will be outlined. These seem to have a powerful hold on people's thinking, at least at the level of 'espoused theory' as opposed to 'theory-in-use' (Argyris and Schon, 1974). Nevertheless, these models can often lead to dangerous assumptions in practice.

The first model is that of the *teamlike group* – a group in which it may be recognized that people differ in the skills and knowledge that they contribute, yet it is assumed that they are identical in terms of their accountability to outside interests. So they are expected to work consensually towards the same ends – to 'work corporately', to use a phrase that often seems to be employed as a means of inspiration in some organizational settings. If differences in value judgement do arise, they are assumed to represent differences in individual values which can be smoothed out purely by allowing them to surface and striving to reach consensus within the group.

The second model is that of the *partnership group* – a group in which the members are drawn from two or more organizations that have separate structures of accountability, yet are assumed to be acting together as partners in some common cause. The presumption is that this cause is important enough, and will thus develop enough momentum, to overcome any obstacles arising from any policy tensions or antagonisms between the partner organizations. Often, the starting assumption is that the partner organizations are in some sense to be considered 'equal'. It is not easy in the early stages of setting up a partnership group to negotiate clear rules to define in what ways some of them are to be considered less equal than others – except perhaps in the classical case where the partnership is seen as a strictly commercial one, in which the partners are investing different amounts of capital which are used to determine precisely how the monetary proceeds are to be distributed.

A somewhat similar but weaker model is that of the *inclusive group*, convened in an ad hoc way not to pursue some enduring joint endeavour, but to tackle some more transient problem in which several organizations are seen as having a stake. The concern is to bring together representatives of *all* these organizations to search for some resolution to the problem in which all their views are taken into account. Some models of participative planning start explicitly from this assumption; but the weakness of this and the partnership model is that it can easily be assumed that the members of the group bring to it full authority to commit their own organizations, however large and complex they may be, and however small a stake those organizations may have in the matters of concern to this particular group relative to other matters on their various agendas.

This last model shades into the model of a multi-organizational group in which the task is seen as one of *conflict resolution*. Here the role of any external decision support consultant can come to be seen as one not merely of facilitation but of conciliation or arbitration – at least in the simple case where the problem can be formulated in terms of arriving at an agreed point of compromise on a monetary or similar numerical scale.

Coming to Grips with Organizational Complexity

It is easy to recognize the instrumental value of the more consensual of these simplified models in helping people in groups make progress towards decisions. The role of facilitator to a group is so much less problematic if the facilitator can behave as if all members were able to act as a team, or as partners in a common endeavour, or at least as fully representative of all the organizational interests involved. Indeed, the practice of working with groups based on the strategic choice approach to decision support (Friend and Jessop, 1977; Friend and Hickling, 1987) rests to some extent on such simplifying assumptions. However, most experienced facilitators gradually adapt their approach in various ways to deal more realistically with the organizational complexities they encounter in their work.

Recent investigative studies by the author have been focused mainly on public policy issues, and have covered fields as diverse as regional development, countryside management, and criminal justice. In this work it has been necessary to search for frameworks of analysis that can offer alternative reference points to those deriving from the pervasive ideology of systems thinking, which seems to rest on a deceptive analogy of organization as organism, as a living body built of a complex assemblage of specialized yet genetically identical cells.

In grappling with the 'inter-corporate dimension' (Friend et al., 1974) of decision-making, the author has found it important to introduce forms of organizational mapping which start with a focus on specific issues for decision or negotiation, and to work outwards from this focus to explore in as much depth as seems appropriate the internal structures of each of the organizations represented, the layers of accountability within each, and the linkages between them – whether through formal channels or more informal personal networks. Such aspects of structure may exercise highly significant influences on group decision-making. Thus it seems necessary to reach out for alternative theoretical concepts which can offer useful starting points in exploring these influences. Most of the concepts developed by the author invert the top-down orthodoxies of policy-making and 'implementation'; an example is the concept of 'policy stress', used to describe a state of conflict between two or more policy guidelines emanating from different sources yet applying to the same area of decision.

Implications for the Facilitation of Group Decision Processes

In this book, it is important to find ways of introducing these insights and methods from investigative work into the practice of group facilitation. Using this experience as a base let us review more generally some of the ways in which any approach to group decision support can be adapted to reflect the complexities of the wider organizational environment in which it is set.

The review will follow what Friend and Hickling (1987) call the A-TOPP framework. This simply identifies four key aspects to any particular *approach to* decision-making and planning, labelled respectively *Technology, Organization, Process, and Products*. The question to address in relation to each of these aspects – which are of course inter-related and the boundaries of which are hard to demarcate with any precision – is as follows:

How far can any approach to the facilitation of group decision or planning processes be enriched by introducing ways of reflecting more realistically the complexity of organizational structure and relations in the wider environment in which a group's work is set?

With the present purpose it makes sense to take the four headings in reverse order – Products, Process, Organization, and Technology.

Products

The simplest assumption when working with a group is that the aim is to arrive at decisions to which all members of the group are equally and fully committed, and to design a set of products accordingly. In the strategic choice approach, the richer concept of the 'commitment package' is introduced. This is a package of incremental steps in a continuing decision process, in which any elements of immediate action are deliberately balanced with other more exploratory steps designed to work progressively towards future commitment. Such exploratory steps may involve a wide range of processes or procedures within the wider organizational or inter-organizational milieu; they can take a variety of forms including technical investigations, political consultations, and inter-organizational negotiations, whether through formal or more informal channels.

Useful as this idea of the commitment package can be, various problems can arise in introducing it into the work of a decision-making group. In some situations, the positive ring of the phrase can be an asset; but in others, a more low key term such as 'progress package' can be more helpful, as it can sound less threatening to decision-makers outside the group who might fear that their authority to commit was being usurped or undermined. More fundamentally, some elements of a commitment package – especially those exploratory steps which involve the exercise of influence through informal channels – may be so sensitive that they cannot easily be brought out for discussion within the group, and are even more difficult to write down explicitly as part of the formal output of the group's work.

Issues of this kind can be dealt with conceptually by drawing a distinction between the 'visible' and 'invisible' products of a group process, along with a cross-cutting distinction between products of substance and those to do with the management of future process. Many of the more invisible products may take the form of learning and adaptation by individual members. Some of them can be brought to the surface by the use of survey methods, or by setting aside time periodically for discussion of matters of process rather than substance.

So there is a range of methods available to help members of groups in conceiving the products of groups working in ways in which organizational complexity is more fully addressed. Yet there remain many challenges in introducing these methods into the practice of decision support with multi-accountable groups.

Process

Anyone who is sanctioned to act as facilitator to a decision-making group starts from a position of considerable influence over the *group process*. For he or she can control the group's use of time through the way in which particular decision support methods are used, and the way in which transitions are managed between one type of activity and another. Periods of individual or subgroup working can be introduced where it is judged useful to do so, and corrective measures can be taken when the dynamics of the group seems to be developing in ways likely to impede progress.

When working with a group for the first time, a facilitator may have little specific knowledge on which to base judgements of this kind. Yet he or she will usually come armed with certain general principles for the use of time, such as a defined sequence of steps used in a particular approach. Friend and Hickling emphasize the value of *process flexibility*, and seek to manage this by introducing to the group a framework consisting of four interrelated modes of activity – called *shaping, designing, comparing, and choosing*. Within this organizing framework, people are encouraged to 'switch' flexibly from one mode to another according to a group judgement on where most progress is to be made – never lingering for too long in any one mode and never neglecting any one for too long at a time.

Useful as such a framework can be, again there are difficulties to be confronted in groups whose members come from different organizations – each perhaps with not only its own particular management procedures, but also its own acquired organizational, professional, and political cultures.

In an interactive group process, normal time scales of decision-making may seem to become compressed; and some group members may resist any idea that they should 'think on their feet' about alternatives to proposed actions to which they have developed substantial commitment. For example, a meeting about alternative schemes for the development of a small country town in a low-lying part of England presents a vivid example. The land-use planners were pressing the engineers from the water authority to suggest alternatives to particular investment projects that were causing difficulties. However, to the engineers concerned, it was inconceivable that any alternative design could be offered without their returning to their desks to carry out weeks of careful technical work.

So here – as in the consideration of products – issues of internal group processes and external processes can become intermeshed. Hickling's consulting work in the Netherlands, which has involved the use of strategic choice methods with project groups meeting regularly over a period of several months, has led to the development of some general guidelines for relating the use of time within group sessions to the use of time in the intervals between group sessions. But there is much scope for the further development of practical guidance in this area.

Organization

A facilitator who is working with a multi-accountable group for the first time will usually start from a position of ignorance about the particular organizational complexities which the other participants see all around them. This position of political naivety can often be used to advantage in the early stages of group work, in helping the participants to focus on the substantive issues that they face. However, as work proceeds, many of the wider organizational forces at work will gradually become more clear to the facilitator – some of them perhaps while the full group is in session, but others only in the course of more informal communications between sessions. In an all-day workshop, the lunch break often provides an opportunity for individual participants to give the facilitator an informal briefing on these wider organizational forces at work – and the tensions to which these give rise among the members of the group. It is worth noting that SODA, in contrast, deliberately sets out to discover these elements of the group through initial rounds of interviews (Eden, 1989), and so reduces the benefits of 'naivety'.

These points are illustrated by a recent experience in facilitating a strategic choice workshop on the topic of information technology strategy for quite a large organization. The workshop brought together several senior managers plus a similar number of less senior staff who had been constituted as an inter-departmental task force on this topic. During the lunch break, one of the junior staff told the facilitator of his frustration at the unwillingness of the seniors to adopt a more rational and purposive approach and one of the seniors expressed his view on the broader politics of the situation and the need to move forward more gradually and selectively. Both pieces of information were extremely valuable in setting expectations about the future management of the workshop and its products.

So a position of naivety can become a wasting asset; and as the facilitator becomes better informed on the *organizational politics* behind an issue, so the responsibilities of the role increase. There will then come a point where the more orthodox working assumptions about shared group task and purpose become a barrier to progress; and it is then that it can be helpful for the facilitator to introduce methods of organizational mapping (see Bryant, chapter 11, this volume) which indicate at least some of the complexities of the wider organizational environment within which realistic levers of influence must be sought. In this way, consideration of substantive choices can gradually be enriched by discussion of more political process choices. But the pace at which this development takes place has to be judged carefully as the group's work evolves.

Figure 2.1 (from Friend and Hickling, 1987) shows a general model of

Figure 2.1   *Organizational responsibilities in strategic choice*

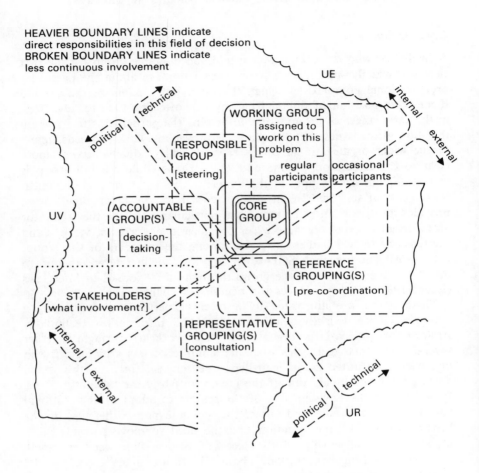

HEAVIER BOUNDARY LINES indicate
direct responsibilities in this field of decision
BROKEN BOUNDARY LINES indicate
less continuous involvement

Source: Figure reproduced by kind permission of Pergamon Press PLC from J.K. Friend
and A. Hickling: *Planning under Pressure* (© 1987)

the wider organizational context of a working group. This model is often
found useful in talking to members of a group, and in helping them to
consider the various other types of group – or 'grouping' to use a
deliberately looser term – which could have a significant bearing on their
task.

Those who are formally accountable for decision-taking in the areas of
choice which the working group is addressing can be seen as constituting
an accountable group (or sometimes groups). In the case of a single

corporate organization, this will often be a high-level board or council; but there may be more than one such if several corporate organizations are represented in the working group.

Those charged with exercising a more direct steering or policy guidance function in relation to the task of the working group can be seen as constituting a responsible group – the membership of which may overlap with that either of the working group or the accountable group(s), as Figure 2.1 suggests. Also shown at the centre of Figure 2.1 is a small core group within the working group, consisting of one or more people with key roles in managing its work and its continuing relationships with other individuals and groups.

Beyond these 'line' responsibilities, it is important to recognize the significance of other important groupings, often less formally constituted. There may be groupings of people representing significant political interests without executive authority over the issues being considered – labelled representative grouping(s) in Figure 2.1 – and others reflecting executive interests whose expertise and co-operation will be important in translating decisions into action – called reference grouping(s). Further out again, there may be various stakeholders in the decision process who are involved only indirectly if at all in the membership of any accountable or representative grouping.

Where a working group is formally constituted in order to work on an issue over several working sessions, then it is more likely that these other significant groups and groupings will also take a relatively concrete form. Whether or not this is the case, it is always worthwhile for a working group to spend some time discussing who the participants in the various other groups and groupings might be within their own organizational – inter-organizational – context. Then they can go on to discuss particular organizational design options, and consider what their implications might be. In practice – as for instance in Hickling's work on environmental policy in the Netherlands – this is found to lead to richer and more productive patterns of participation on the part of people outside the immediate working group.

Technology

The way in which the technology of group decision support is adapted to organizational complexity is bound to be more specific to one consultant's practice, here based on the strategic choice approach, than what has been offered for discussion under the other three headings. The strategic choice approach introduces particular methods to do with the mapping of interrelated areas of decision, and the conscious management of uncertainty through time; and experience has gradually led to these being adapted in particular ways in situations where the 'ownership' of decisions – and the ownership of uncertainty as well – is less concentrated than in the simplified context of a teamlike group.

Various marginal adaptations have already been introduced into the basic technology of strategic choice to reflect differences in the ownership of decisions. For instance, within a 'decision graph' – which is essentially a map of the relationships among interconnected decision areas, usually built up through interactive working in a group – it is possible to introduce symbols representing differences in the extent to which decision areas can be influenced by the group, or overlapping zones of influence for different organizations.

However, as pointed out by Bennett and Cropper (1989), the basic method does not treat the ownership of decisions as a central feature of the analysis as do some other approaches – for example those which derive from the theory of games (see chapters 6 and 7 of this book). This may not be altogether a drawback, especially in so far as it encourages members of a newly convened group to think and act in a non-competitive way. But it is important that the repertoire of the facilitator should include ways of breaking out of this assumption as and when it seems productive to do so.

The issue of technology for working with uncertainty raises in practice challenges of a more subtle kind. For any concept of 'group uncertainty' can be a very elusive one. Lately, Friend and Hickling have been dealing with this difficulty by stressing the concept of the uncertainty area; an area of uncertainty which can be seen as 'owned' by a group wherever there is a state of disagreement within the group about assumptions – on the environment, on values, on intentions or whatever – which they are unable to resolve by reference to some authoritative source.

Of the three basic categories of uncertainty used in strategic choice – labelled UE, UV, and UR, relating to the Environment, Values, and Related decisions respectively – the second and third offer direct routes into the consideration of organizational complexities beyond the boundaries of the group. This can lead into discussion of important issues to do with the dynamics of wider decision processes. Yet members of groups often seem to feel more inhibited when working with these ideas than when participating in the comparatively 'safe' activity of mapping relationships between decisions. So the facilitator must learn to exercise caution in the way such ideas are introduced, especially when working with multi-accountable groups.

One point of agreement between those who use the strategic choice approach and others who are involved in the business of group decision support would probably be that the heading of 'technology' has to be seen as embracing not just the specific techniques used to structure problems, but also the physical devices used to facilitate communication and interactions in groups – whether in the form of flipcharts and well-designed working spaces (see Eden, chapter 15 and Hickling, chapter 17), or more advanced computer aids (see Phillips, chapter 13 and Ackermann, chapter 14). The concept of an 'open technology' – accessible not just to the expert but to all members of a working group – is one that many of us would share as an ideal. Yet it is important for us to develop an appreciation of the limits to its application in group settings where there may be severe organizational inhibitions to the free sharing of perceptions, and to have other less open alternatives up our sleeves for use as and when it seems appropriate.

Learning about Complexity

Any progress made in learning how to handle organizational complexity in personal practice tends to come about in an incremental and even opportunistic way. Indeed it seems to be highly dependent on the continuing interplay between experiences in active and investigative roles. The active role involves working with groups in a facilitating role to help them work on particular decisions. The investigative role involves carrying out research into the complexities of decision-making in particular organizational or inter-organizational settings. This means interviewing individuals, observing groups at work, studying relevant background documents; using each type of experience to help decide what line of enquiry to pursue next in a highly adaptive way.

It is in this latter type of work that there is more opportunity to learn in depth about the organizational complexities that influence the behaviour of people working in multi-accountable groups. For example, when working actively with a group whose members are drawn from four different organizations or departments A, B, C, and D, an external facilitator can quickly become aware of the breadth of accountability represented within the group. But there is another dimension to the organizational complexity of the group – the dimension of depth – which is likely to take longer to uncover through active involvement with the group alone.

For example, it may be important to appreciate that organization A is large and internally complex, with many nested levels of accountability; yet with a stake in the issues of importance to this working group which may be quite marginal relative to A's stakes in other issues on its own current organizational agenda; and with interpersonal and inter-sectoral political pressures which, though not easily discussed in settings where other organizations are represented, may profoundly influence the way in which A's representatives behave. Organization B, meanwhile, may be much smaller, with a much more intense local interest in the matters the group is discussing, yet with a significant micro-politics of its own. Organization C may be more cohesive, with a strong technical or professional bias, while Organization D may be no more than a loose coalition of interests within which there is difficulty in forming any cohesive policy. . . .

There is no limit to the time that could be spent endeavouring to learn more about the organizational and political complexities that surround any set of issues – especially where those issues impinge on the interests of several stakeholder groups. So there is a skill to be learnt in judging just how far to go in exploring in depth the organizational milieu of the issues facing a group – especially where there are insistent real-time pressures for decision, and the issues themselves may forever be changing shape.

There are many possible approaches to the understanding of organizational complexity, only a few of which have been touched on here. Sometimes these approaches can be introduced openly into the group process itself; at other times, the risks will be too great. As a group develops its own sense of identity, the level of risk that can be taken in exposing organizational politics to discussion within the group will tend to increase. Yet these risks will never disappear. *However hard the facilitator may strive to develop an open and 'teamlike' group culture, the surrounding organizational complexities will persist, and can never be ignored.*

Directions for Future Progress

In this chapter the aim has been to articulate a little more clearly some of the more important things learnt from the author's working experience, so that they can be shared with others who have had similar opportunities.

Further progress in building the recognition of organizational complexity into professional practice will inevitably be incremental and opportunistic. Most of us have too much investment in a particular way of working to make it easy to contemplate more radical departures. Also, it is important to recognize the value of starting work with a group without challenging too early the more orthodox assumptions about how a task-centred group should work. Nevertheless, opportunities to challenge these assumptions invariably begin to surface as soon as the group process gets under way, and the more we can bring ways of exploiting these opportunities into our various decision support repertoires, the more effective our future practice will become.

3
The Complexity of Decision Support Practice

STEVE CROPPER

A neglected area in decision support research is simply the description of the ways in which methods are used in practice – the ways in which decisions about the choice and use of methods in practice are made. With some notable exceptions, we are left with highly generalized statements describing seemingly replicable procedures and techniques and the relationship of these to different types of problem (eg Jackson, 1986). These statements fail to convey a sense of how the methods work in practice, of the decisions faced by consultants in setting the methods to work. In short, they divorce the methods and the problems from their contexts. As a consequence, we hear little about the ways in which the use of methods varies in practice, and why. Such knowledge would be the very essence of a theory of decision support practice and a necessary part of the successful transfer or acquisition of decision support methods. To make progress toward a theory of decision support practice, we need to take as our focus the idea of *methods-in-use*. And, as a corollary, we need to place at the centre of enquiry those people who use the methods – the consultants – and the theories-in-use (Argyris and Schon, 1974) that guide their practice.

Contingencies and Differences in Practice

The aim of recent research (Cropper, 1984) has been to bring the people and their ways of framing the contexts on which they act back into the picture as significant elements of methodology. Others are also taking this as a starting point for research into OR consultancy (Jones, 1989). The aim has been to understand and to compare how individual consultants work with their methods. Initial forays were driven by the question, posed to individual consultants, 'What do you actually do in practice?'. Actual practice, it emerges, is highly contingent. Choices as to the purpose and direction of an intervention, and the tools and processes that are appropriate are framed through the relationship with a client. Different situations require different responses, different tools or combinations of tools, and different ways of using them. These choices are made by consultants in the light of a whole host of considerations. Comparisons of and generalizations about specific practices are difficult and dangerous, then. Descriptions of actual practice – for example through case studies – while a useful first step, nevertheless are unable to provide the full story; comparison is an essential part of the research strategy.

If analysts vary their practice – the design and execution of their methods-in-use – according to the problem with which they are engaging, and if they see this variation as an essential part of their practice, then we are faced with the question of the bases on which they make decisions about practice. This is a central concern of this chapter. It is important, also, for an understanding of decision support to address the limits to consultants' willingness or capacity to adapt their way of working and method to the problem situation. For the consultants interviewed, these limits are set by clear, prior conceptualizations of the decision support task and by rules of thumb concerning the 'right way to go about things'. These rules are very much individually based; consultants' styles or ways of working differ considerably (Cropper, 1984).

In order to make sense of these contingencies, differences, and similarities, we need a framework that identifies the elements which constitute and delineate the consultant's way of working.

The Decision Support Consultant – a Rough Working Model

Two broad types of influence can be distinguished (see Figure 3.1). The first derives from the theoretical and modelling structures that are used in tackling problems – the cognitive maps and repertory grids used within SODA, the component parts of analysis of interconnected decision areas (AIDA) of strategic choice, and so on. These technologies are, in effect, publicly known, definitional conventions that serve to distinguish approaches. For example, the game theoretic notion of an option is quite different to the idea of an option as understood within the strategic choice or SODA frameworks. Clearly there are differences between individual practices, which stem from differences in the method or methods used. But it is noteworthy that *there are significant differences in practice between consultants using ostensibly the same methods*; and there are certain significant features of practice that may be shared by consultants using different methods. Method, then, is not all.

We should emphasize that not all decision support consultants restrict themselves to exclusive use of a single method. Many prefer to develop and draw on a varied repertoire of methods according to personal rules of choice. Indeed, the focus on individuals' approaches to decision

Figure 3.1 *Outline model of the individual decision support consultant*

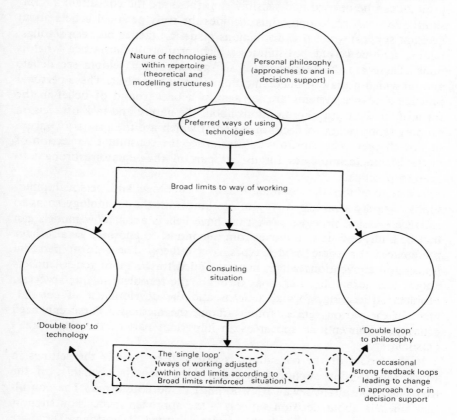

support revealed precisely these rules – in the form of a multitude of personal preferences. These make up the second type of influence on decision support practice and include firm ideas about choice of clients and choice of members of the client group, about the relevance of particular techniques and ways of organizing the enquiry process, about working with the client group, about the input of effort (both consultant's and client's) over time, and so on. Some of this can be found encoded in the more public forms of guidance (see the case studies of Checkland, 1985, and Eden, 1985, reporting decisions about the design of interventions made in practice and Friend and Hickling's, 1987, painstaking attempt to agree a set of rules of thumb for practice using the strategic choice method) but much cannot. Interestingly, the position of the boundary between public and private guidance varies widely between methods.

In short, the element labelled 'Personal philosophy' in Figure 3.1 encompasses both consultants' *'approaches to'* decision support and what might be contrasted as their *'approaches in'* decision support. The latter consist of the rules held by consultants about the way decision support projects can be devised and sensibly run: these are the consultant's 'craft skills'. Personal philosophy thus includes the truly personal beliefs about decision support – the fine distinctions made in practice between settings, remits, and perceived possibilities which profoundly influence what is done. These are the fragments of self-guidance that seldom see debate and on which it may be uncommon or difficult to reflect. These personal practice guidance systems are set against a background of belief in the form of fundamental presumptions about the nature and task of decision support (approaches to decision support) which are the primary concern of this chapter. These profoundly influence the consultant's selection of methods and technologies for use as part of the repertoire brought to bear in practice.

Taken together, the combination of technology and personal philosophy suggests a preferred way of working with the technology so as to enhance decision processes. We thus have beliefs about how models can best be built, and how to move from one model to another; we also have preferences for some model types over others. These form personal procedural conventions which may be added to the more general beliefs about, for example, iteration through the problem-solving process, problem structuring, formal analysis and the development of commitment in the various guises found among the methods. These enhanced procedural conventions appear as an important part of the consultant's personal style.

If the model of the consultant is extended to include the settings in which the decision support consultant acts, then the dynamics of the individual consultant's way of working can be considered. The consultant's beliefs about decision support – the approach *to* decision support – set broad limits to individual consultants' ways of working. These are in effect the boundaries within which the consultant feels it possible or appropriate to vary his practice. The adaptation of an intervention within these bounds represents what Argyris and Schon (1974) have called 'single loop learning'. This is analogous to the control of a heating system by a thermostat. Adjustments fall within the analyst's anticipation of the event and within his or her beliefs about appropriate practice. The 'control device' itself – the system of beliefs and rules held by the consultant – is adequate and requires no adjustment. These rules may, however, be challenged. As Spink (1980) notes, decision support continually involves the testing of a repertoire against a setting and this process

> . . . may lead those going into the applied setting to alter their own personal option bars; to try out something different, to go into something they feel less skilled about, to have an experience which may radically shift some of their ideas.

Occasionally, then, 'double-loop learning' (Argyris and Schon, 1974) will occur whereby a consultant's *broad limits* are adjusted or subjected to radical change. The remainder of this chapter considers what it is that might constitute radical change – that is, reviews some fundamental presumptions underlying decision support practice.

Filling in the Model: 'Approaches to' Decision Support

It is convenient to arrange these presumptions as ideal types. Figure 3.2 reveals two chains of dialectically opposed reasoning about decision support. These provide alternative views of complexity, the technology required to manage that complexity and the way in which these technologies can be used by consultants to assist groups of decision-makers in practice. The difference between them may be characterized as one between

- intervention as an analytical or intellectual process of problem-solving involving a focus on abstraction; and
- intervention as a process of assisting social interaction and commitment making.

Any actual approach and individual way of working will represent a synthesis of the two positions. Indeed, a common response from consultants as the various component features of either chain of reasoning have been identified has been to suggest that their approach to decision support swings from one side to the other.

Each ideal type is briefly characterized in terms of its position on three issues: the conception of the client and the problem (of both client and decision support consultant); the aims of intervention; and the role of the consultant. For each position, particular leverage points are implied. These are features of problem situations which are defined as opportunities for the consultant to intervene powerfully to assist the decision process. Beliefs about the location and the nature of relevant leverage points will clearly affect what choices are open to the consultant in practice.

Conception of the Client and of the Problem

Within the context of this book it is useful to identify the client as a group. That said, one type of approach – the analytical – starts, often by default, from a view of the client as singular; the client grouping is assumed to have a common purpose, if not a common view, and to form from the start a distinct, whole decision-maker and actor. The opposing approach – the social – starts from a model of the client as diverse or pluralistic in its purposes and views; the grouping is *conceived* as a set of individuals with their own personal and organizational agendas, beliefs, areas of responsibility and power.

There are a number of implications for the design and use of methods

Figure 3.2   *Filling in the model of the decision support consultant: approaches to decision management*

Two ideal-typical views of *complexity*, the *technology* required to tackle it and the *way in which technologies can be used* to assist problem-solving in teams

Problem-solving as an intellectual process involving manipulation of abstract sets of variables	Problem-solving as a social and political process of enquiry, negotiation and commitment-making
⬇	⬇

CONCEPTION OF A CLIENT: locus of problem

Conception of client – client group conceived as	Singular (single view, single voice, concerted locus of power, interest and responsibility)	Pluralistic (multiple view, multiple voice, plural contribution of power, interest and responsibility)
Locus of problem (leverage point) as	(Representation and analysis of) problems 'external' to the client group	(Management of complexity) internal to client group through a social process of problem negotiation
	Clients provide relevant data for analysis and act upon conclusions	Problem cannot be abstracted from the *people* forming the client group

that stem from these divergent starting points. In particular, we can identify crucial differences in the way adherents of each conceive the *leverage points* for interventions into the decision process. The consultant is looking for points of leverage by attention to which he or she can assist the client group to move forward to take decisions and actions, to 'finish' with the problem (Eden, 1986).

For the analytical approach, the analyst treats the leverage points as problems external to the client group and it is assumed that the problem can be abstracted from its context and specified in a model for collaborative treatment by the consultant and the client group. For example, uncertainties can be represented as probabilities that external events will occur. The client's problem is also the problem to which the consultant addresses himself or herself and the appropriate techniques. Attention is focused outwards on to a problem as represented and manipulated by a model through which the client group can be helped to decide how to move from the problem situation. If they do not have the power to change their circumstance, at least they may be helped to understand how it has come about. For the type of approach we have labelled 'social', the presumption is that the problem (the consultant's point of leverage) resides inherently within the people in the client group. Attention is thus focused on the internal, social process of problem negotiation. From this presumption stem clear and important implications for practice including, for example, a need for information about the individuals forming the client group, their aspirations, motivations, status and so on. It is a fundamental principle that 'the problem' cannot be abstracted from the people forming the client group.

Aims of Intervention

We can pursue the two ideal types further down the chains of reasoning that stem from these presumptions by examining the aims of intervention found in each respectively.

A shared claim is that methods are designed and used *to assist in articulation, definition, and clarification of a 'messy' problem*. Decision-making is characterized as a learning process in which expression itself is seen to be problematic. However, there are significant differences both in the reasoning behind this assertion and in the way the process is conducted in practice across the two types of approach. These are best exposed in considering some further aims of decision support.

Framing and Modelling

A second shared claim in decision support, as undertaken by management science and operational research consultants, is that expressed concerns about a problem should be transformed into an explicit representation or model. There are clear differences in the process by which information is elicited and used, however. The explicit aim of the analytic position is to establish choices for the client group conceived as a whole. The process is such that bits and bobs of information are elicited from all members of that group and assembled to form a group picture of the problem. This encourages and uses group synergy, piggy-backing, and argument on the spot. From the opposing position, the concern is to listen to and elicit individuals' points of view as wholes and thereby to understand the clients' various constructions of their problem. This implies that interventions should start with an opportunity for each member of the client group individually to explain their view.

Technology and Negotiation of the Problem

These positions have clear implications for the techniques required to give form to these presumptions. The aim of either approach is to *use a modelling technology to move to a shared group view of a problem*. From the view of decision support as levered by intellectual analysis of a problem, the body of technique provides a conceptual framework

Figure 3.3   *Aim of intervention*

Common aim
to aid the articulation
definition and
clarification
of issues to
be addressed

Framing and modelling	Privileged frame defines the salient features of problems in particular ways	Individuals' points of views as wholes elicited 'Natural' frames
	Group construction (synergy etc)	
Negotiation of problem definition	Modelling the problem in terms of privileged frame allows debate in common language but model structures are rigid	Natural frames counterposed provide vehicle for generation of dialogue and *negotiation* between clients
Development of decision scheme	Clients input data on content of problems: this is then held constant to allow analysis	Debate and negotiation implies problem structure is constantly changing
	'Cycling' round the modelling process to provide dynamics	Use a model form and process that allows for absolute fluidity in problem definition
Choice and commitment	Privileged frames as powerful structures for thinking about choice, but the link between analysis and action is ill-defined	The whole process of problem negotiation and option generation related to the generation of commitment to act
	Action arises where analysis reveals one option to be 'self-evidently' the 'better' scheme	Action arises from a process of individual commitment and social persuasion that options can and should be taken up

which is put forward as normatively privileged – especially relevant – as a way of putting order on and boundaries around the information being proffered by members of the client group. The consultant's role is to encourage and enable the clients to use the power of this framework as a way of selecting relevant information, concentrating minds on critical features of the problem and so on. We can contrast this with the view of problem-solving as a social process which is firmly linked to an attempt to devise and use technology which will capture and reflect individual clients' own concerns, language, and framing of a problem (Schon, 1983; Eden, 1989). These then form the basis for negotiation of a group-developed and owned vocabulary for describing and bounding the problem. Here, the consultant's frame is undeclared or implicit; it emerges much as those of the clients, in a process of problem negotiation.

Development of Decision Schemes

A third shared aim is to develop alternative decision schemes or options for action. Where intervention is conceived as an intellectual process, client involvement in the process tends to be in the form of input to a model which is then driven by an internal logic. A decision tree, for example, as used in both strategic choice (Friend and Hickling, 1987) and decision conferencing (Phillips, 1989a) yields decision schemes by logical, systematic combination of elements or options. Clients can influence the input to these schemes by specifying the options (encoded for them by the consultant) and can further influence their combination by specifying incompatibilities between options and so forth. That the input generally needs to be redefined implies procedural manoeuvres – deliberate cycling back through the process, for example. Where the process is treated as social in nature, the concern in devising and using technology being to assist the *constant redefinition of the problem as the clients negotiate between themselves*, the problem structure, not held artificially constant by the needs of the model, is fluid. Decision schemes emerge from creative synthesis of proposals and from changes in clients' views rather than from model manipulation.

Choice and Commitment

Based on the development of alternative ways forward, the concern of either position is, above all, with assisting choice. Again, however, there are different views about the development of commitment to one scheme or another that lead to differences in the nature of technology as a support to decision-making and in the way of working with technology.

Frames introduced as 'privileged' do indeed provide powerful structures for thinking about choices. However, the mechanism that allows a choice among competing schemes is theoretically unattended and therefore practically ad hoc. Techniques may be used to evaluate different options, but there is no presumption that leads the consultant to attend to the link between such evaluation and the process of commitment and choice. It is presumed that following an acceptable definition of the problem, decision schemes and evaluation criteria, analysis will reveal the scheme that self-evidently is preferred. From the opposing position, the implication is that less imposing technologies of analysis should be devised and brought to bear: commitment is presumed to result from ensuring that individuals' views as wholes form the basis for problem definition, that problem definition involves a shift in those individual views such that on crucial issues there is an agreed, negotiated structure, and that throughout the process of option definition and evaluation, the possibility and process of implementation is a paramount consideration in the consultant's support of the process of debate and analysis.

The Role of the Consultant

To summarize, we can identify two opposed sets of presumptions about decision support. The first sees *problem solving as an intellectual process*: a series of presumptions about appropriate practice for consultants follow which identify the crucial leverage points to which the consultant should attend. The second sees *problem solving as a social process* from which standpoint a different set of imperatives is implied for consultancy practice. The differences can be characterized as between enabling analysis of a problem (as an abstract set of elements) and assisting communication and understanding of clients' concerns as a means of driving a process of negotiation and commitment making. Learning about the problem contrasts with learning about co-clients' beliefs, will, and ambitions.

The two roles for the consultant which accord most closely with the two processes suggested are that of *expert conceptualizer* as the provider of a privileged framework and manager of an intellectual process of enquiry, and the *facilitator* as the manager of a social process of enquiry. To conclude this characterization of positions, we re-emphasize that any actual approach will represent a synthesis of the two chains of reasoning. In terms of consultants' roles, the reality is one in which *consultants find a happy medium between facilitation of human interaction and intellectual analysis of a problem*. Helping clients articulate their beliefs goes alongside attempts to order or conceptualize the 'data'; framing the problem becomes a way of sparking debate and analysis which reveals counter-intuitive results which may, through raising questions, be beneficial in challenging premature group commitment.

Conclusion

In much the way that Bunker (1980) has argued for 'a theory of practice for experiential learning', there is a need for a theory of practice for decision support, a theory which addresses the complexities of practice brought by people and contingency. Research into the ways of working of a number of decision support consultants has suggested a framework which would serve to organize their current best knowledge. This would incorporate both approaches in decision support and the basic presumptions that guide consultants' work – their approaches to decision support. Other reports (Huxham, Cropper and Bennett, 1989) address consultants' approaches in decision support – the craft skills of practitioners. Here the focus has been on the elements of a framework concentrating on consultants' approaches to decision support, on the background presumptions that inform ways of working in practice. Two sets of internally coherent presumptions were presented as dialectically opposed approaches to decision support. Examination of these sets of presumptions revealed those leverage points to which adherents should attend in practice.

In summary, four significant new issues arise from this work:

1 The contingency or variation of practice across different situations by individual consultants' practice is clear – this adaptation of the method-in-use is guided by often implicit theories about appropriate responses to problem situations.

2 The influence of the individual consultant on the method-in-use is highlighted; this finding dispels any notion that techniques and their associated procedures are reliable in any scientific sense. Differing sets of presumptions about appropriate leverage points and differing individual styles mean that differences in practice are inevitable across consultants. The style of a consultant is an important variable which is relatively independent of the body of technique used.

3 This raises questions about the type of knowledge that must be made explicit if the transfer or acquisition of methods and techniques is to be successful. On the one hand, it would seem desirable to pass on the craft skills of successful consultants, as in the traditional apprenticeship model. On the other hand, we need to recognize that these will not necessarily endure in the face of new, individual needs, preferences, and styles.

4 The range of convenience of methods is not set by their relationship to problems in the abstract, but by their relationship to consultants' theories-in-use. Methods-in-use are highly individual creations. We need to understand more about their origins, their role in consulting performance and the ways in which they can be monitored for purposes of reflection, reaffirmation, and change.

4

Using the Competing Values Approach to Explore 'Ways of Working'

JOHN ROHRBAUGH AND COLIN EDEN

A strong argument has been made for decision support consultants better to understand the mix of method, consultant style, and client setting that in combination define their 'ways of working' (Cropper, 1984). Whatever technique is selected for such self-appraisal should be consistent with contemporary organizational theory. One helpful framework for understanding this complexity is provided by the competing values approach (Quinn and Rohrbaugh, 1983; Lewin and Minton, 1986).

The Competing Values Approach to Organizational Analysis

According to the CVA framework (as shown in Figure 4.1), four middle range models of organizational analysis exist: (a) an internal process model that focuses on *information management and co-ordination* as the means by which stability and equilibrium can be developed as organizational outcomes of primary interest; (b) a rational goal model that focuses on *planning and objective setting* as the means by which productivity and efficiency can be improved as organizational outcomes of primary interest; (c) an open systems model that focuses on *flexibility and readiness* as the means by which source acquisition and growth can be increased as organizational outcomes of primary interest; and (d) a human relations model that focuses on *cohesion and morale* as the means by which the value of human resources can be made greater as an organizational outcome of primary interest.

The CVA framework makes clear the parallel relationship between these four models of organizational analysis and the four functional prerequisites of any system of action identified by Parsons (1959): (a) the integrative function; (b) the goal attainment function; (c) the adaptive function; and (d) the pattern maintenance and tension management function. In combination, the open systems and human relations models reflect instrumental concerns, that is, the *differentiation* of organizational

Figure 4.1   *The competing values approach (CVA) framework*

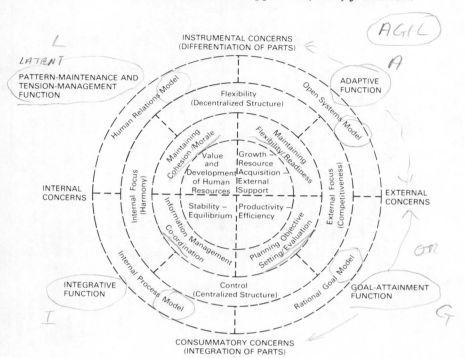

parts. These two pairs are reflective of Gouldner's (1959) two general models of organizational analysis: the rational model with an emphasis on formal, planned behaviour and the natural system model with an emphasis on flexible, spontaneous behaviour.

Stratification of Competing Values within Organizations

The work of Jaques (1976, 1982) on stratified systems theory provides a useful basis for more thoroughly exploring the presence of competing values in organizational decision-making. Jaques has proposed a common structure for all organizations, large or small, public or private, located in the East or the West, providing goods or services. This structure has up to eight strata or levels, with boundaries between strata representing qualitative shifts in the nature of work within each level. For job promotions within a stratum, the change in the position of decision-makers merely means 'more of the same', but promotions across boundaries result in quite different, more abstract, and far greater responsibilities. Jaques's basic structure of work in organizations is shown in Table 4.1. The strata about which Jaques has written can be

Table 4.1 *Basic structure of work in organizations*

Stratum	Organizational level	Individual position	Time span	Main activity	Task characteristics
I	Shop floor	Clerical worker	1 day to 3 months	Concrete shaping	Following well established rules that are seen as inflexible; improvement occurs by gaining more practice and greater experience
II	Section	First-line supervisor	3 months to 1 year	Reflective articulation	Clarifying goals while working towards them; improvement occurs by reducing ambiguities with more workable definitions of the job
III	Unit	Department manager	1 year to 2 years	Linear extrapolation	Planning for work requirements by responding to predictable trends; improvement occurs by more accurate forecasting with existing technologies and more timely preparation
IV	Division	General manager	2 years to 5 years	Alternative subsystems	Identifying a variety of known approaches to the current work in search for better ways to enhance performance; improvement occurs by finding methods that increase efficiency
V	Subsidiary	Managing director	5 years to 10 years	Shaping whole systems	Redefining goals and objectives by creating plans and allocating resources; improvement occurs by increasing one system's responsiveness to opportunity and to threat
VI	Corporate group	Executive vice-president	10 years to 20 years	Reflective articulation whole systems and the world	Creating long-term strategies for direction that can better guide relations between systems and their environments; improvement occurs when whole systems become less vulnerable
VII	Corporation	Chief executive officer	20 years to 50 years	Linear extrapolation whole systems	Anticipating the need for initiating, extending, or eliminating systems; improvement occurs as human resources are developed more effectively to direct long-term initiatives
VIII	Super-corporation		50 years to 100 years	Alternative systems whole society	Conceiving of new social orders; improvement occurs as the quality of life in the society is enhanced

Figure 4.2 *Organizational strata and the CVA framework*

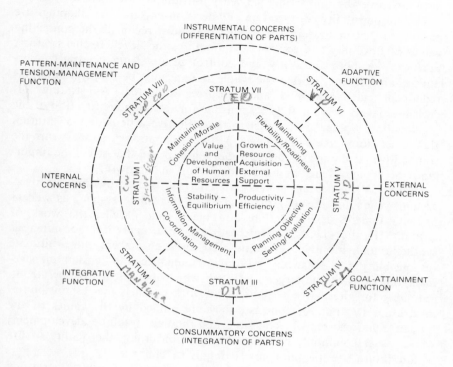

understood better when juxtaposed with the CVA framework. As shown in Figure 4.2, the dominant values that receive expression in each stratum are linked directly to alternative models of organizational analysis described by Quinn and Rohrbaugh (1983).

Stratum I decision-makers, while focused on the day-to-day demands of their work within the organization, must reconcile their own job satisfaction with the task specifications that explicitly direct their employment; their self-interest as employees spans the human relations and internal processes models. Stratum II decision-makers, called upon to perform the integrative function for an organization, have the primary responsibility for basic co-ordination as first-line supervisors. For this reason, they are guided essentially by the values of the internal process model alone: maintaining control over the short-term, internal operations of the system.

Stratum III decision-makers take on responsibility for anticipating and preparing for predictable events external to operations that may attenuate the unit's performance; their interests span the internal processes and rational goal models. Stratum IV decision-makers are charged with the goal attainment function of the organization. As general management, these individuals most embody the values of the rational goal model alone: planning and implementing work programmes that are expected to most improve the mid-term (2–5-year) profitability of their divisions.

The responsibility of stratum V decision-makers for shaping are parallel to that in stratum I, although they must reconcile the competing values of flexibility and control at a more abstract level. In this stratum, the need for both flexibility and control results from external opportunities and threats, so that the whole system must be shaped: situations redefined, rules generated and resources allocated. At stratum VI, decision-makers become fully responsible for the adaptive function of the organization. Somewhat parallel to the reflective articulation of stratum II, the decision-makers must develop 10–20 year strategies that assure the competitive advantage of their corporate group and that stress the importance of open systems' resource acquisition and growth.

Stratum VII decision-makers are charged with providing an overarching vision for the long-range good of the whole system, as well as its environment. Extrapolations are made that parallel the work of stratum III, but here the forecasting is not analytical so much as synthetic and intuitive. Stratum VIII decision-makers have ultimate responsibility for enhancing pattern maintenance and tension management functions of the larger society in which many systems operate. In searching for alternative systems, their work parallels the responsibilities in stratum IV, but, in contrast, they are guided by the values of the human relations model (cohesion and human resource development) where issues commonly come to the fore concerning the quality of life within future societies and how it might be enhanced.

Of course, the specification of client setting offered by stratified systems theory is only one of many conceptual schemes available that improve our understanding of differentiated organizational requirements. Nevertheless in conjunction with the CVA framework it is suggestive of more advantageous (and more disadvantageous) matches between client setting and both consultant's style and method (i.e. respectively, both the *approach in* decision management and the *approach to* decision management, to borrow Cropper's terms).

The Relationship between Styles and Methods of Consultancy

In addition to the observed diversity of styles and of methods, it is important to emphasize that single methods of consultancy practice (i.e. alternative approaches to decision management) can vary almost as greatly within types and across types. Unlike off-the-shelf product lines for which strict manufacturing specifications apply, the use of decision support techniques is far from standardized. For example, decision conferences have been conducted for three or three-score participants by one, two, or more decision analysts in a consultancy team who may construct a resource allocation model, a multi-attribute utility model, or both during a one-day, two-day, or three-day meeting.

Often, the selection of a type of method is prescribed substantially by a specific and explicit commitment to values by which the consultant chooses to structure what 'data' will emerge (and in what form) from a group. A significant part of the variation in a particular type of method also may be associated with the consultant's style (i.e. alternative approaches in decision management); the two are integrally intertwined. How large should the client team be? How large should the consultant team be? What model(s) should be used? What length of meeting is appropriate? The answers to these and many other questions depend not only on the values embedded in the consultant's approach *in* decision management, but also on the values embedded in the consultant's approach *to* decision management. No approach *to* decision management is entirely free of the approach *in* decision management. (Cropper, chapter 3).

Consistent with the CVA framework, a consultant's method will reflect predominant concerns for certain effectiveness criteria. The method may stress differentiation (with more divergent thinking) or it may stress integration (with more convergent thinking). The method may be designed to increase individual cohesiveness (inviting participation), or to decrease organizational inefficiency (limiting participation). The method may emphasize the need for process centralization and control (with a fixed agenda of carefully preplanned activities), or decentralization and flexibility (with an open agenda that responds dynamically to changing concerns). Why do some consultants fault certain methods for being too ambiguous in approach, too unspecified? Why do other consultants fault certain methods for being too mechanical in approach, too automated? The answer lies in the competing domains of effectiveness differentially valued in the style of their consultancy practices, that is, their differing approaches in decision management.

The Match between Client and Consultant's Style and Method

The appropriateness of the match between the client setting and the consultant's style and method can be understood, at least in part, with reference to the CVA framework. The values of the consultant, reflected in the approach in decision management and the approach to decision management, must be consistent with predominant concerns of the organizational stratum involved. Stratum V and VI clients will not be well served by consultancy practice that views better co-ordination and information management as a primary solution principle. Similarly, stratum II and III clients would be expected to reject consultancy practice that emphasizes maintaining flexibility and continuing adaptations.

As an example, the consultant method and style of Eden will be taken to illustrate the usefulness of the CVA framework for this purpose. The explicit focus of SODA as a method is that the model is a 'facilitative

Figure 4.3   *Match between client and consultancy practice in the CVA framework*

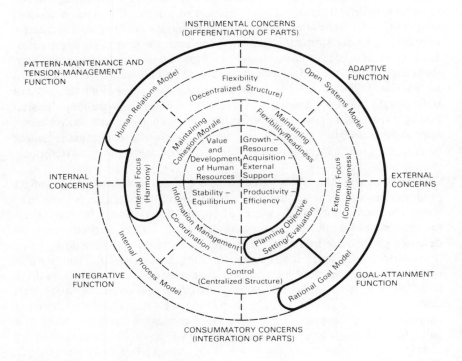

device' (Eden, 1989) designed to help a small team *negotiate* consensus and commitment to a strategy, where that strategy is a new way of construing the world. The goal system for a recent SODA project placed *maintaining cohesion and morale* as a significant subordinate goal to *maintaining flexibility and readiness* with a *competitiveness* focus. Some adaptation and change was anticipated. There was little explicit interest in co-ordination, stability, or control; the outcome expected was a 'system of actions' involving a substantial element of objective setting. The method clearly focused on goal attainment and the 'structuring' was cognitive mapping (rational goal model). What of consultant style? Eden has a background in operations research (OR), an early commitment to the rational goal model of organizational interventions. Nevertheless, his interdisciplinary academic setting has been close to the human relations model of the organizational development (OD) paradigm. Additionally, his commitment to strategy as a way of construing the world as a learning instrument rather than as a plan would suggest a developing interest in an open systems model. Figure 4.3 reflects these emphases in a more graphic manner.

The implication of this illustration is that Eden's particular consultancy practice is better suited to organizational clients at stratum IV and above, wherein goal attainment, adaptive pattern maintenance, and tension management functions predominate. Since cognitive mapping is intended to manage complexity rather than reduce it, clients must be willing and able to work with relatively large structural representations. Eden has noted that a characteristic of 'budding' clients is an inclination to see strategy in predominantly qualitative rather than quantitative terms, not characteristic of stratum II supervisors and stratum III department managers.

The previous chapters have acknowledged the need for more research into the nature of the match between interventions of one sort or another and the decision processes they are supposed to support. If this is to be done in a manner that will provide real insights then researcher/consultants must be clearer about how they approach an intervention. In this respect the conceptual frameworks provided by Cropper and by CVA applied to each consultant's way of working, an assessment of client group attributes, and the method may give a greater clarity to research questions and to practice (Argyris and Schon, 1974).

5

The Unfolding Nature of Group Decision Support — Two Dimensions of Skill

COLIN EDEN

It is a basic premise of supporting decision-making that the method will direct the user to a way of handling the complex content of an issue. That is, the business of the facilitator is to help in the intelligent analysis of data that describes a problem; the form of the analysis will be guided by the method. If we accept the argument Cropper makes (in chapter 4) for understanding analysis in the context of the style of the facilitator/ analyst then we can be assured that the form of the analysis will also be guided by the personal skills of the analyst. These personal skills will rarely be reflected in statements about the method itself.

However it has also been suggested by Churchill and by Friend (in chapters 1 and 2) that skills in the management of process are crucial to the success of group decisions. In addition Cropper discusses the importance of personal style to the effectiveness of a method, thus implying that the nature of the process orientation of the decision support consultant significantly influences outcomes.

These two propositions are in themselves relatively obvious. What is not obvious is the need to formulate method so that it adequately accounts for the *two skills acting in tandem*. Indeed within the professional world of the consultant the organizational development (OD) consultant specializes in using behavioural science expertise to help a group better manage its processes, and the management science/operational research (MS/OR) consultant specializes in offering to help a group analyze its problem from the standpoint of formal model building. It is rare for these two professionals to work together. There is little overlap of the literature – for example *Process Consultation* by Schein (1969) is rarely read or referred to by OR/MS people and operational research or even 'soft' systems literature rarely read by OD consultants. It is also rare for the behavioural science specialist to take on the skills of the formal model builder – they are usually 'frightened' by mathematics and computers. Operational researchers most often have a background as a mathematician, engineer, or physical scientist, and consequently regard behavioural science skills as 'common sense' or intuition, or at least something that cannot be learned formally.

Process Multiplied by Content?

In the field of group decision support it seems obvious to suppose that these skills must come together. Decision support to a *group* of persons depends upon an astute analysis of the nature of the group, the political dynamics within the group, and the interpersonal agendas that will influence the behaviour of members of the group. It also depends upon the model building skills of a management scientist. However, if experience suggests that it is unlikely that management scientists will take on organizational development skills and perspectives, or vice versa, then it is possible that future group decision support *systems* can be specifically designed to create a way of bringing these together. In other words group decision support system (GDSS) methodologies and technologies (such as those discussed in this book) provide an opportunity for designing methods which fully reflect theories of process management *and* content management.

The proposition may be illustrated symbolically. Consider the success of the *O*utcome of an intervention in group decision-making as represented by 'O', the extent of *P*rocess management skills represented by 'P', and the extent of *C*ontent analysis skills represented by 'C'. The combined effect of the two skills as practised currently may be shown as,

$$O = P + C$$

that is, they act in an additive manner. If OD consultants added to their skills those of management scientists, or vice versa, an increase in overall effectiveness might be expected.

Within the context of group decision support it may be suggested that the two skills can become integrally tied together so that they are fully interdependent. By so doing it is likely that their impact will be multiplicative:

$$O = P \times C$$

where the multiplier is the imposition of a *designed* intervention that explicitly accounts for process and content issues together. Process management is informed by the analysis of content, and the analysis of content is informed by the analysis of process issues, thus,

$$O = P \times C$$

In this text the two support systems that explicitly address the theory of process and content are 'Decision Conferencing' (Phillips, chapter 14) where Phillips trains facilitators in group processes which derive from the Tavistock Human Relations school; and SODA (Ackermann, chapter 13) which specifically argues that the method itself derives from a political perspective of organizations and an interpersonal perspective on the consultant–client relationship (Rosenhead, 1989).

By using 'P' to indicate process management it conveniently suggests the analysis of *p*olitics, *p*ower, and *p*ersonal agendas. However it should also include issues relating to work group sizes, inter/intra-organizational issues (Friend, chapter 2), timing, time management, design of the physical environment (Eden, chapter 15 and Hickling, chapter 17), and other so-called 'trivial' aspects of process management (see Huxham, chapter 16).

In this way the *multiplier* emphasizes the total *social* event intended to address the substantive *content* of the issue faced by a group. Thus rather than creating two separate streams of activity, one focused on team development and the other on backroom analysis, the multiplier suggests that *process and content are treated together*.

The implication of attempting to design a multiplicative effect between attention to process and to content is that the multiplier becomes the impact of a *designed* group decision support *system*. Such a system need not be too formalized or driven through the use of computers, indeed the term may be used following a 'common-or-garden' English-language interpretation of the four words acting together.

Group Decision Support with or without Computers?

Chapters 13 and 14 focus on the role of *computers* in providing decision support, indeed most of the literature on GDSS presumes that computers are an essential part of such support (Huber, 1984). The introductory chapter to Part IV on computer support, by Eden, will argue that there are good reasons why we are only just beginning to envision a scenario where computer-based DSS will have a significant impact on senior decision-makers.

A scenario which sees computers as the main focus for group decision support is a form of self-deception on the part of technocratically oriented decision supporters. It is relevant to ask why it is that non-computer-supported methods of the sort reported later in this book by Bennett, Huxham and Eden, and Bryant, as well as strategic assumption surfacing and testing (Mason and Mitroff, 1981) and the well established soft systems methodology (Checkland, 1981b) and strategic choice are so obviously successful. And concomitantly the computer orientation of SODA (Eden, 1989) and decision conferencing (Phillips, 1989a) are not outstandingly more successful. Is the computer-enhanced method a 'puff-ball' – full of promise, until pushed hard, when it explodes into a cloud of nothing? The purpose of this discussion, at this stage of the book, is to lead to a suggestion that a group decision support system should not be seen as dependent upon computer support.

'Group decision support' clearly need not be computer dependent – the phrase must imply any designed process or method that has specific characteristics that attend to the particular issues of providing support to a group rather than an individual. However the method must aim at *supporting* a decision situation that belongs to the *group*, a problem over which the group has some power to act rather than being of service to a group concerned to evaluate a situation as analysts rather than actors. Thus process-oriented methods such as nominal group technique (Delbecq et al., 1975) or 'metaplanning' provide GDS only if they are used to provide support to the *decision-making* group. However in contrast, methods such as strategic choice are specifically designed to provide GDS by using a *system* of concepts and tasks focused specifically on a *group* to *support* their *decision*-making.

It is within this definitional framework that progress can be made towards the *effective* role of computers and special purpose software in providing support to groups. The reason for suggesting a broader view for GDSS is that it provides important clues to the issues of developing computer-aided GDS. Later in this volume, Eden discusses the history of computer (support?) in organizations, a history which has undoubtedly influenced the expectations of both users and designers of decision support software.

The Future of Computers in GDSS

Most application software has tended to ape manual activities that are well established; for example word processors and payroll packages ape activities established decades, or even centuries, ago. Even so-called decision support software such as financial packages and spreadsheets are copies of well established manual activities. And yet there are powerful arguments to support a view that GDSS software should, on the one hand, computerize the subtleties of well established manual techniques. On the other hand GDSS software should be a result of conceiving of a creative and original use for computers.

The second view supposes that the use of computers to provide decision support to groups is a new opportunity rather than the development of decision support techniques that were intended for use in backroom analysis. GDSS software such as COPE (Eden and Ackermann, 1989) does not replicate any established way of recording or manipulating data, and consequently a lay user cannot expect to use the software without a prior knowledge of the conceptual framework and practicalities of the cognitive mapping techniques that underpin the role of the software for GDS. The same would be true for software being designed to replicate most of the strategic choice methodology. In both of these cases the method itself is highly contingent, as Cropper reported in chapter 3, and cyclical rather than well structured and sequential. Thus it becomes difficult to prescribe the use of replicative software other than by the possible use of an embedded expert system that can ape the decision support consultant. This is in contrast to decision-analytic based GDS software which is able to provide more of a menu-driven structure (e.g. Hiview, Fuzzy, SAMM).

In a more fundamental form Eden will later capture the key elements of this differentiation and imply that future GDSS software will reflect different attitudes to the sort of model likely to be of use to senior managers and, if Cropper is right, different ways of working of decision support consultants.

The work of Vari and Vescenyi (1984) affirms experiences that senior managers are more concerned to question key assumptions and tackle more fundamental aspects of the problems they face, rather than optimize within those assumptions – the strategic issue is not one of working with estimates of the probability of a rise in oil prices but of creatively inventing options to control oil prices. Put another way, group decision support to senior managers involves them not in predicting the future but in managing and controlling the future. Whereas the lower levels of an organization have the task of responding to forecasts of sales, the higher levels are concerned to manage and control the level of sales. *GDSS models must exhaust empiricism and place no bounds on rationality.* Doing this is the challenge of the next decade.

If such computer support is to place no bounds on rationality then it is probable that it must be unbounded by menus or an ordered structure; the user must be able to take the support in the direction of the rationality of the group. Thus the contingency model of consulting that Cropper discovered must perforce be more explicitly a part of GDS methodologies and software that is developed to support such method-ologies. This means the user of methodologies/software must know their capabilities intimately, and so *the 'drivers' of GDS events are always likely to be trained facilitators rather than lay members of the group.* The research reported by Cropper seems substantially to support the view that methodologies and therefore GDSS software are well connected with consultant style or ways of working. Interestingly, this constraint is counter to the objectives of many computer-supported GDSS projects under way or about to start in US universities.

PART II
CONSIDERATIONS IN PROVIDING DECISION-MAKING SUPPORT TO GROUPS

Introduction

COLIN EDEN

Chapters 6 to 8 will set out some of the key considerations for providing decision support to groups. They act as an introduction to the issues that are then addressed in Parts III and IV, on 'mixed methods' and computer-supported methods. In chapter 6 Mitchell et al. discuss the concerns that arose from their study of the use of one of the perspectives that influences many of the approaches discussed elsewhere in the book, that of metagame analysis. Many attempts have been made to refine the ideas that derive from metagame and hypergame analysis, and the developments reported by Bennett (chapter 10), Bryant (chapter 11), and Huxham and Eden (chapter 12) are intended to address the sorts of issues raised by Mitchell et al. in this section.

Chapter 6 raises some general issues about the problems of providing support to groups. A primary concern is with an evaluation of the nature of the client. Their experiences in the use of the 'metagame theory' decision support software, CONAN, lead them to argue that the willingness of decision-makers to understand and utilize decision support techniques depends in large part on their personal characteristics as expressed in management style and philosophy. They offer a typology of four different management styles which impact upon the likely success of group decision support. Their discussion strongly reinforces the views expressed in Part I of the book about the fundamental importance of the client personality and style combined with that of the consultant. It is also worth recalling that in Chapter 4 Rohrbaugh and Eden used the CVA framework to reflect on the style of the consultant within the context of method. While Mitchell et al.'s typology can provide the basis for an initial analysis of the probability of success, CVA might also be used for a second, more detailed exploration.

It is thus important to note that everything that follows this part of the book must be seen in the light of an understanding of the *client style and personality* as well as consultant style and organizational context.

The success of group decision support depends upon the ability of the consultant-facilitator to undertake the analysis which gives this understanding.

Mitchell et al. also point to the importance of simplicity, 'hand-holding', and a method that is not threatening. The first two of these are most likely to lead to the third. They also suggest (an observation which may be US dependent) that the rational actor model 'is rooted in Western business culture'. One implication of this appears to be that decision-makers have a need for 'closure' rather than 'milestones'. Mitchell et al. report that in their study 'completion of the decision process was equated with closure' and that there seemed little inclination to use the 'organizational memory' generated by the intervention as an on-going tool. The observation is interesting when considered in the light of Friend's experience that some groups do not incline to closure and want continuing opportunities to research the situation from the 'back-room'. This may be a contrast between private sector and public sector groups. For example, Eden has observed that public sector users of SODA seem to want to develop their decision support models whereas private sector move to closure and action.

In the second chapter of this part (chapter 7) Radford explores the analysis and resolution of decision situations using the metagame analysis of outcomes. His work addresses some of the issues that arise from the research of Mitchell et al. by its adoption of a less formalistic framework which involves clients in simulations of the unfolding dynamics of interaction rather than simply formal analysis. While these dynamics increase complexity, Radford argues for managing complexity through a more client-driven and 'hand-holding' environment, where the facilitator is guided by a conceptual framework rather than by a particular analytic technique. Thus Radford devotes the early part of his chapter to the literature that informs his framework. The literature extends the views expressed by Churchill in chapter 1, by exploring the nature of cyclic understanding of situations within incremental moves towards action.

Mayon-White (chapter 8) carries forward the debate about the role of the facilitator. The intellectual threads of the debate were found in Part I, where Churchill discusses in broad terms the potential role for facilitators to senior management groups, Cropper considers their role in relation to method, and Rohrbaugh and Eden identify the conceptual parameters of a number of different ways of handling the role. Mayon-White considers the practical issues that a facilitator faces when working with a team. He considers the relevance of the nature of the group for success (hints of Mitchell et al. taken into a group context), issues of the facilitator disengaging from the group and issues relating to the choice of technique. He also provides a historical and comparative view of the development of group decision support which builds from the predominantly content analysis approach to a more dynamic and process-oriented approach.

Thus, while Part I expressed views about the context for decision support in terms of organizations and groups, multi-organizational settings, decision support methods in relation to their consultants, and the relationship between process and content, Part II amplifies some of these views through the eyes of specific methodological stances. Mitchell et al. do so through the stance of metagame analysis, Radford through a broader view of the analysis of options, and Mayon-White through facilitating systems analysis from the stance of organizational development. We see an appraisal of the effectiveness of content-related decision support, originally provided to give power to the consultant, translated into a more user friendly support *to a group* (Mitchell et al.); to a more developmental view of analysis *by groups* of the outcomes and options open to interacting actors (Radford); through to an overt interest in a more process-oriented approach to working on content *with groups* (Mayon-White).

6

Observations of Complex Decision-Making Situations Utilizing Metagame Analysis

TED MITCHELL, CHARLES POWELL, WARD CHING
AND CHARLES BENJAMIN

Recent developments in computer-assisted decision support methods have created the opportunity to evaluate game-theoretically based decision-making approaches in several applied contexts. Employing a combination of the CONAN (Co-operation and Conflict Analysis) software (Howard, 1989) and manual techniques, it was possible to observe, record, and evaluate the reactions of business bargaining and negotiation participants to 'metagame analysis of outcomes' methods.

For the most part, the participants were male business decision-makers who were placed, either involuntarily or by choice, in situations where bargaining and negotiation was required to achieve a specific business objective. In most cases, the decision-makers had limited or no prior exposure to alternative decision management approaches. Most, if not all, of the observed decision-makers had received traditional business school training in decision-making, in which the dominant decision-making approach was the rational actor/value maximization variety, discussed at length in Ching et al. (1987).

Description of Management Styles and Philosophies

It is useful to keep in mind from the start that getting decision-makers to understand and utilize analytical techniques, especially new and developing ones, is in itself a problem in persuasion and negotiation. As such, the personal characteristics of decision-makers, especially as expressed in terms of management styles and philosophies, are at least as important as the instrumental relevance of the techniques to the decision process. A guide to the management styles and philosophies can be seen in Figure 6.1, which displays a rough typology generated by cross-tabulating two sets of distinctions, analytic–intuitive and reactive–proactive:

Figure 6.1 *Types of management style and philosophy*

	REACTIVE	PROACTIVE
ANALYTIC	Product life-cycle marketing strategies	Aggressive marketing strategies
	Sophisticated farm management	
INTUITIVE	Rule of thumb farm management	Entrepreneurs, hustlers, movers, shakers
	Small public agencies managing rapid change	Local government interested in economic growth
	Small retailers	

The four descriptive components include:

Analytic/Reactive Business decision-makers with quantitative finan-cial analytical skills who employ historical information to forecast future business conditions which may directly affect company performance. Examples of this type of decision-maker include those with advanced business degrees, usually MBAs, focused on financial management, accounting, production control, operations research or company valua-tion activities. These decision-makers will tend to make use of product life cycle or PIMS (profit impact of marketing strategies) methodologies. This type of management style is also characteristic of sophisticated farm managers who try to forecast weather and market conditions and to posi-tion themselves accordingly. While they may believe that they cannot do anything about these conditions, they can try to take advantage of them. This approach could cynically be called 'going bankrupt on a farm with a PC'.

Intuitive/Reactive Decision-makers who utilize more informal decision-making approaches and employ reiterative experiential approaches. Examples of this type of decision-maker are those who rely on business 'rules of thumb' and 'gut feeling' or instinct. They are usually operating in an environment in which the resources and training to engage in more sophisticated analysis do not exist. Such decision-makers perceive themselves as being too busy 'playing the game' to worry about overall strategy. This kind of decision-making style is typical of farmers who have smallholdings and rely on intuition. It is also characteristic of small public agencies trying to manage change; for example small cities experiencing rapid growth. These decision-makers perceive themselves as having power and believe that they can get people and events to react to them. They are just not very sophisticated about predicting what will happen.

Analytic/Proactive Business decision-makers who employ aggressive marketing strategies. They see themselves engaged in market warfare and as being capable of creating demand for their product. They also have considerable control over the supply of raw materials. They tend to think globally. They will often hire consultants to evaluate alternatives, pros and cons, and evaluate strategies.

Intuitive/Proactive Decision-makers who attempt to take advantage of perceived business opportunities and quickly commit sizeable amounts of capital and other business resources to explore and exploit possible market niches. The principal objective of the proactive business decision-maker is to move into an immature or emerging market, create a profitable presence, and establish a realistic opportunity to increase market share. Examples of this management style appear in the high technology, financial services and leading-edge consumer products markets where the entrepreneurial culture is allowed to exist. This type of decision-maker 'shoots from the hip', is myopic and thinks that because he enters the market, he will automatically succeed. This style is also characteristic of small governments trying to create and attract economic growth.

While the 'obvious' market for decision support products and training would be the 'analytic/proactive' type of decision-maker, this perception may no longer be valid. For one thing, the entry 'port' for expertise has typically been operations research and other technical staffs. Recently, these corporate staff functions have tended to be phased out or significantly scaled back as organizations shift operational emphasis to 'profit centre' structures. Additionally, the advent of distributive data processing has reduced the need for centralized computing and computer support staff. The immediate effects of these two developments are: (a) the decay of the traditional market for expertise support; and (b) the possibility of unmediated contact with the actual locus of decision-making, either directly or indirectly via software and data support. To come clothed in the garb of the 'high priesthood' of applied mathematics and operations research seems less likely to work as a marketing gimmick (assuming that it ever really did) in these changed circumstances.

This is not necessarily a bad thing. Contemporary game-theoretic approaches and their component analytical techniques generally depart to a varying but considerable degree from the classic value-maximizing models, and, it can be argued, represent a broad 'paradigm shift' away from *homo economicus* toward *homo psychologicus* (Simon, 1985; Powell et al., 1987). The sorts of method outlined in this book are partly the result of this shift. What was usually regarded negatively as 'reactive' and, especially, as 'intuitive' may well include complex elements of decision-making behaviour which more simplistic (linear, static, non-interactive models do not take into account.

To say that we must have a more adequate image of the decision-making process which specifically includes 'psychological' elements is not to say that this approach is 'softer' (as in 'soft' operations research) in some pejorative 'hold hands and hum' personal development sense. Neither does it mean that systematic motivational analysis of personality assessment is required to proceed analytically. Nor does the primary focus have to be diverted from the 'hard' choices and consequences in decision-making over to 'alternative currencies' (how to schmooze in various corporate or national/local cultures). It means rather that techniques are now being developed which go beyond crucifixion on a PERT chart and capture the non-linear, dynamic, and *interactive aspects* which characterize bargaining and negotiation. 'Intuitive' and 'reactive' management styles contain elements which are not just problems and obstacles in marketing analytical techniques, but which may also be instructive in the development of complex techniques.

The Metagame Analysis of Outcomes Approach

While most analytical procedures are initially intimidating, game theory has maintained (and probably fostered) a mythically formidable reputation in social science. The contemporary reality is considerably more user friendly (Benjamin and Powell, 1988).

In providing his strategic solution to the 2×2 formal game Prisoner's Dilemma, Howard (1971) argued for the use of a more analytically convenient notation than the game-tree or pay-off matrix which had traditionally been used to describe game theoretic situations. Even the use of the decision tree in 'departure game' analysis, (Brams and Wittman, 1981; Zagare, 1985) which has certain advantages, especially representationally, requires a great deal of the user. In contrast, the procedures derived from the Howard metagame analysis of outcomes approach require relatively less of the user.

Howard suggested that concrete choice alternatives be represented by 'yes–no' *options*, using a simple (1,0) set notation to indicate whether the option was taken (1) or not (0). In doing so, a particular set of 'yes–no' choices (a set of 1s and 0s; for instance: 00110) can be used to define a specific player's *strategy*. Taking all players' particular strategies together constitutes the definition of a *particular outcome* of the situation. Thus, two actors, one with a five-option strategy 00110, and the other with a three-option strategy 010, produce an outcome 00110010. There is a consequent brevity of notation, since n options, across all players, implies 2^n outcomes. Our two players have 8 options between them so 2^8, which means that 00110010 is one of 256 logically possible outcomes.

These outcomes are then analyzed to determine which logically possible outcomes are strategically stable given the decision-maker's definition of the situation (particularly the assessment of player preferences in pairwise comparison of outcomes). The set-theoretic analysis can be constructed and displayed in terms of a 'strategic map' of the situation, based on and driven by the decision-maker client in interaction with the analyst.

The metagame approach now utilizes microcomputer technology which allows for the identification of actor options, preferences, and strategic choice without cumbersome loss of information or frame of analytical reference common to manually recorded techniques (Fraser et al., 1985, 1987; Fraser and Hipel, 1984; Ching et al., 1987). This means that a decision-maker does not have to understand very much of the computational procedure.

Conceptually, this computationally enhanced game-theoretic approach captures the complex nature of strategic decision-making in bargaining and negotiation situations. It also takes into account the emerging descriptive cognitive psychological model of human beings (including expert decision-makers and analysts) as *limited information processors* (Dyson and Purkitt, 1986; Powell et al., 1987). This approach to modelling and structuring an interactive conflict situation should hypothetically constitute a significant cognitive aid in at least three significant ways:

The approach allows for situational simplification – since the real world can be more complex than any model could ever fully represent, the metagame analysis of outcomes modelling process facilitates simplification. Structuring a bargaining or negotiation event could help a decision-maker by forcing an identification of the pertinent aspects of the situation.

The approach forces the recognition and evaluation of the opponents' perspective – if the decision-maker is missing important information, the metagame model's requirement of completeness forces either the necessary situational assessment or the recognition that action must be taken without it. Decision-makers are likely to know their own options, and usually their own preferences for outcomes, but are less likely to consider either the options available to other players in the situation or other players' preferences. The analysis of outcomes technique should force the decision-maker to take into account the point of view of the other players, which is crucial from the standpoint of achieving better outcomes and stabilizing them in strategic interaction and bargaining.

The approach allows the analyst to deal with complex decision situations – bargaining and negotiation situations beyond the very simple and obvious are virtually impossible for any human being to think about in a comprehensive, simultaneous manner. Structuring a situation utilizing the analysis of outcomes technique should permit a decision-maker to be consistent and comprehensive, while still considering a situation in processible chunks.

Observations: Positive Responses

The observations of business decision-makers who were exposed in one form or another to metagame analysis of outcomes exhibited both positive and negative reactions to the techniques. The positive reactions included the following:

- Many decision-makers found it refreshing to think in terms of other 'players' rather than simply reacting to a 'conflict' environment.
- Decision-makers were explicitly able to develop alternative strategies and policies. The ability to do so was for the most part a function of the technique of 'slowing down' the bargaining and negotiation process. Decision-makers saw themselves as 'players' and looked for opportunities to 'evaluate their options'. Recognition of alternative strategies for themselves proved useful and constructive.
- Decision-makers were able to begin the process of thinking through outcomes as possible future scenarios. They were able to look at multiple strategies that they or the other players might use and see the consequences of their contemporary judgements and strategic employment of options. (The successful achievement of short-term objectives, however, remained critical to the process.)
- Decision-makers were able proactively to evaluate scenarios and outcomes at least on first best decision choices.
- Decision-makers came to realize that proactive and analytical decision-making required sufficient 'intelligence' about other players' preferences, levels of problem understanding, and resources that could be devoted to a protracted or limited bargaining activity and 'level of commitment'. Thus, decision-makers recognized the need for intelligence concerning the opponent's wants, goals, and threat/ promise capabilities in advance of the actual initiation of the bargaining or negotiation process.
- Decision-makers built upon their own and their organization's observations and 'experiential wisdom' (organizational memory, personal and professional histories, and opponent-directed expectations) to think about what factors would materially contribute to a co-operative, co-intended, and stable outcome. (It was difficult, however, for decision-makers with considerable experience to understand that co-operative solutions could be the first best of the *available* outcomes, and, as such, more feasible than first best zero-sum (we win, they lose) outcomes. Co-operative approaches were often treated as decisions of last resort.)
- The usefulness of the technique was enhanced when the decision-maker voluntarily identified with an alternative co-operative strategy.

Needless to say, this research indicates that the 'Hawthorne effect' is alive and well. If decision-makers are set down in a trusting setting and helped to think through their problems, they seem to make better decisions. Does it, however, matter very much *what* analytical technique is used? If it does *not*, and 'something good' happens regardless of what you did, then it would seem at least intellectually intriguing to discover *how* this works. Alternatively, if the technique *does* make an instrumental difference, how did this happen? In both cases, the key research question is the same: does a technique such as the analysis of outcomes help limited information processors process a greater variety and amount of relevant information, thereby achieving improved problem definition and decision-making effectiveness? (It would seem useful to work towards a common research agenda at least to the extent of concurrent and successive experimentation and field research bearing on this basic question.)

Negative Responses

As pointed out earlier in this chapter, alternative analytical decision-making approaches are usually resisted by first-time users. Successful employment of the metagame analysis of outcomes approach was more likely where decision-makers maintained a proactive/analytical decision-making philosophy. The following negative reactions were primarily from decision-makers who did not display proactive/analytic styles of management.

Non-analytical decision-makers in particular resisted or were unable to use the technique. The use of a more rigorous methodology often represented a personal 'threat' by exposing experiential or judgmental vulnerabilities to others. Bargaining and negotiation were also seen by some intuitive decision-makers as dramas of personalized confrontation requiring non-cooperative behaviour and a zero-sum decision-making approach. Indeed, sometimes intuitive decision-makers seemed to use amazingly low-grade approaches to decision-making, in effect employing what might uncharitably be termed 'lobotomized incrementalism'.

None the less, these negative reactions should not be dismissed *a priori*. They may be viewed as an extremely useful source of information about the limits of the technique in its present form. Both positive and negative reactions may also contain valuable insights about the nature of the decision process in bargaining and negotiation.

The amount of *time required to perform simple problem definition appeared overly long*. In many instances, decision-makers were uncertain as to what the bargaining 'problem' was or how to characterize the problem in a fashion so as to produce possible analysis of outcomes and cross-actor preference orderings.

The *decision-maker's definition of 'player' tended to be limited* to those people with whom the decision-maker ordinarily talked, negotiated, or bargained. Players who were not included in the decision-maker's set of 'communication points' tended to be lumped together as part of the general environment of the problem.

Many *decision-makers exhibited an inability to identify specific goals* and objectives associated with a negotiation or bargaining situation. Zero-sum perspectives were intuitively obvious, but co-operative solutions were not quickly identified.

Decision-maker identification and assessment of both their own and other players' options and preferences tended to be either constructed *post facto* to the completion or discovered in the midst of the bargaining process.

Decision-makers wanted specific solutions and certainty. The metagame analysis of outcomes approach reduced the opportunity to achieve specific solutions and policy/outcome certainty in the short term. The technique produced more questions and policy/outcome uncertainty.

Decision-makers wanted simplicity. Even analytical decision-makers have been conditioned by formal training to rely on forecasting models that generate simple, linear, single-point estimate answers. The technique often showed the situation to be more complex, not simpler, which did not fit their expectations of what an analytical technique should accomplish. Metagaming created what they felt to be an artificial and unnecessarily complex representation of the decision environment, even though they saw that this complexity was inherent in their own definition of the situation.

Decision-makers wanted to think in terms of a process that brings about a particular 'final' outcome. *Completion of the decision process was equated with 'closure'*, which is closely linked with 'certainty' or 'getting the problem behind us'. Analysis of outcomes forced the decision-makers to think in terms of outcome stability *after* an outcome had been achieved. The question of stability once the negotiated outcome had been achieved was extremely difficult for decision-makers to comprehend.

Because the start-up and the initial phases of the analysis of outcomes took a great deal of time and mental effort in information gathering and organization, practical considerations of time (also very likely problem avoidance and strong needs for closure) tended to preclude 'what if' or 'what's best, second best, third best' analysis. This was particularly the case with respect to assumptions and predictions about other players' options, preferences, and alternative strategies. Cutting off further exploration of the modelled definition of the problem situation meant an effective failure to utilize the major advantage of this *technique as a support facility for on-going negotiations*, or 'organizational memory' (Eden, 1989).

The successful use of the metagame analysis of outcomes was reduced when the decision process was in its advanced or 'terminal' stages or if the decision implementation process had been set in motion, even though, as indicated in the previous point, it should be quite useful in monitoring and supporting an on-going process. Again, the failure to see outcomes as on-going processes seems to be at the root of this problem.

Decision-makers exhibited considerable difficulty simultaneously linking the analysis of 'internal' games between players in their own organizations and 'external' games in which the organization is treated as a single player.

Where considerable *'hand holding' in a trusting environment* with the analyst was not possible, the analysis was severely limited or failed.

Decision-makers found the *interrogatory method of the metagame approach to be very threatening*, because they usually had not thought about the problem 'in that way'. Not having answers to specific questions produced perceived or real vulnerabilities which could affect future promotions, salary increases, or other business opportunities.

Comments: Non-trivial Issues and Solutions

As the observations listed in this previous section would indicate, there is significant value in continuing to use alternative decision-making methodologies such as metagame analysis of outcomes in business decision contexts. The technique allowed decision-makers to be more specific about what and with whom they were conducting negotiations. The technique sharpened problem definition activities. Co-operative solutions, not normally part of the businessman's negotiating vocabulary, were recognized as viable and stable outcomes. Outcome stability was becoming just as important as process completion.

While the negative observations need to be considered intensively, a preliminary review points out three important issues. First, because basic and applied research in the area of metagame analysis of outcomes is relatively new, no current consensus exists concerning methodological application. How one analyst uses the technique can vary significantly from the next (following Cropper's observations in chapter 3). In particular, within the author group, use of the technique varies to some degree depending on whether or not the CONAN program produced by Nigel Howard is employed. Thus, a partial, causal explanation for some of the negative observations could be attributed to 'pilot error'.

Second, each of the authors noticed varying degrees of cultural resistance to the approach by the decision-makers. It was clear that the prevailing rational actor/value maximization model had 'culturally conditioned' their response to new approaches. Dislodging or replacing the prevailing decision-making paradigm proved extremely difficult. *The depth to which the rational actor model is rooted in Western business culture is extraordinary.*

Finally, use of the CONAN program proved difficult at times. The decision-makers exhibited a reluctance to rely on new and test-stage computer technology. Their experience with 'systems that failed' limited its acceptance both as a valid decision aid and as a reliable analytical technique. Howard (1989) has since upgraded to CONAN 3.0 which is considerably more user friendly than earlier versions.

Attempts were made to develop ad hoc solutions to some aspects of these issues. It is difficult to say with certainty at this point that the following solutions directly contributed to improved decision-making on the part of the decision-makers, but it seems to us that these practical changes did smooth out some of the methodological rough edges of the analysis of outcomes approach. Perhaps this was more 'tinkering' than formal solution development. Only further observation and testing will tell.

The first solution dealt with the problem of building credibility and trust with the client. The introduction of alternative decision analytical techniques required considerable amounts of 'pre-work' activities by both consultants and clients. 'Pre-work' means activities conducted prior to the actual analysis of outcomes. These activities include client profiling, financial analysis, circulation of an 'expectations' questionnaire or client interviews with specific protocols. The purpose of the pre-work phase was to build trust and credibility in order to enable the decision-maker to engage in the analytical process more honestly and readily. These negotiations seemed to reduce or eliminate the 'we–they' syndrome. Pre-work became a way to learn how alternative decision-making methods would or could be accepted in a working environment which tends to be both point-specific and zero-sum.

In addition, because of the complexity of the problems being analyzed, *no single decision analytical support technique could be used as a 'stand-alone'*. In most instances, analysis of outcomes was masked by financial, operational, or strategic planning activities. These ancillary decision support activities assisted in keeping decision-makers engaged in and committed to the analysis of outcomes technique.

The second solution to many of the difficulties that decision-makers had with the analysis of outcomes approach was to have the 'line' decision-makers actively and intimately involved in the decision process as early as possible. This was achieved through role playing (adopting the positions of both sides of the negotiation), crisis simulation and intelligence evaluation (both of their own and their competitor's position – see Radford (1984) and Huxham and Eden, chapter 12 in this volume). We discovered that it was *not* important for the decision-makers to have a comprehensive appreciation of the technique they were employing, but *very* important for them to participate actively in the process. Too much information or pre-work dedicated to making the decision-makers sufficiently aware of the working of the analysis of outcomes technique proved counterproductive. By getting the decision-makers to become actively involved in the 'doing' of the analysis, it was possible to construct and achieve limited objectives. Achieving these preliminary objectives of problem definition and options identification generated a sense of accomplishment ('moving forward'), as well as the crucial commitment to decision strategies generated by them through personal involvement in the analytical process.

Conclusion

Nigel Howard's metagame analysis, and its computerized version called CONAN (Co-operation and Conflict Analysis), should constitute a significant cognitive aid to decision-makers in at least three ways: (1) situational simplification; (2) the recognition and evaluation of the opponent's perspective; and (3) processing complex decision situations.

The willingness of decision-makers to understand and utilize decision support techniques depends in large part upon their personal characteristics as expressed in management style and philosophy. The four styles identified earlier seem to be a useful framework: analytic/reactive, intuitive/reactive, analytic/proactive, and intuitive/proactive.

Analytic/proactive decision-makers responded positively to the CONAN method in several ways: recognition that they must think in terms of other players; development of alternative strategies and policies; thinking through outcomes as possible future scenarios; proactive evaluation of scenarios and outcomes; recognition of the need for intelligence concerning the opponent; and thinking in terms of co-operative, co-intended, and stable outcomes.

Reactive and intuitive decision-makers' negative reactions to the technique included: perception that problem definition took too long; difficulty defining players; difficulty identifying specific goals and objectives in the bargaining situation; timing of own and other players' options and preferences; desire for situational certainty and simplicity clashing with a technique that produced uncertainty and complexity; perceived time limits and desire for closure limiting the willingness to engage in open-ended analysis; difficulty linking internal and external games; and the fear that interrogatory methods might expose personal vulnerabilities in an organizational-cultural context of zero-sum competitiveness.

Thus, the acceptance of this type of computer-aided group decision support system will first require the development of a proper science protocol for its use and evaluation. A more difficult obstacle is the limiting conception of a non-interactive, myopic value-maximizing 'rationality'. Even proactive/analytic decision-makers may have 'rational'/technical expectations about the nature of 'proper' decision-making which hamstring their capacity to function in complex dynamic negotiations.

The success of a metagame analysis of outcomes approach (using CONAN) lies in its ability to recognize and process the complex structural elements of strategic interaction in bargaining and negotiation situations. These elements constitute an important (and valid) part of the resistance thrown up by intuitive and reactive decision-makers to the use of systematic planning and intelligence techniques. That such elements are captured in the analysis to the satisfaction of decision-makers is crucial in winning their commitment to these techniques.

Given negative experiences with systems that failed to meet

expectations, new computer-based techniques are inherently viewed with suspicion. These difficulties can be overcome with sufficient trust-inducing activities between consultant and client and the utilization of multiple analytic tools including role playing, simulation, and intelligence evaluation.

Most importantly, the client/decision-maker must have a *sense of ownership* of all phases of the analytical process, without necessarily having technical mastery of the technique itself.

7

The Analysis and Resolution of Decision Situations with Interacting Participants

JIM RADFORD

A number of authors have suggested approaches to the resolution of what we now call complex decision situations. Herbert A. Simon is generally credited with the introduction of a procedure described under the title of the 'principle of bounded rationality' (March and Simon, 1958; Simon, 1960). In describing this principle, Simon stated that managers often are not able to conduct an exhaustive search for solutions to a decision problem in the manner in which those seeking an objectively rational solution do. Instead, they use as much time and apply as much resources as they think appropriate in the search for a solution. They then choose a course of action from among those that seem to apply to the decision problem which is satisfactory or good enough in their opinion. Simon called this method of proceeding 'satisficing'. He recommended it instead of optimizing under conditions in which optimization is impossible due to circumstances such as incomplete information, multiple objectives, or lack of quantitative measures of benefits and costs.

Braybrooke and Lindblom have recommended a different, but complementary, procedure for dealing with ill-structured decisions, which they call 'disjointed incrementalism'. (Braybrooke and Lindblom, 1965; Lindblom, 1959, 1979). After reviewing the deficiencies of 'synoptic' or comprehensive analytical models in the context of the resolution of social problems, these authors suggested that analysis should be limited to consideration of alternative policies '. . . which are only incrementally different from the status quo'. A longer-term solution to a problem is approached by a series of steps rather than by one large change. As Lindblom (1979) put it, the process consists of 'a sequence of trials, error and revised trials'. Incrementalism may be seen as similar to 'piecemeal social engineering' as discussed by Popper (1945). Braybrooke and Lindblom did not recommend the procedure for all types of problem. They specifically recognized that certain fundamental decisions, such as a major policy change, should probably not be approached incrementally. However, they pointed out that incrementalism is not necessarily slow moving. In fact, a fast-moving sequence of small changes can on occasion accomplish a major alteration of the status quo more speedily than an occasional major policy change.

Etzioni (1967) sought to combine the characteristics of the rationalistic-comprehensive approach with those of incrementalism. He proposed a 'mixed-scanning' strategy which included study of a decision situation at two or more levels. One of these levels of study would be such as to cover all aspects of the situation, but not in great detail. The second level would zero in on areas revealed by the broader study to merit more in-depth examination. Etzioni stated that while mixed scanning might miss areas in which only a much more comprehensive approach would reveal a need for attention, it is less likely to miss obvious trouble spots in unfamiliar areas.

All of these approaches provide some insight into the manner in which a solution to a complex decision situation can be sought. They do not, however, provide a comprehensive approach to such decision problems nor do they deal explicitly with the salient characteristics of many of the most complex of decision situations; namely, the *existence of two or more participants with different preferences with regard to a final outcome.* This chapter outlines an approach to decision support when a client group naturally focuses on the interactions between several participants.

In his early work on decision-making, Simon (1960) proposed a simple three-stage model for the process consisting of intelligence (or data gathering), design, and choice. This model relates to situations in which a single participant carries out the three activities. It does not contain an activity especially related to interaction between two or more participants. A modification of the Simon model has therefore been proposed (Radford, 1978) which retains the three stages, but redefines them in terms of intelligence (as before), analysis, and interaction between participants (as illustrated in Figure 7.1).

The arrows returning back from the later stages to the earlier ones in Figure 7.1 are meant to indicate that the decision-making process consists of several cycles of the three-stage model over a period of time.

The second stage of the model consists of analysis in two broad categories:

1 *Strategic analysis*, which is concerned with possible final outcomes of the decision situation under study (or stable, interim outcomes of the situation) and with participants' preferences for them;
2 *Tactical analysis*, which is concerned with the choice of courses of action for a participant to use in one or more forthcoming inter-actions with other participants.

The distinction between strategic analysis of final outcomes and tactical analysis of more immediate courses of action is in some ways arbitrary

Figure 7.1 *Three phases of the resolution of a complex decision situation*

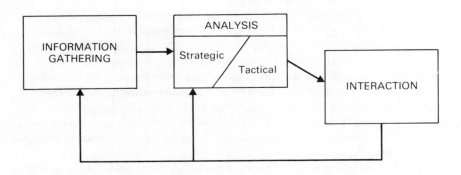

and it is one that is not necessarily universally observed. However, it is in many ways consistent with Etzioni's recommendation to engage in 'mixed scanning'.

The third stage of the model consists of interaction between two or more of the participants in the decision situation. The objective of each participant in this stage is to persuade or coerce the other participants to agree to the outcome that is most preferred by that participant, and at the same time to prevent being persuaded or coerced by other participants to proceed to an outcome that is less preferred by that participant.

The most important factor in the interaction stage is the relative power of the participants because it determines the ability of the participants to persuade each other to agree to an outcome. The most important activity in the interaction stage is communication, because it is by this activity that participants become aware of the views and possible actions of the other participants involved. Communication in this sense can be achieved by direct oral exchanges, by exchange of written material, by other actions designed to convey a message, or by a combination of all three methods.

The eventual outcome of the decision situation is one to which all participants agree, some possibly reluctantly. In some cases, a participant may agree to an outcome that is not initially his or her most preferred, in order to dispense with a time-consuming or costly argument and to proceed to other matters that are considered more important.

The outcomes of complex decision situations are similar to equilibria in game theory. They are solutions to a situation from which no participant can gain by moving as long as the other participants do not. However, the outcomes of such situations do not normally arise naturally as do pure strategy and mixed strategy equilibria in game theory. Instead, these outcomes are constructed as a result of interactions between the participants. The penalties and disadvantages that discourage participants from moving from an agreed outcome derive from those interactions. These penalties and disadvantages are usually contained and described in contracts and other agreements that result from the interactions. They guarantee the stability of the outcome, at least until the situation changes to the extent that one or more of the participants chooses to reopen negotiations with regard to a different solution of the decision situation.

The process of resolution described earlier may be swift or it may take months or years. Many complex decision situations in a variety of fields are resolved in the course of a few days and an intensive series of interactions between the participants. Others that are more intractable may take a year or more to resolve; for example, the numerous interactions surrounding the release of the US hostages in Iran (Radford, 1988). Others again, such as the Arab/Israeli conflict and the dispute in Northern Ireland have already lasted a very long time without final resolution.

The three phases of resolution illustrated in Figure 7.1 will now be described in detail.

Information Gathering

A first necessity for those involved in the resolution of a complex decision situation is to build up a base of information about the situation and about the environment in which it is situated. Managers in organizations can contribute substantially to this base from their own personal knowledge of the situation. Much of this knowledge can be brought into general circulation and organized into an information base by posing questions of the following nature to those involved in resolution of the decision situation:

- Who are the participants in the situation? What persons, organizations and other entities have the potential of becoming participants in the situation?
- What are the characteristics of actual and potential participants? What is the history of their participation in situations of this sort in the past? What are their likely actions in the situation at hand? What is their power to influence the outcome of this situation?
- What have been the past relationships between the participants? Might these relationships influence their actions in the situation at hand? Are the participants likely to form any coalitions in the context of the present decision situations?
- Are there any laws, policies, agreements, or precedents that may affect the actions of the participants in the situation at hand?
- Are there any economic, technological, geographic, or other factors that may place limitations on the actions of the participants in the situation?
- Are there any natural events such as weather, tides, or length of

daylight that may affect the environment in which the situation must be resolved?
– Are there any possible actions that might be taken by people or organizations in situations apparently unrelated to the one at hand that could affect the outcome of the present situation?

Gathering this information is greatly facilitated if the organization involved has an on-going strategic information system (Radford, 1978a). If not, the information gathered in this first phase of resolution of a complex decision situation can be a useful starting point for the establishment of such a system.

Strategic and Tactical Analysis

A major task in the analysis of a complex decision situation is a detailed consideration of possible future outcomes and of the participants' possible preferences for them. This detailed consideration is called *strategic analysis* because it deals with eventual final or interim outcomes of the decision situation. A simple model of a complex decision situation that is useful in strategic analysis is shown in Figure 7.2. In this figure the participants are shown in the box at the top. They are involved in the 'present situation' which surrounds an issue. The situation is shown unfolding down the page.

Each of the participants in this figure is engaged in estimating possible future final or stable interim outcomes of the decision situation. Four such outcomes are shown in the figure as being available at some time in the future as a possible resolution of the decision situation. The participants each have different initial preferences for the outcomes, as indicated in the table at the bottom of the figure. Since all the participants must agree on a final outcome, it is not possible in the situation shown for each participant to obtain the outcome that they most prefer initially. The final outcome must therefore be determined after some amount of interaction between the participants.

The model shown in Figure 7.2 is only a very simple representation of a decision situation. It does not take into account all of the complexities that are encountered in many such situations. Nevertheless, it is a starting point for consideration of the manner in which these situations can be resolved. It has proved in practice to be a framework within which managers can concentrate their thoughts and construct an initial exploration of a complex decision situation. In practice, we have found that even those who have had no prior exposure to the method can produce a first strategic analysis of a situation in some three to six hours' work. Such an analysis can then be modified continuously as the experience of those involved with the method increases. Such modification is usually concerned with the possible outcomes that may be envisaged by other participants and their preferences as the realization increases that all participants' perceptions are not exactly the same.

Figure 7.2 *Strategic analysis of a complex decision situation*

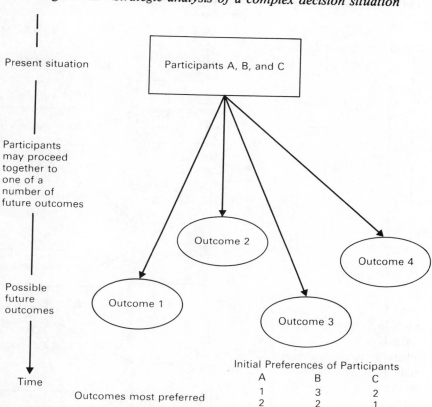

Having conducted some initial strategic analysis, each participant must concentrate on the choice of tactics for use in the first and subsequent interactions. Tactics must be chosen as methods of achieving progress towards the desired strategic outcome in the particular interaction for which they are designed. Tactics may be direct or indirect. For example, in some cases it may be judged desirable to make an open statement of intentions in order to persuade others of the virtues of a particular outcome. In other circumstances, it may be thought better to refrain from such statements and, instead, gather information on the intentions and attitudes of others. Whereas the strategic outcomes preferred by a participant may remain essentially unchanged over a number of interactions, tactics are specific to a particular encounter. Furthermore, the choice of tactics in one particular interaction depends upon the participants' perceptions of likely developments in future interactions. The choice of tactics to be used in any one interaction may therefore be

Figure 7.3   *Resolution of a complex decision situation as seen by one participant*

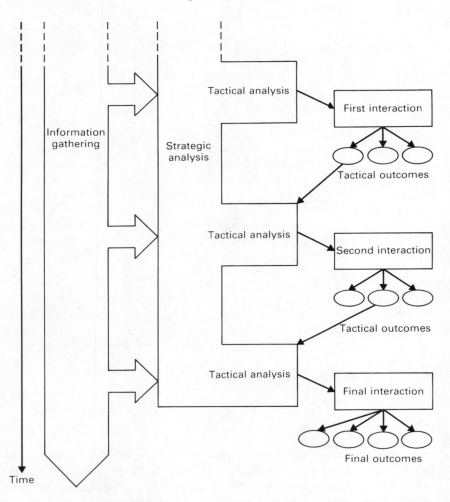

dependent upon a chain of such choices related to the later interactions. The problem involved in the choice of tactics is to ensure that the tactics used in a sequence of interactions leads to the outcome specified as most preferred in the strategic analysis.

With these considerations in mind, the model of the resolution of a complex decision situation from the point of view of one participant can be visualized as shown in Figure 7.3. Here both information gathering and strategic analysis are shown as on-going activities. A period of tactical analysis is indicated prior to each interaction. The purpose of this analysis is to assess tactics for the immediately ensuing interaction and to form a basis for choice of tactics for that interaction.

When searching for a methodology to be used in tactical analysis, a similarity emerges between the process of resolution of a complex decision situation, as illustrated in Figure 7.3 and play in the game of chess (Radford, 1981).

Development of this idea suggests that tactics to be used in each interaction should be evaluated in terms of:

1. *The immediate consequences of use of a tactic* in terms of such factors as:

   - the cost of implementing the tactic in dollars;
   - the degree to which future tactics might be impaired or enhanced;
   - the effect of the use of the tactic on the reputation of those involved;
   - the effect of the use of the tactic on future relationships with the other participants involved;
   - the possible cost of reversal of the tactic at some future time;
   - the possible effect of the use of the tactic on the time required to obtain an interim or final settlement of the issue involved.

2. *The effect of the use of the tactic in the longer term* in terms of:

   - the facilitating effect of the tactic in bringing about outcomes that are preferred by the participant using the tactic; and/or
   - the constraining effect with respect to outcomes that are not preferred by the participant using the tactic.

Choice of tactics is therefore a multi-attribute decision problem for which there is no readily available analytical procedure. However, experience shows that the human mind is able to deal with such problems with some degree of capability.

Interaction

This third step in the process of resolution is the part that all the work in the first two steps prepares for. Having done all of the information gathering and assessment possible in the time available and having used this information in strategic and tactical analysis, the manager should be well prepared for the interactions with the other participants. Despite this preparation, however, some unexpected developments may occur. Other participants may have unforeseen and different objectives than had been assumed. Their perceptions of conditions and events that are common knowledge may be different from those assumed. Whatever the case, the outcome of each interaction provides information and material that adds to the store of information available and to the appreciation of the situation.

Simulating Involvement in Complex Decision Situations

A useful technique for preparing managers for participation in the resolution of a complex decision situation consists of simulating the resolution prior to the actual process. The simulation procedure requires that those taking part in the resolution on behalf of a participant be brought together in a series of meetings prior to the event. In the first of these meetings, the representatives of the participant are divided into two, three or more teams, each of which is instructed to take the position for the purpose of the exercise of one of the participants in the situation under study. Each team is instructed to represent only the views of the participant assigned to it (as far as the team understands them). The team members are encouraged to embrace the position of the assigned participant and to take on the role, to the best of their abilities, of leading personalities related to the participant being represented. The teams are provided with previously prepared information packages in which such items as speeches by leading personalities concerned with the issue are included, along with such of the participants' real-life position papers and policies as are available. These information packages are made up from material that is available in the press, in news magazines and in the participants' own published documents. The teams are given a period of time to study the information package and to prepare their strategic and tactical analysis prior to an interaction with the other participants in the near future (Radford, 1984, 1990).

This interaction takes the form of a 'hearing' before an impartial chairperson or facilitator during which each participant (team) is given 10 or 15 minutes to express its position on the issue. These presentations are followed by a 15–30-minute free interchange, during which participants are free to question or challenge others, subject only to the direction of the chair. At the end of the first 'interaction', the chairperson adjoins the meeting and calls for a second interaction to take place after the teams have had the chance to reconsider their positions. Sometimes direct negotiations are allowed or encouraged between interactions. These negotiations often provide useful experience for the team members.

The simulation may be allowed to run into two or three interactions (or more) depending on the progress made on the issue. At the end of the last interaction, the teams are instructed to retire and to report later on the following topics: (1) how well did our team do in furthering our participant's cause? (2) how well did each of the other teams do? (3) what are the lessons from the exercise for our organization? and (4) what policies should our organization adopt in the light of the exercise? The team members then reconvene (now restored to their normal position in their organization) to discuss these questions.

The benefits of a simulation exercise are manifold. Actual participation in the process of considering and resolving an issue seems to heighten the interest of those involved. The learning process is facilitated by the interest in role-playing. The requirement to speak about a situation before an audience of one's peers provides a major incentive for learning about the issue involved and for preparation of arguments for and against positions that are generated in the simulation.

One of the most valuable aspects of a simulation is the rehearsal of interactions and negotiations that may occur in future. Managers who have been involved in a simulation often have a sense of being there before once the actual negotiations begin. The experience in a simulation often gives a unique advantage in that the possible positions and reactions of others have been studied in advance.

8

Problem-Solving in Small Groups: Team Members as Agents of Change

BILL MAYON-WHITE

Drawing upon experience in the use of an intervention method developed by Mayon-White (1986) this chapter discusses the role of a facilitator in a task force or study group engaged in group problem-solving. The facilitator is seen in relation to the client in the framework of trans-actional analysis. In addition the development of several approaches to problem-solving is discussed. Many of these methods attempt to blend the hard disciplines of systems engineering and operational research with soft approaches.

One such transferable framework is the systems intervention strategy (SIS). This is taught over a six-month (50-hour) part-time Open University management course in the UK and is designed to overcome the limitations of traditional approaches to problem-solving and change management. From the client's point of view, the attraction of this framework derives from its role as a common language and way of working for resolving problems which can be put into place across a whole organization.

It has proved extremely difficult to extract a clear description of the processes which take place inside any group engaged in change management. All the dynamics that one would predict from an understanding of the theories of group behaviour are present, but it is more difficult to pinpoint the ways in which a team uses particular techniques within the methodology. Figure 8.1 shows some of the processes used by a number of the authors in this book, and in practice they seem to be easy for change management teams to learn and to use.

The Facilitator's Role

One way of attempting to model the role of the facilitator as he/she works alongside a team of managers is to call on transactional analysis (Berne, 1964). The ideal form of communication between team and facilitator is 'adult–adult', in which any advice is sought, not offered and

Figure 8.1 *A 'family tree' of hard and soft approaches*

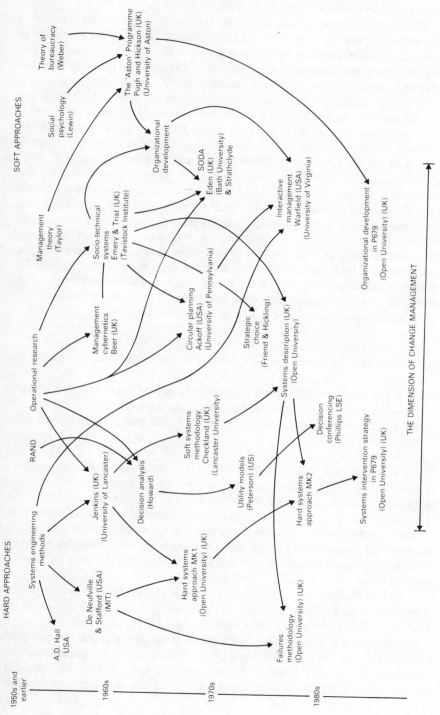

the facilitator increasingly becomes a 'sounding board' for ideas and a source of clarification, not a source of directives.

In the early stages of analyzing the setting of a change problem it is common for the facilitator to find him/herself in the 'parent' role of tutor as the methodology is first explained. However it is usual for this role to disappear once an initial iteration through the methodology has been completed. Some methods demand more initial explanation than others. For example soft systems methodology (Checkland, 1981a) uses special-purpose language which must be understood by the client group. Other methods are designed to be as transparent to the client as possible.

Much of the response is determined by the behaviour of the team of managers. With a self-confident team of middle-level managers (that is, section heads or equivalent) who are able to bring a range of skills and experience to the common task of solving an organizational change problem progress can be rapid and exciting. In such a setting, the facilitator quickly settles into the role of adviser and acts as a 'sounding board' for new ideas. In addition he or she may be able to contribute as a member of the team instead of restricting the role to that of impartial chair and facilitator. When members of the organization take on the role of facilitator, this transition is usually immediate and other team members seem to respect the dual role played by their colleague.

This discussion leads us to several new questions:

- Is an internal facilitator to be preferred?
- Should the facilitator be of senior status compared to the team members?
- Does the team need a senior executive to act as a patron and to give the team some protection within the organization?
- Should all members of the team be of equal status within the client organization?

The facilitator may play several roles: tutor, chairperson, controller, counsellor, recorder, initiator, summarizer, or rapporteur. An internal facilitator may be preferred if he or she (a) attracts respect from the team, and (b) is seen to be unbiased and fair to all views. If these two conditions can be met, the questions raised above can be resolved. Status becomes irrelevant for the facilitator, though from the viewpoint of other parts of the organization, it may be advantageous to be seen to have a senior person in control.

A skilled facilitator is also able to manage status differentials between group members and elicit effective contributions from the most reticent, while containing the more extroverted members of the team.

It is sometimes argued (but usually by consultants!) that an external facilitator brings an objective view to the organization and that he or she can avoid becoming enmeshed in arguments about content by focusing on process. It is also fairly common for organizations to use such consultants as scapegoats when things do not work out as planned, thus avoiding the need to allocate blame internally!

Against this must be set the knowledge of a firm and its workings which a good internal consultant has in addition to a knowledge of the personalities of the team members and of other personnel in the organization. It is this knowledge which must always give the good internal facilitator an edge over an outsider, providing that the skills needed can be made transferable.

A stronger argument in favour of the external consultant is that the demands of the 'process' of running a group or team are so high that it requires a long apprenticeship to understand and cope with the pressures that this generates. Running a meeting then demands the full attention of the facilitator or process consultant during a session, leaving little time for other forms of intervention or contribution to the debate. Some methods, notably decision conferencing (Phillips, 1989a) and SODA (Eden, 1989), use more than one facilitator in order to counter this problem. In these methods one facilitator concentrates on managing process and one on managing content analysis.

Despite the increasing tendency for organizations to use some kind of computer support for planning, simpler methods are sometimes the best way of helping an organization to plan and make decisions. Those methods which rely heavily on computer support have been defined by Huber (1984) as group decision support systems (GDSS). At the present time some facilitators argue that there are advantages in the client organization having a robust process that is known and understood by internal staff and is not clouded by the 'magic' of computer support, whereas other authors in this book argue that computers can help a group manage more complexity without recourse to 'backroom' work.

Encouraging Experiments

From the preceding discussion it is clear that a facilitator needs a formidable set of skills. She or he needs to understand and operate a methodology and also will need to be able to deal with new questions of procedure intuitively. For example:

- When to use particular techniques from within the methodology.
- When to abandon the framework and ad lib.
- When to use well known in-house methods which are familiar to team members.
- When to suppress discussion and move the debate in a new direction.
- When to break off the discussion and call for a pause and refreshments.

The courage to experiment with group processes is derived from self-confidence and experience rarely seen in the leaders of the 'occasional'

Table 8.1 *The key features and methods of the change management strategy*

The three phases of the strategy	The steps of the strategy	What kinds of actions are appropriate to each step?	What tools and techniques are available to help?
	Remember that iteration is helpful when using this strategy		
	0 Entry	Start by recognizing that change is a complex process.	Make use of the concepts of 'mess' and 'difficulty'.
	1 Description	Structure and understand the change in systems terms. Get other points of view on the change problem or opportunity.	Use diagrams. Set up special meetings (NGT, DELPHI, etc.). Create a model of things as they are.
Diagnosis	2 Identify objectives and constraints	Set up some objectives for the systems you are examining. Think of the objectives of the change itself.	Set up an 'objective tree'. Prioritize your objectives for change.
	3 Formulate measures for your objectives	Decide on ways of measuring if an objective is achieved.	Use '£s' or quantities where possible. Scaling or ranking methods elsewhere.
	4 Generate a range of options	Develop any ideas for change as full options. Look at a wide range of possibilities. Your objectives may suggest new options.	Brainstorming. Idea writing. Interviews and surveys. Comparisons with best practice in other organizations.
Design	5 Model options selectivity	Describe the most promising options in some detail. Ask of each option: What is involved? Who is involved? How will it work?	Diagrams are simple models. Cost-benefit analysis. Cash flow models. Computer simulations.

Table 8.1 *contd.*

The three phases of the strategy	The steps of the strategy	What kinds of actions are appropriate to each step?	What tools and techniques are available to help?
Implementation	6 Evaluate options against measures	Test the performance of your options against an agreed set of criteria.	Set up a simple matrix to compare the performance of your options. Score each option against the measures. Look for reliable options.
	7 Design implementation strategies	Select your preferred options and plan a way of putting the changes into place.	Check back to the 'problem owners'. Plan time and allocate tasks.
	8 Carry through the planned changes	Bring together people and resources. Manage the process. Monitor progress.	Sort out who is involved. Allocate responsibility. Review and modify plans if necessary. (Critical Path Analysis etc.).

task forces and committees which spring up in organizations in times of crisis and change. All too often, such work groups follow a sterile process of debate loosely based on the conventional committee protocol. Creativity is stifled and contributions are frequently assessed by the status or rank of the individual from whom they derive, and are not studied for their value to the organization and its problems. A simple framework which is easily learned could transform such groups and make them much more effective.

Table 8.1 is one guide which has been used to help the facilitator choose a technique for a given stage in the analysis. Its limitation is that it can become restrictive if it is simply used as an algorithm and not as a means of generating learning and understanding about a set of changes for an organization. The good process consultant will take cues for moving to another stage in the analysis from the group and not from a table of instructions.

The Consultant as Trainer and 'Parent' to the Group

An added dimension to the business of being a facilitator is the change of role demanded by the process of analysis. At an early stage in the diagnosis, a more directive instructional role (in transactional analysis the 'parent' role) may be permissible (Harris, 1973). Later in the design phase a more 'laid back' approach is needed to encourage creative thought. Finally, in the implementation phase, a new sense of leadership is needed as the project moves ahead with a programme of changes being put into place. For the facilitator this third phase of implementation may take place some time after the two previous activities. If an external consultant is being used, he or she may become detached from the project at this stage as the organization takes over and begins to drive the change forward. It is also fairly common for a project leader to emerge from amongst the group members as the earlier phases of analysis and planning proceed. The processes help to build commitment to the theme of a change and for some individuals this may lead to a decision to commit their careers to the management of a particular set of changes. Clearly the consultant has a crucial role in helping such individuals with these choices, and in training them in the methodology.

This may, in effect, amount to a change in facilitator and brings with it two new ideas. Those of the 'leaderless', but autonomous, group and the notion of rotating leadership as the initiative and responsibility for process is handed from one group member to another.

In all groups or teams all these things happen to some degree; the concern of those involved in designing methodologies should be to recognize this and to help teams to use it to its best advantage. Each member of a group brings a set of skills to the activity. Part of the facilitator's role is to recognize these skills and bring them to bear on the problems being reviewed.

Facilitating and Managing the Client

Throughout this discussion is the implicit assumption that there is a benefit for the project team to think of the parent organization as its client. Thus the team is in effect an internal group of advisers and problem-solvers, drawn from across the organization and not from a single specialist department. This has implications for the choice of project team, the choice of venue for the working sessions, and the frequency of meetings.

Members of a project team or task force are expected to be prepared to forgo their departmental loyalties in favour of a commitment to the 'best interests' of the organization. This is rarely easy to achieve since the role of task force member will be seen as a temporary one and the gains and losses of any change to a 'parent' department are readily assessed. Thus all too frequently the wrong individuals are put forward as task force members. Instead of putting forward individuals who are imaginative and open in their attitudes, individuals who can be trusted to defend a department's interests at all costs are offered instead. A good facilitator will use the patron inside the client organization to prevent this from happening.

The choice of venue and frequency of meetings will be affected by the urgency and importance of the task in hand. Ideally an off-site venue should be used to ensure that the group is free from distractions. It also helps to create a sense of identity amongst the members of a group. Comfortable surroundings, good lighting and ventilation, and ample wall space for charts and displays are essential (see chapters 15 and 17). Most company boardrooms tend to fall short on all of these requirements. Special environments for decision support work are now being created and even the simplest of these increases the effectiveness of group interaction.

Finding enough time for group work is difficult. Ideally two to five days are needed to work through complex problems effectively. These sessions may need to be repeated at fortnightly or monthly intervals over a period of up to six months. Persuading busy executives to keep their diaries clear is difficult. When the initial meetings are being set up, some direction from senior staff in the company may be needed. For example, the initial approach to individuals could be made by the patron, but after that the commitment and intrinsic challenge of the problems should be sufficient to maintain momentum. In many circumstances the group is self-selecting as individuals will already have an interest in the issues being considered; in such circumstances the more usual task is that of identifying any other interested parties which should be represented in the work group.

Letting Go

The external consultant faces one unique problem, that of letting go and accepting that the later stages of the project can be managed with a diminished or zero contribution from the facilitator. Indeed one criterion of success may be the ability of the organization to do without external help in the final stages of the implementation of changes. If this happens, the ideas of change and methodology have indeed been transferred. One of the earliest signs of this occurs when a task group reconvenes and the facilitator discovers that the debates have been progressed by informal meetings and discussions. This can be disconcerting to the consultant but shows that a commitment to the work has been achieved.

A Model of Change Methods

In the course of developing these ideas it has become clear that some kind of framework which encompassed several methods would help in understanding the relationship between the work of different practitioners and the context in which some of the well known so-called 'rational' approaches to managing change have developed.

One way is to look at the origins of methodologies and at the predecessors to the present generation of methods. A 'family tree' which attempts to do just this is offered in Figure 8.1. It shows how parallel developments appear to have taken place more or less simultaneously on both sides of the Atlantic and within different academic fields. There seems to be convergence between various systems engineering methods as they have progressively been 'softened' by practitioners who appear to have been working independently of one another.

The two poles of 'hard' and 'soft' approaches in Figure 8.1 are a scale in which the figure is set. The figure must be interpreted with some care. The links mean 'influenced the development of', which in some cases means: 'as a result of difficulties with "x", we came up with "y" as a more promising way of dealing with certain kinds of issue'.

But in most instances the reasoning is simple. Thus for example Warfield originally worked as a systems engineer at the University of Virginia and developed his approach as a means of dealing with the complex management issues which frequently emerged from the technical projects with which he was concerned.

In a similar manner Checkland (1981a), Eden et al. (1983) and Ackoff (1974) appear to have developed their respective approaches as a reaction to the shortcomings of systems engineering and OR methods. In the work of Ackoff it would seem that it was the limitations of operations research and statistics that spurred the development of his ideas, which now have wide application to the areas of corporate planning and management.

The right-hand side of the figure is deceptively simple, for in reality there are a very large number of practitioners of organizational development (OD) each following the tenets of slightly different schools of thought. For the purposes of illustration only those which relate directly to the ideas presented in the Open University course, 'Planning and Managing Change' (Open University, 1986), are shown. This course teaches both OD and systems methods to its management students.

The scale on the left-hand margin is approximate, but serves to illustrate the manner in which consultants, managers, and the academic community have been able to respond to the practical problems of managing change as they are presented in industry, in corporations, and in public sector bodies. Over this same time scale, we can also argue that social norms have changed, along with the nature of the technology employed by organizations in every aspect of their work. Both of these trends are generating new kinds of problem for the manager.

Organizational Development is shown in the figure, and increasingly OD seems to be dependent on the formation of teams within the workplace for the successful conduct of particular stages in the change process. This emphasis on participation is also present in SIS, and prompts the question: 'why so?'

The most appealing reply would be that it reveals some important theory about organizations. In fact the probable answer is less sanguine. It seems more likely that a change in social behaviour has changed the nature of the control process inside organizations and groups. Rigid organizational hierarchies are now less common, higher levels of education prevail, and in some cultures the traditions of trade unionism have led to management styles which employ negotiation and consensus, and avoid management by dictat. Together these ideas may add up to an important statement about communication and control in the 'evolution of the organization'.

Success in managing change is not achieved by chance, and a positive proactive approach is clearly important. Often this can be achieved by relying entirely on resources within a company or organization but sometimes outside help is needed. All the approaches in Figure 8.1 attempt to help those who use them to control their own destiny, and to know the boundary of the areas over which they do have control. With these approaches there seems to be a tendency to use consultants near either pole, whilst towards the centre some 'self-operating' or 'consultant-free' methods may be emerging.

Again this could merely reflect social and cultural norms. The 1960s and 1970s may have been a time in which organizations willingly followed the advice of 'experts'. The 1980s and 1990s may be the time of the internal change agent and of the 'do-it-yourself' OD practitioner. The background to some of these approaches is explored in articles by Pritchard (1986) and Rickards (1986). These tend to suggest that many organizations do have considerable skills available to them; the facilitator merely helps the organization to make good use of its human resources.

Hard versus Soft

The main argument behind many of the methods developed by authors in this book (including the systems intervention strategy method) is that both 'hard' and 'soft' methods have weaknesses which can be overcome by using methods that draw from both. For example, the basic structure of SIS reflects its origins in systems engineering. The delineation of three distinctive phases of work and the use of iteration to refine and test the output of each stage set it apart from the traditional formal methods for systems analysis. Superficially the early stages of description appear to match Checkland's rich picture construction. Both build models of the situation as perceived by the task force. However SIS makes explicit use of systems concepts in this stage whereas the rich picture explicitly avoids using the concept of system. This is an important distinction. Checkland claims that his soft approach avoids the assumption that systems exist 'out there' and await discovery by not using the terminology of 'system'. SIS uses the concept of system to impose a shared structure on the problem setting and so makes the initial analysis possible. Once the debate is under way this representation may be modified or discarded but remains as a common reference point. In SIS the use of diagramming enables the participants to build an agreed, shared model of problems, thus immediately creating a sense of shared ownership.

In its later stages SIS can make direct use of several well-known techniques such as brainstorming and objective setting. However, these techniques are used precisely because they are familiar and can thus be adopted and used efficiently by any task force.

Qualitative Methods

The importance of process cannot be overestimated. The idea of a change methodology as a learning system is captured by Churchman's concept (1971) of an 'inquiring system'. As the company evolves, organizational learning is taking place. Any team attempting to manage change will itself be learning about the organization, its environment and about the skills possessed by the team itself. Thus a team acquires confidence in its ideas and proposals, rather than verifiable proofs which state that their preferred course of action is the best.

For example, the SIS process makes extensive use of qualitative techniques to test agreement and to search for common ground. Nominal group technique (Delbecq et al., 1975) and its variants is always used together with a variety of voting procedures.

Wrap-round: phenomenology and positivism in the world of engineering and the social sciences

Another interpretation of Figure 8.1 is that the two extremes reflect a reductionist view of the world, with positivism and a mechanistic world view emerging in the 'hard' paradigm, and the social sciences attempting to use the methods of the natural sciences to explain their objects of study. If this deterministic world view is associated with the earlier methods shown at the poles, then those methods shown in the centre of the figure reflect the outlook of phenomenology, even though most of the practitioners would admit to being reconstructed positivists. The two ends of the continuum thus reflect the same outlook and the central area represents a contrasting paradigm. It may be helpful to think of the figure as representing the surface of a cylinder in an 'evolutionary space' in which ideas and paradigms spiral through time.

If we pursue this idea further it becomes clear that if we choose other slices through this space some of these will intersect the cylinder, others will touch, and other slices will not have any contact with the surface described. We can then imagine that those intersecting surfaces include artificial intelligence, expert systems, and other emerging fields such as software engineering.

Conclusions: Where Next?

Possible future developments of most methodologies in the 'soft *and* hard' categories may be (a) in the direction of computer-aided decision support; and (b) some simplification of the methodology so that it can be used by an individual manager to help with problem structuring in the course of day-to-day work.

The skills of the consultant are vital and more work is needed to understand how the processes of decision are helped by the facilitator. Some internal consultants are very successful, others fail when using well established frameworks and more investigations are needed to understand the mix of craft skills which are needed to ensure success for most work groups (Cropper, 1984, chapter 3).

The team members themselves are the main source of ideas in any change exercise. It is perhaps appropriate that the balance of thinking shifts from focusing on the consultant as the change agent to give the team members greater recognition for their role in the process of managing change.

PART III
MIXING METHODS

Introduction

COLIN EDEN

Each of the chapters that make up this next part report on experiences of mixing methods. In all cases there is an element of cognitive mapping mixed with some element of game analysis. Bennett (chapter 10) sets up his approach within the additional context of *uncertainty* as guided by strategic choice. Bryant (chapter 11) develops his own approach to mapping within the overall context of exploring the *perceptions of different actors* within a hypergame format. Huxham and Eden (chapter 12) demonstrate how game-like considerations can help in the identification of *competitor dynamics*.

Cropper (chapter 9) suggests, at the beginning of this part, that the 'mix approaches' attempt to be more flexible and contingent in approaching messy problems than each of the approaches that are the constituents of the 'mix'. However it is only Huxham and Eden that explicitly address issues of process design in the use of mixed approaches. Thus whereas Bennett and Bryant explicitly recognize that their intention is to facilitate the thinking of the client group rather than proffer solutions, they do not describe procedures but rather focus on formal analysis. Churchill argued earlier that decision support should aim to *make issues clearer* so that, in effect, the group could construct a new problem in which all could have an interest (Eden and Sims, 1979). It is the role of formal analysis to do this; attending to process issues alone will not do it. In the 'P × C' equation it is the coupling of both aspects that provides the pay-off.

The role of mixing methods must be contingently to move a group towards clarity of issue faster than would have otherwise been the case. But is this not simply saying that the different approaches to dealing with messy problems must be seen as a part of a 'tool box'? This has always been argued in the case of the more traditional mathematical techniques of operational research. Is it not the case that Bennett, Bryant, and Huxham and Eden are simply taking one step in the direction of demonstrating the argument for using a mix of different tools from the tool box? If so there is nothing special about doing so, indeed they might be taken to task for not expanding their tool kit well beyond two methods.

Bryant may make matters worse by labelling his mixture as if it were a new method. However while Bennett clearly identifies himself as being in the mixed method camp, he nevertheless probably sees his work as extending his own 'hypergame analysis' method. Similarly Huxham and Eden seem to have explored an extension to SODA. In other words, of the chapters presented, one builds off a hypergame perspective, the other off SODA, and the third is a possible bid for a new 'stand-alone' method. Given Cropper's earlier statements about the link between proponent and method these comments are probably not surprising.

What does seem important is that attempts to mix methods are undertaken with considerable caution. While the standard techniques of OR can be seen as tools in a tool box to be selected and mixed as appropriate, methods for dealing with groups working on messy problems are likely to be embedded in more complex theories, explicit or implicit, about organizations, groups, and consultancy practice. For example, SODA is described as being a *method* which derives from an explicit *theoretical framework* about organizations, groups, and problems, which informs a *conceptual framework* about the nature of the consultants' role. It is also seen as a method that uses and designs the *technique* of cognitive mapping, which in turn uses and designs the *tool* of COPE (computer software for group support). This relationship between theories, concepts, method, technique, and tool is apparent to a greater or lesser degree in game theory/hypergame analysis (Radford, chapter 7 in this book; Bennett, 1980), strategic choice (see Friend and Hickling, 1987), decision conferencing (see Phillips, 1989a), and Mayon-White's approach to systems analysis (see chapter 8 of this book).

The implication of this recognition is that when different methods reflect different 'theories-in-use', it is unlikely that they will sit happily together in practice. The decision to mix methods needs always to be informed by an awareness of their theoretical underpinnings. It is interesting to note that Checkland and Eden have both expressed concern that the method developed by the other is atheoretical! Checkland, not surprisingly for someone committed to the systems movement, expects to talk about grand theories about the nature of the world, whereas Eden uses and synthesizes relatively micro-theories about problem-solving by individuals, groups, and in organizations.

9

Variety, Formality, and Style: Choosing Amongst Decision-Support Methods

STEVE CROPPER

The aim of this chapter is to sketch out some current thinking on key dimensions of the choice and use of decision methods in practice. This is particularly important where consultants are tempted to mix and match among a repertoire of methods and their component techniques. The main theme of this chapter concerns the variety of method that is evident in this and previous parts of this book. The argument is essentially that we need to take stock of the tools that we, individually and as a community, use in the analysis of problems interactively with client groups.

To this end, a number of dimensions by which to explore methods and their use are suggested and related to the other chapters in this section. Within this theme of variety, then, are three subsidiary concerns. Firstly, does the purpose of a decision support episode – the nature of the problem or task being addressed – have major influence on which methods are used and how they are used? Secondly, when and how is it appropriate to make use of formal analytical methods in supporting group decision-making rather than to use such methods informally? Thirdly, and closely related to the second concern, what are the differences between enactment of situations compared with modelling such situations in decision support?

On the Variety of Methods and Mixes

Many of the chapters in this book include models which have some basis in the game-theoretic framework and each of them attempts to address the critique of such approaches set out by Mitchell et al. in Part II. Whilst there is agreement that game theory and the analytic methods derived from it are of use in addressing problems in organizations, there are considerable differences in the claims and conclusions about what precisely it is that they offer and how they should be brought to bear. The combination, in a variety of ways, of these game-based methods with other tools (notably cognitive mapping) serves to accentuate, but also to confuse, the differences. It is interesting, then, to reflect on why such variety should emerge. It is interesting also to attempt some clarification of the roles such methods can play in the analysis of complex decision situations with senior managers.

While the methods concerned have gained some exposure recently as new methods of analysis in management science (Rosenhead, 1989), the practice of the methods is as yet not widespread. As this practice has spread, it is clear that the methods have been adapted and used to tackle new types of problem. Further, methods have been mixed and a variety of procedures have resulted. This is healthy, but it means that it is difficult to keep track of developments, to evaluate applications and developments and to codify or appreciate where mixing methods is taking methodology.

What, then, are the important dimensions along which practice and method have varied and which frame the possibilities for future practice? Three aspects of decision support practice which act together to constrain the use of methods either singly or in combination are proposed. These are:

- the nature of the problem or task being addressed;
- the degree to which a formalism is employed; and
- the personal style of the consultant and the way in which the method is used with clients.

Nature of the Problem or Task being Addressed

In chapter 10, Bennett presents a clear contingency approach to the choice and use of methods based essentially on the analyst's understanding of the situation the clients are addressing – that is, the nature of the problem. There will be times when the match between problem and method is glaringly obvious. The problem may clearly be one of conflict, or it may be one of managing uncertainty through time. At other times, more usually perhaps, there will be no clearly dominant structure, but rather one or two themes which particular methods might help us explore more systematically. Thus, Bennett argues, it is helpful to be able to mesh methods as appropriate, using them sequentially or in parallel. But Huxham and Eden's chapter (chapter 12) reveals some difficulties in implementing such an approach. Exploration of these difficulties suggests why a simple contingency theory of choice of method is insufficient as a methodology for group decision support.

From a conflict perspective, one would expect the actions and stances of competitors (or partners) to be important considerations in the development and execution of business strategy: indeed, one would normatively insist that they should be so. It is clear, however, and

Huxham and Eden make the point, that many existing methods of strategy development miss the dynamics of competition, or, more precisely, of competitive interaction. These dynamics are precisely the concern of game theory and its derivatives, hypergame analysis, the analysis of options, and the strategy and tactics model (Bennett et al., 1989; Howard, 1987; Radford, 1986). Such models should, according to simple contingency theory, be helpful.

In discussing their experiences with game-based methods to complement and bolster the SODA approach to strategic management, Huxham and Eden describe a series of difficulties in bringing the methods to bear. Their observations about the nature of strategic management suggest that 'competition' is relatively intangible, something which, whilst a clear concern, is difficult to pin down in a form amenable to formal analysis. The task of the analyst, Huxham and Eden suggest, is to assist the process of defining strategic thrusts, to define the issues, to choose the arena in which to play and thereby to be able to anticipate the competition to be faced – in short to choose a 'seat' in one of many possible games. It is difficult to conceptualize and represent this complexity in game-theoretic terms. The situation they describe is some way from interactions in which competition is direct and intense, or well defined. Here, the game and the issues are set, perhaps even thrust upon the client; the competition is known. What is required is a strategy of response – there is the pressure to (re)act described by Churchill in chapter 1 of this book.

There is thus a difference in the purpose of analysis from the start. The difference might be summarized as follows: for Huxham and Eden and the type of situation in which they were concerned to intervene, competitor analysis might form the primary process of strategic management: for the better-defined type of situation, the use of game-based methods to provide strategic analysis (in the sense coined by Schelling, 1960) might inform the management of competition. It would seem helpful, at minimum, then to refine the categories used to describe the situations which a consultant might encounter and which would influence the choices of method(s) the consultant might consider. The dimension highlighted here is that of the primary management activity which analytic help is to support.

A Spectrum of Ways of Using Formal Game-Based Methods

There has been a failure to distinguish *ways of using* a method that has allowed the differences between the uses of methods suggested by other authors to go unmasked and unexplored.

It will be helpful to pursue a line of enquiry, started earlier, by sketching some points along a spectrum. The spectrum points up some ways in which conflict-analytic methods can be brought to bear by consultants;

in particular, it relates to the question, 'Just how formal to go?'.

At the least formal end – closest to substantive theories of decision-making – we find that game theory and its derivatives offer a poorly articulated theory of the world. Nevertheless, some assumptions are embedded in the theory and these are increasingly being surfaced (e.g. Bennett et al., 1989). Here the idea or label of 'the game' enters problem-solving activity as an analogy (Bardach, 1977; Long, 1958) or *generative metaphor* (Schon, 1979) – a way of looking at the world or 'seeing as' which can prove illuminating. The idea of a 'game' suggests players with whom one is competing or co-operating, the options faced at particular points, the importance of considering the effects of choices made by different players on one another's welfare, and so forth.

The second point on the spectrum sees conflict-analytic methods as providing the consultant with *a conceptual framework*. A sensitizing framework comprising formal concepts bound together more systematic-ally than in the game analogy specifies which features of situations are of relevance and what, therefore, to abstract from the complexity. Game-theoretic frameworks suggest such features as actions, options, outcomes, preferences and so forth. Similarly, strategic choice sensitizes the consul-tant to features including areas of choice, options, uncertainties, and criteria or comparison areas. But the situations may not be modelled explicitly in these terms – they are conceptual rather than representa-tional tools. It is at this point, Huxham and Eden argue, that the most appropriate use of conflict-analytic methods can be made. Bryant's hypermaps may also be located here.

Point three on the spectrum can be labelled quite conventionally as *problem structuring*. Here, the conceptual framework is supported and given form by models. These are used to represent problems abstracted from the mess and to assist in the process of abstraction. With the intro-duction of models, the methodology of use starts, at this point, to become a distinctive feature. Different models will highlight different aspects of a problem and its context. Choice of technique or 'tool' thus becomes a critical factor in working on the problem with clients.

A fourth point which it is helpful to distinguish can be labelled *preparation for analysis*. This corresponds to stages 1–3 identified by Mitchell et al. (chapter 6). It is often included under the label of formal analysis, but it consists of a distinct, prior step in which models are *systematically* 'filled in' with information which they define as relevant and which they require, minimally, in order to 'work'. An example would be the systematic development and combination of options to form a decision tree or a game matrix together with the specification of probabilities or preferences respectively needed to give the model analytic potential. It is possible to use the models semi-formally, then; to examine the dynamics around a game matrix and possible bargaining strategies, for example. It is interesting to note that Radford (1984) in a similar procedure, found that the most useful part of the whole exercise is often the preparation of the preference table forming part of the analysis of options method. Huxham and Eden, however, report difficulties at this point due to the mix of methods of representation and enquiry. This is unlikely to be purely a problem of technique, however, as is suggested in the following section of this chapter.

Fifthly and finally, we can pick out formal analysis as a significant point on the spectrum of uses of formal conflict-analytic methods. This corresponds to steps 4–6 as defined by Mitchell et al. and implies, in the game-theoretic derivatives for example, bringing to bear such formal concepts as dominance, improvements, sanctions, and stability.

Huxham and Eden's message is clear, and shared to some extent, by Radford; a denial of a strong role for the formal, analytical side of the game-theoretic approaches in strategic management. Such approaches, they argue, can and should provide only a backdrop or loose, guiding framework to the more detailed and creative work on problems that can be achieved using cognitive maps and allied models. They are primarily *conceptual aids to a social process*. By contrast, the approach reported by Bennett will, where appropriate to the problem situation, involve the full use of the formal apparatus of game-theoretic models either as stand-alone models or in conjunction with other methods of representation. Indeed, the work reported by Bennett has led to links between methods which are not just at the conceptual level but also at the level of the modelling technology – most notably in the 'arenas' model.

Enactment versus Representation as Ways of Working with Methods

The degree of formality with which methods are used by the consultant is, then, a clear distinguishing factor between the mixes of methods reported in Part III. Another important factor is the manner in which clients are exposed to and interact with the methods used by the consultant. For Huxham and Eden, and for Radford, work with client groups is extensively through *enactment*: game-based modelling media, at least, are kept at a distance for use by the analyst alone. Enactment makes use only of the broad sensitizing concepts to structure the game and the enquiry – the formal models are little used, if at all. For Bennett (and in the work reported by Mitchell et al.), by contrast, enquiry with clients into a problem they are facing is conducted through a process in which questioning and analysis are mediated or carried out through *explicit representations* or models of problems, whether game matrices, options analysis tableaux, strategic choice decision graphs or cognitive maps. This may be more or less softened by the use of the most transparent model types with clients, as Bennett tends to argue, but nevertheless models are centre-focus in problem-solving activity. Recourse to arguments about the relative effectiveness of the different manners of use are unlikely to be conclusive especially if the different purposes to which they are put are not acknowledged at the outset. But there may be more important factors at play.

Conclusion

The mix of cognitive maps and hypergame analysis has attracted practitioners of each of these methods, even if the contrast between the actual syntheses in the following chapters is strong. Mixing the two approaches can lead to a dilemma. Hypergame analysis tends to encourage abstraction of one aspect – conflict – from a mess and its treatment apart from the client group. The approach has the advantage of allowing analysts to focus on issues that hypergame analysis proponents believe important without constant buffeting by the variety of concerns of the clients. The essence of the approach is to hold these concerns constant. This contrasts starkly with Huxham and Eden's beliefs about their clients' needs and with their own aspirations to assisting the strategic management process. Game-theoretic concepts thus serve only as a backdrop to the gaming activity and experience. Models, they claim, cannot provide an effective means to manage a learning process. Bennett argues equally forcefully that modelling is a powerful vehicle for learning rather than just serving an analytical role.

Rather than explaining this contradiction purely as a function of the different type of problem situations that each author is addressing and proceeding thereby to make normative statements about the appropriateness of methods in the abstract, it is also helpful to look to the style of the consultant as a way in. Style thus corresponds to the craft skills that a consultant builds over time and experiences – the personal method-in-use (see chapter 3 of this volume). This, it is proposed, relates closely to three layers of competence which accumulate one on the others – repertoire, mastery, and performance. At its most constraining level, that of performance, competence is indicated by the ability of a consultant to fit a method into a personal way of working with clients that is nevertheless responsive to the particular situation of which the clients are a part. One significant concern is the possibility that mixing methods, at least *naive* eclecticism, may hold hidden costs or dangers. While the view that the methods are primarily tools, and therefore readily adaptable to different purposes and styles, is plausible, we should nevertheless bear in mind that these tools are based on quite different theoretical foundations. Ultimately, they may not mesh as we would wish. To use concepts, models, and techniques without their framework or to use concepts for their commonsense, face-value meaning, may cause loss of the significance and power that they derive from their place in a coherent and system-like approach to decision-aiding. Care in the choice, mixing, and use of methods, then, is critical. And that will depend on the level of commitment to the conceptual and technical languages associated with methods. So it is not just a matter of appropriateness of fit to a situation, but also of fit of method to method and ultimately to the personal style of working of a consultant that establishes the tools that we have.

10

Mixing Methods: Combining Conflict Analysis, SODA, and Strategic Choice

PETER BENNETT

The various contributions to this book all reflect a common concern to develop ways of helping with problems variously described as 'wicked' or 'complex', or as 'messes'. While specific definitions differ, there are several intertwined themes. Situations of concern are those in which subjective factors play a vital role, where quantification may be difficult or inappropriate, and where conditions of conflict and/or uncertainty prevail. Each decision problem will have its own peculiar difficulties. There may be no 'solution' in a strictly logical sense – perhaps not in the sense of a generally acceptable plan of action. Such problems are not only intellectually difficult: they also often fall outside the normal patterns of organizational responsibility, and so call for novel ways of working.

Given this commonality of interest, the question arises of how and when different approaches might usefully be combined. This chapter specifically reports some efforts to combine ideas taken from three: *'conflict analysis'* – a term used here to cover a set of modelling methods derived from game theory, including analysis of options and hypergame analysis – *cognitive mapping*, as incorporated within the SODA methodology, and elements of *strategic choice*. The last two are described elsewhere in this volume, and introductions to all three can be found in Rosenhead (1989). This chapter is written in three parts. The first sets out a general rationale for trying to link the approaches. The second part introduces one possible form of linkage that shows some promise in practice. This uses a combination of approaches, especially in starting off the process of working with clients. The third section outlines and compares two contrasting applications.

A Rationale for Linkage: Similarities and Differences

One natural enough question to start with is why one should think of combining these three particular sets of ideas. Why not others – as well or instead? Although an element of happenstance cannot be denied, at least a partial rationale can be given within a more general discussion of linkage.

The intellectual case for linkage derives from considering both similarities and differences across the approaches. Let us first consider the common ground. The most fundamental point is that all are designed *to help small, relatively autonomous groups of people to make non-routine choices*. This has consequences both for the sorts of client one might seek to help, and for the sorts of help on offer. A first presumption of these 'decision-based' approaches is that clients are able to take – or at least influence – actions they see as significant. Rather than just carrying out instructions or routine tasks, clients have choices available and some degree of autonomy in making them – though cases where others also have some power are of interest.

A second similarity is that all the methods are designed primarily for a style of working in which consultants work *with* clients, rather than producing analysis *for* them. Consequently, the stress is on working with small, informal groups, within which debate and discussion can be encouraged. Not all potential clients are amenable to this – though sometimes a feeling that 'all else has failed' can lower resistance to trying something new. In general, the most likely customers are those with the freedom to bypass or adapt normal bureaucratic procedures. These tend to be found either at the very top of organizational hierarchies, with responsibility for strategic management, or in positions affording a good deal of local autonomy, especially where responsibilities cut across established bureaucratic boundaries. Informal methods are also particularly suited to clients acting outside any large, well-established organization – individuals or small groups trying to manage their own choices and responsibilities more effectively. These are the intended customers for 'community OR' – Rosenhead (1986) has already pointed to parallels between community OR and work done with very senior managers.

Though this constitutes an important common ground, it would be a grave mistake to suppose that conflict analysis, strategic choice and SODA are really just 'all the same, expressed in different ways'. Admittedly, some formal parallels can be established between analysis of interconnected decision areas – AIDA – and analysis of options (Fraser and Hipel, 1986). But the equivalence is very limited and, much more importantly, the approaches are not just collections of formal models and techniques. Each has its own distinctive theoretical rationale (for example, SODA is primarily based on ideas about decision-making as a social process, conflict analysis on problem-solving as an intellectual process). Within each, there have developed distinctive ways of working with clients – ways that are often personalized by different practitioners of the 'same' approach.

By asking what sorts of 'help' the approaches offer, one uncovers a patchwork of similarities and differences. Taking four general forms of help relevant to 'soft OR' (Bennett and Cropper, 1986), it can be seen that in practice, mapping, conflict analysis and strategic choice all commonly contribute to each, but in different ways and to different extents.

To summarize briefly here, the first form of assistance is to help clients articulate and think through their problems, surfacing both the consequences of shared assumptions and sources of disagreement. In this, the consultant acts as 'process manager', helping along discussion, debate, and decision. He or she may take some responsibility for the 'mechanics' of the decision process, especially for time management within meetings (Friend, chapter 2 of this volume). But the emphasis is not on contributing to the content of discussion. This has long been recognized as a major role for practitioners of both mapping and strategic choice, but has been a very secondary consideration in conflict analysis.

The second form of help is that of setting problems in a structured format. The consultant comes armed with ways of conceptualizing particular sorts of problem, to provide a structure for discussion and decision. Such models also draw attention to specific aspects of problems – most obviously, when using the more 'directive' structures of strategic choice and conflict analysis. Using the former will automatically bring up questions about quite specific types of uncertainty, while conflict models 'force' attention on other actors, their aims and possible actions. At least to start with, mapping tends to reflect whichever issues the clients see as most central. But as work proceeds, the 'structuring' role comes to the fore in SODA too, for example in serving to differentiate high-level goals, assumptions, options, and so on.

Thirdly, the consultant can be a valuable generator of new ideas, perhaps challenging clients' current thinking. He or she brings a fresh view to bear, and may have more freedom to raise awkward or 'too-obvious' questions. To deny this possible role would be a prime example of 'wasted freedom'. Practitioners of all three approaches do in fact take this role, while trying to avoid being cast as an expert on problem content. While the existence of this role does not depend on the particular approach used – useful suggestions can come from experience of analogous situations, or from 'common sense' – specific suggestions are inevitably also influenced by consultants' general theories (for example) about the nature of conflict or uncertainty, or about organizational decision processes.

Finally, more formal analysis of key aspects of the problem can be undertaken. This can lead to 'non-obvious' conclusions about the problem, not necessarily correct, but providing valuable food for thought. The form such conclusions are likely to take directly depends on the types of model used. An idea worth exploring is that each approach tends to bring up characteristic sorts of surprises. In strategic choice, for example, a solution tree might be built that turns out to contain outcomes intuitively dismissed as unworkable. Analyzing a hypergame model may suggest that an apparently powerful threat can be evaded, or that some apparently trivial misunderstanding could have disastrous consequences. Surprises in mapping seem often to involve virtuous or vicious loops.

This admixture of similarities and differences makes linkage something of a minefield (Bennett, 1985). It also provides one answer to the question of 'why just these three approaches?' Considering three generates more than enough complexity! A less superficial reason is that linkage can only be realistically pursued through practical, collaborative research, and it is with practitioners of these approaches that the main opportunities have so far arisen.

For all that, the promise inherent in linkage can be set out quite simply. Game-based methods offer a view of decision problems based on options controlled by specific actors. They stress conflict of aims and differences in perception *across* (rather than within) decision centres. The analyses of uncertainty within strategic choice provide an important complementary emphasis to that on conflict. Meanwhile, a major focus of SODA is on the variety of problem constructions typically held *within* decision-making groups, and on ways of accessing and using this variety. All these concerns are perfectly compatible with each other. Were one deliberately to conjure up a situation designed to ensure the relevance of them all, it might well be described as follows:

> An analyst is called on to help a group having responsibility for certain decisions. As the shape of the problem emerges, it appears that the group faces both uncertainties about its own goals and available choices, and conflicts with other actors. Furthermore, each member of the group seems to have a different view of what the problem is. The analyst believes it important to elicit and use these individual views as fully as possible. But internal agreement on a way forward has to be reached. The group has to make its decisions, and these must command the necessary commitment from individuals to carry them through.

Far from being far-fetched or self-contradictory, this situation will probably be all too familiar. Furthermore, each approach would be able to make a distinctive contribution not already offered by the others. It is this that makes the prospect of linkage in practice so enticing.

Towards a Combined Methodology

Clearly, methods and models can be put together in different ways (Bennett, 1985). They can be used at different stages, or for different functions. One can select from existing models, or try to design hybrids taking account of more than one existing focus (for example, conflict and uncertainty). The methodology discussed here incorporates several forms of linkage. Its overall shape can be pictured as in Figure 10.1. This

Figure 10.1   *Components of a decision-aiding methodology*

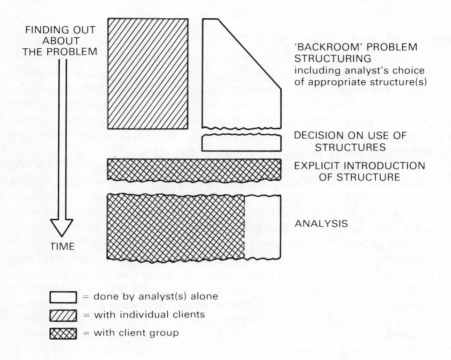

shows four main activities taking place as time unfolds 'down the page', also noting whether these are carried out with individual members of the client group, with the group as a whole, or in backroom work. The activities are:

(a)   a process of *problem exploration* – of finding out about the problem from the clients – working primarily with individuals;
(b)   initial 'backroom' *problem structuring*, done in parallel with (a), preceding a provisional choice of types of model to use with the clients;
(c)   *explicit introduction of problem structure* with the group as a whole; and
(d)   *more detailed analyses* (as well as continued and revised problem structuring), done predominantly with the whole group but with backroom work interspersed.

This forms a framework for using various methods and models. It is not a rigid, linear scheme, but varies in response to features of each individual intervention. Its elements will now be described in a little more detail, concentrating on two specific points: the initial use of separate methods for problem exploration and structuring ((a) and (b)), and the choice of model referred to in (c).

Problem Exploration and Problem Structuring

An important early task in almost any decision-aiding project is to explore how clients see the problems. Though one would certainly expect these views to change as a result of a successful intervention, this starting point is of paramount importance. Otherwise, it is all too easy to start off some 'clever' piece of analysis that actually has very little relevance to clients' worries. In tackling this task, our methodology is strongly influenced by our preferred answers to two questions.

Firstly, assuming that there is a client *group*, should one work with the whole group from the word go (the normal practice in strategic choice), or start by exploring the views of each individual (as, usually, in SODA)? Having tried each approach, the author's preference is strongly for the latter. This is based on two premises. The first is that there will be at least as many definitions of the problem as there are members of the client group. Accessing and using these – quite apart from any extra ideas injected by the consultant – can help avoid the pitfalls of 'group-think'. The second is that one should try to ensure that each member of the group has a fair chance to be heard, and knows this to be so. Perhaps with sufficient process management skill, these aims can be achieved working with the whole group throughout. But this is very difficult indeed. Despite one's best efforts, discussion tends to be dominated by a few, and clients remain reluctant to bring up issues that might provoke embarrassment, internal disagreement, 'mission crisis'. At least in the early stages of a project, clients do seem to be more forthcoming when given undivided and individual attention.

The second question is that of whether to introduce (mildly) technical representations (for example, hypergame 'problem structuring' models, or AIDA diagrams) straight away as vehicles for exploring the problem. It can be argued that these can suppress variety within the group, and force the problem into some preordained mould. Yet they can also be seen as powerful ways of addressing questions about choices. Usually, one can see the possible applicability of particular sorts of model early on ('this really looks like two interlinked games, between . . . and about . . .'). But is plumping for such a representation straight away too directive? Will it discourage anyone from exploring other aspects of the problem, and other sorts of model that might be just as fruitful? There are strong arguments for delaying any explicit introduction of theoretical structure until clients have had plenty of opportunity to describe and discuss problems in their own terms.

A response to these points is to develop the notion of treating problem exploration and structuring as two (initially) separate, parallel activities, in what might be called a 'twin-track' approach (Bennett and Cropper,

1986). Along the exploration track, work is with individual clients, to elicit their views expressed in their own terms. Cognitive mapping provides a most convenient and effective vehicle for doing this, in a relatively 'neutral' way. In working on-line with clients, the start is roughly as recommended by Eden et al. (except in special circumstances noted later). Following a short group meeting to explain the aims and intended form of the intervention, the views of each individual are explored and modelled in some depth over two rounds of interviews, using cognitive mapping as a medium. (If this is impossible for reasons of time, small subgroups provide the next-best alternative.) In practice, one important difference has been a greater reliance on pen-and-paper mapping, rather than on computer programs such as COPE. This personal preference comes partly from a desire to keep representations simple. It also reflects the point that maps are generally only used to capture individual views, rather than to help generate a common perspective for the group, as in the SODA methodology. In the latter case, it becomes necessary to merge individual maps, and a computer becomes virtually indispensable.

Along the other track, problem structuring starts as a backroom activity. This allows one to experiment with different structures as the story unfolds, in ways that clients might find too time consuming. One major exception to this preferred pattern exists. On occasion, a recognizable structure – a set of conflicts between identifiable actors, or a set of decision areas – leaps out from clients' initial descriptions. If clients are already thinking in terms very close to a framework that the consultant is happy to use, this can be introduced straight away, as a vehicle for further problem exploration (Huxham and Bennett, 1985). Provisionally at least, there is no need for two separate styles of working.

Choice of Structure

In starting work with the whole client group, the intention is to bring together the two previous 'tracks', marrying up the content of the clients' description with the analyst's attempts at structuring. This is done by introducing provisional models to the group – for example, diagrams of decision areas in the AIDA format – whose content – decision areas and options, links and uncertainties – comes from the maps already produced with the clients. The hope is that clients will have enough 'ownership' of the models to take them as a good starting point for further work. As work proceeds, the specific models initially offered may well be altered almost beyond recognition (as noted later, even the general types of model used may be changed later on). But the first choice of framework is still important, and recognizing that there is no single 'correct' way to model a problem makes that choice less than straightforward. When, for instance, 'should' a situation be formulated in terms of hypergames?

When in terms of strategic choice? When would it be more productive to carry on using maps/SODA?

If the frameworks provided by conflict analysis or strategic choice can be introduced successfully, they give particularly neat and direct ways of analyzing decisions. The choice between them is primarily a matter of judging the relative importance of conflict with identifiable 'other actors', as opposed to the forms of uncertainty addressed by strategic choice. However, problems are not classified as involving either conflict or uncertainty exclusively. Rather, a dominant framework is selected within which other forms of analysis can be nested (Bennett and Bussell, 1986). For example, some problems are most naturally defined primarily in terms of managing uncertainty, but the implementation of certain (AIDA-type) options would lead to potential conflict with other interested parties. Conversely, some problems can best be defined primarily in terms of conflict, but within this perspective uncertainties also arise – for example, about the feasibility of certain options, or about one's own values. In each of these two cases, there is an appropriate choice of dominant (not exclusive) framework. A further possibility, however, is that the problem as described bears no coherent resemblance to either framework. In particular, discernible, reasonably specific options (in either an AIDA or conflict analysis sense) may be hard to find. This is interpreted to mean that the client's problem, at least for the present, is not primarily one of choice. Rather, the need may be for ways of helping clients reflect on a situation, exploring it in a more general way, and elaborating their own hopes and fears regarding it. In this case, suitable methods are provided by the continued use of mapping, and by methods (for example, means-ends analysis) forming further elements of strategic choice.

The provisional nature of framework choice has been stressed, and the choice is influenced by the need for flexibility in switching from one to another if appropriate. For example, analysis of a situation initially structured in terms of uncertainty may suggest that the key uncertainty concerns conflict with another party over a certain proposal. The flexibility to change the types of model (rather than just the specific models) used should be enhanced with the current development of hybrids going some way towards a unified treatment of conflict and uncertainty (Bennett and Cropper, 1989). In addition, maps may well be used again in these later stages in an 'embedded' role. Having developed an overall problem structure, piecemeal mapping around particular outcomes can help to uncover the rationale underlying preferences, or to explore sources of uncertainty (Huxham and Bennett, 1985).

Two Examples

Various applications of this combined methodology have already been undertaken: two examples will serve to illustrate some of the points made here.

Maps and Strategic Choice

The first example involved the use of mapping as a precursor to elements of strategic choice. The clients were staff of a university teaching department, and the problem concerned the future (if any) of a postgraduate diploma course. From the clients' initial descriptions, multiple uncertainties existed, as did competing criteria on which to base decisions (including academic and financial criteria, and considerations of job satisfaction), and it had proven difficult for the group to come to any agreed decision. Mapping provided the means to explore the views of the four individual lecturers most closely involved. Backroom structuring of this material suggested – or rather, confirmed – the existence of linked decision areas in the AIDA sense, but no obvious conflicts with other actors. The material in the maps was therefore used in drawing up a preliminary set of perceived decision areas, options, uncertainties, and criteria, and diagrams showing these prepared. (As a rule of thumb, disagreements within the group, as evidenced by the maps, were translated into uncertainties for the group.) To start off the first plenary meeting, this material was used so as to 'prime' the process of strategic choice – short-cutting the usual process of starting with blank flip charts. From there, the meeting reverted to a 'normal' strategic choice workshop. The exercise was successful, in the sense that a new course was designed and introduced which went a long way towards meeting the apparently irreconcilable criteria expressed within the group (Matthews and Bennett, 1986).

'Maps, Games and Things In-between'

Our second example involves a more ambitious attempt to bring together the use of maps, conflict analysis and, to a lesser extent, elements of strategic choice (Bennett and Cropper, 1987). The clients were a group of planners in a London local authority, attempting to push forward a programme of local economic development in a generally hostile political environment. As before, mapping was used to elicit each officer's view of the situation. At the same time the problem was structured in terms of a linked set of hypergames – this seeming to be the most appropriate structure to express the complex web of conflicts emerging from our clients' descriptions. These two strands were then brought together by presenting the group with models incorporating the hypergame structure, but maintaining much of the content of the maps. This was done by interpreting the latter as input to, and output from, a set of linked

Figure 10.2 *Extracts from a 'decision arena' model*

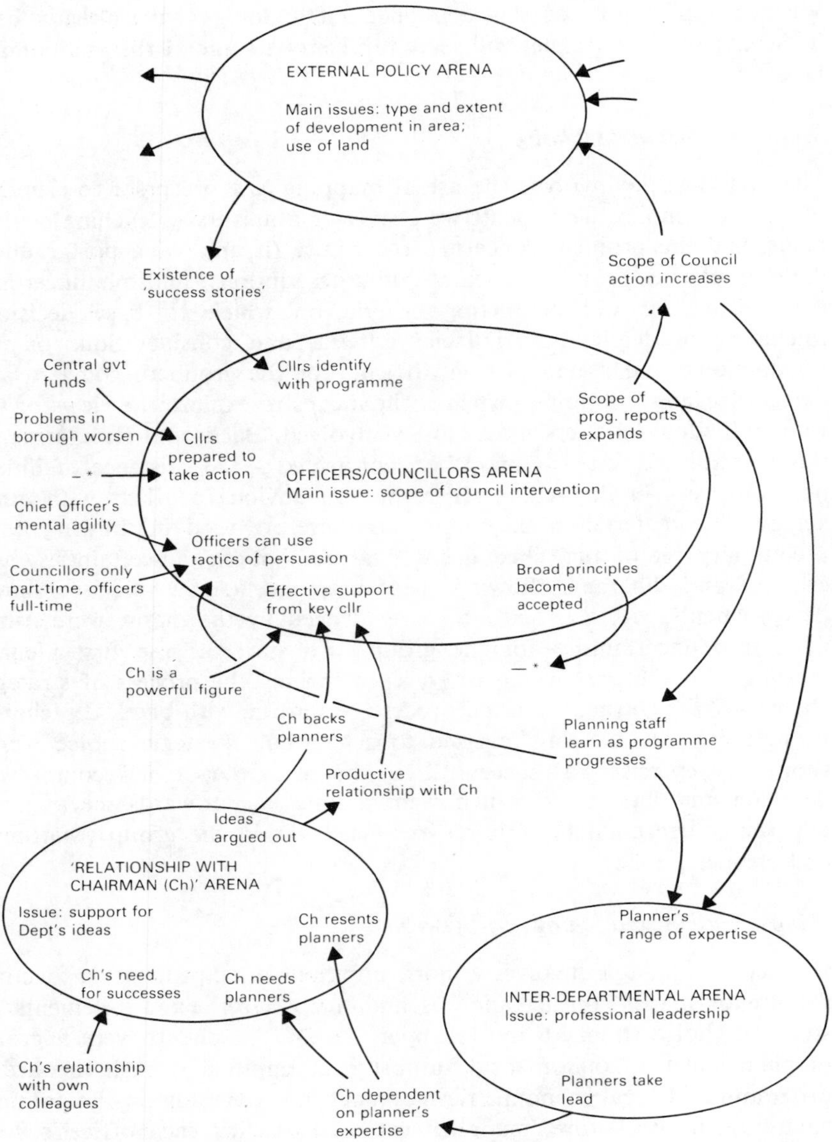

EXTERNAL POLICY ARENA

Main issues: type and extent
of development in area;
use of land

Existence of
'success stories'

Scope of Council
action increases

Central gvt
funds

Cllrs identify
with programme

Scope of
prog. reports
expands

Problems in
borough worsen

Cllrs
prepared to
take action

OFFICERS/COUNCILLORS ARENA
Main issue: scope of council intervention

Chief Officer's
mental agility

Officers can use
tactics of persuasion

Councillors only
part-time, officers
full-time

Effective support
from key cllr

Broad principles
become
accepted

Ch is a
powerful figure

Ch backs
planners

Planning staff
learn as programme
progresses

Productive
relationship with Ch

Ideas
argued out

'RELATIONSHIP WITH
CHAIRMAN (Ch)' ARENA

Issue: support for
Dept's ideas

Ch resents
planners

Planner's
range of expertise

Ch's need
for successes

Ch needs
planners

INTER-DEPARTMENTAL ARENA
Issue: professional leadership

Ch's relationship
with own
colleagues

Ch dependent
on planner's
expertise

Planners take
lead

'decision arenas' corresponding to hypergames at various levels. An example of such a model is shown in Figure 10.2. Shown in much simplified form here, this represented one planner's view of how the political system operated in his area of responsibility. Bringing together the individual views within this common format provided an effective way of starting a group discussion of the various facets of the situation in hand.

These two examples show both similarities and differences within the combined approach outlined earlier. Both cases involved use of mapping as a precursor to other forms of model. The choice of the latter differed, being primarily determined by deciding whether uncertainty or conflict seemed to dominate the situation described. Further work in this vein continues, and should lead eventually to a set of 'rules of thumb' for the productive intertwining of the three hitherto separate sets of methods.

11

Systems of Perceptions: Developments in Hypermapping

JIM BRYANT

No one faces problems in a social vacuum. There will always be people who are seen as playing some part in creating our problems, as having some influence on our handling of them, or as having some interest in the outcome. Thinking about these others is usually managed purely intuitively, and they are often treated as part of the taken-for-granted backdrop of a situation. The basic premise of this chapter is that a more self-conscious and explicit consideration of those who are regarded as significant in a problematic situation can help us to act more effectively.

Such a large proportion of the time and energy of individuals in organizations centres upon the handling of relationships with others that it is hardly surprising that it is a topic which has attracted much attention. In particular, the manipulation of these relationships is the material of inter- and intra-organizational politics, a subject that has spawned an impressive literature (Pfeiffer, 1981; Pettigrew, 1973). However, little of this work has proposed the use of a structured framework to support individuals as they try to gain an understanding of those others with whom they interact. Eden, Jones and Sims (1979) have indicated one way in which this could be done: through the construction of a set of cognitive maps intended to illuminate the worlds of others. This chapter puts forward a related but distinct approach to providing cognitive assistance, involving a rather more elaborate methodology that augments the language of mapping with dramaturgical and game-theoretic concepts.

The central artefact of the methodology outlined here is a device called a hypermap, which depicts the relationships between the mental models of others held by an individual. The use of this device channels the whole process of problem exploration and decision support, by causing a specific set of questions to be asked about the situation faced, and by suggesting a particular way of structuring the potential outcomes for consideration. In the next section of this chapter the key concepts of hypermapping are introduced. These are then illustrated through a succession of cameos excised from practical studies. Throughout, the emphasis chosen has been on the role of hypermaps in problem structuring, since it is here that the mixing of the parent methodologies of hypergames and cognitive mapping is most evident.

The Concept

The hypermap concept is most simply seen as a generalization of hypergame ideas. In brief, hypergame analysis (Bennett and Huxham, 1982) posits a world in which the central feature is conflict (in its most general sense of a difference of intentions or interests) between autonomous players or actors. It further assumes that these players make considered choices which inform their deliberate actions. Each player may be active in a number of arenas (Bennett and Cropper, 1987) in which they become engaged over different issues with a variety of other actors. In each arena there is usually a range of potential outcomes of the interaction and these depend upon the starting conditions (individuals' beliefs, preferences, perceived options, etc.) of the conflict. Hypergames extend traditional game theory by removing the usual assumption that all players see the same game: subjectivity is taken seriously, and it is recognized that the options and preferences perceived by each player for himself and for the others involved will not necessarily coincide. From this standpoint, hypermap analysis (Bryant, 1983) takes the issue of subjectivity one step further by recognizing that each player may also see a different set of 'others' caught up in this conflict, and that each of these others will have an idiosyncratic view of what is going on, a view whose richness is unlikely to be captured by the extreme and dry abstraction of formal hypergame analysis.

A Textbook Approach

The use of a hypermap as core concept leads to a process of enquiry that sensitizes the individual to certain features of his subjective world. These may be summarized as issues, participants, exits, and development. It also suggests a process through which these features may be explored by a consultant working to support a client or client group. The treatment of the highlighted features will be discussed here in the context of an overall approach summarized by Figure 11.1, where, for the sake of exposition, it is assumed that a client group is involved.

Typically, the process begins with a round of individual interviews with members of the client group. In each one, an exploration of the history and antecedents of the situation which they perceive is carried out; what is amiss, and how did it arise? A graphic device called an *ideagraph* (see Figure 11.2) has been found useful for capturing these discussions. Here key assertions, facts, choices, or opinions are set down and linked connotatively or causally by lines or arrows respectively. There are obvious similarities to cognitive mapping, but these are less formally

Figure 11.1   *Idealized group process using hypermaps*

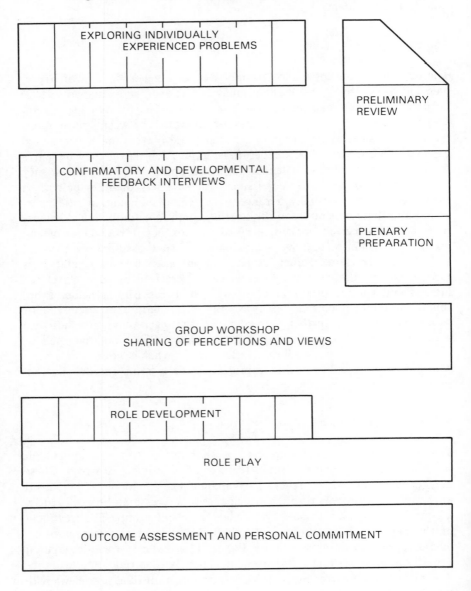

constructed and are not intended to act as a direct problem-solving device. Word elements within items may be highlighted for linkage when they, but not the whole, are specifically related.

Special care is also taken at this opening stage to log the main stakeholders (Mason and Mitroff, 1981) who are seen as being involved in what is going on, and to note the issues over which they apparently

Figure 11.2 *Specimen ideagraph: a view of the management centre (MC)*

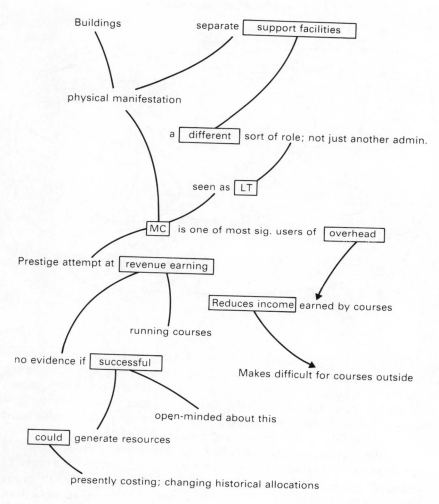

interact. Here a simple enumeration of individuals may suffice, though it is likely that a more structured *cast list* may be used: the example in Figure 11.3 uses Venn notation to indicate multiple membership of groups by individual actors. A cast list can be a revealing personal statement as Jones (1983) has demonstrated.

From these data, the consultant may construct a preliminary review of the issues and participants that each person sees as important, perhaps even using preliminary problem structuring (PPS) (Bennett and Huxham, 1982) or arenas notation (Bennett and Cropper, 1987). Significantly, this review will include the informant's pictures of how things probably

Figure 11.3   *System diagram displaying specimen cast list: the symposium (individuals are signified by their initials. Labels in boxes apply to set members)*

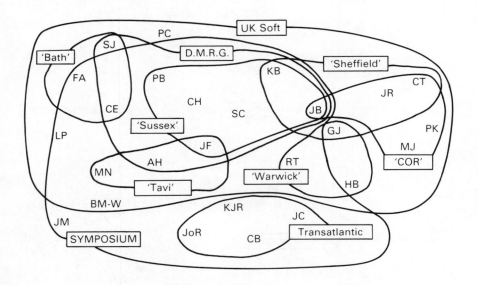

appear from the perspective of each of the others caught up in the conflict. Essentially fragments of a hypermap are being recorded, as the example in Figure 11.4 (based on an idea by Boothroyd, 1978) shows: this depicts three individuals A, B, and C, and each 'bubble' shows how things are seen by the corresponding person (note the possible differences across individuals in cast listing and elaboration of ideas).

It is then usual for the consultant to conduct a further round of individual interviews to confirm and elaborate the earlier records. In particular, the use of argumentation analysis (Toulmin, 1958) to probe links in the ideagraphs, and the consideration of the perceived exits from the problem arena for all concerned might be included. Following this stage, the consultant then prepares for a plenary session with the client group. This preparation involves examination for *motifs* – recurrent themes across individuals – and the composition of provisional merged cast lists.

Within the group session, run as an open workshop involving all the clients, the early stress is on a sharing of views and ideas, feeding these in through the artefacts produced from the earlier interviews. Depending upon the divergence of views emerging at this point, the time taken for sufficient mutual understanding to develop varies. The group is then led through a structured consideration of the region within which feasible

Figure 11.4 *A specimen hypermap*

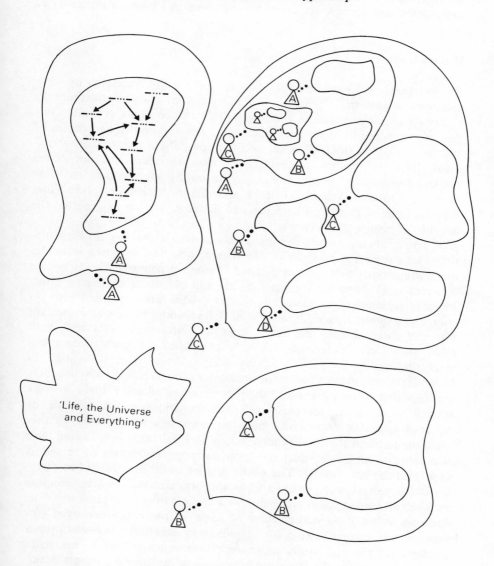

'Life, the Universe and Everything'

outcomes seemed to lie, at the same time noting any assumptions or conditions that might be associated with these. Not unnaturally, given the game-theoretic antecedents of hypermapping, these outcomes are generated and expressed in terms of the selection of combinations of options or policies by individual actors. However, not surprisingly there is little prospect of (or indeed much point in) conducting any formal analysis of the situation. Instead, the move towards committed action takes place in a more experiential way, the use of role play to work out the interchange between actors being one possible method, this leading to a subsequent plenary review of the outcome as shown in Figure 11.1.

Realizations

The perspective offered by hypermaps is most readily illustrated by some examples drawn from practice. These have been chosen principally to demonstrate the structuring framework that the concepts provide. Only one of the examples comes anywhere near the complexity and extent of the idealized twin track (Bennett and Cropper, 1986) approach just outlined. This emphasizes a feature common to many decision-aiding methodologies: that simple, technically unsophisticated models are often all that is required. What is critical is that the theoretical perspective that they enshrine is permitted to direct the enquiry, and so to generate the insights of which it is capable.

A matter of importance for many clients is to appreciate how a situation looks from the perspective of other actors. The first two examples illustrating hypermap ideas are based in such a context. The first case concerns work done for the paternalistic and dictatorial managing director of a regionally important UK brewery, who was concerned with his company's public image. A cast list of actors whom he saw as important was elucidated during the initial meeting. Subsequent interviews with other staff, in which each subject's perception of present company marketing policy and of company image were discussed, varied in content and emphasis. The trade managers' conversation ranged widely and included word pictures of their perceptions of competitive brewers as well as a venting of their own preoccupations and a grinding of personal axes: the commercial manager painted a far broader picture, while the publicans' stories related mainly to local features affecting their own takings, although touching upon more general issues of image as seen from the bar counter. The whole process could be regarded as carrying out a partial perceptual audit of the organization; that is, building up a set of related cognitive pictures (a hypermap) of the situation. The outcome was a good appreciation of some of the issues perceived (for example, the annual assessment of pub rents negotiated between brewer and landlord was highlighted as an important, sensitive, and by no means peripheral, issue for the company in seeking to promote a stronger advertising image) which informed subsequent conventional market research.

In a second example involving a perceptual audit, the client was the academic head of faculty within an institution of higher education. The faculty had recently established a management centre which was intended to act as a 'shop window' for its skills as well as providing a focus for interaction and collaboration with external commercial and industrial organizations. However, all was apparently not going smoothly, and there was concern that the initiative might have to be aborted if the situation persisted. Astonishingly, the client opened the first meeting by saying, 'I expect you'd like a list of actors' so it was easy to set down his cast list on a flip chart. It was interesting to see that the list featured no business interests outside the institution. The subsequent discussion of the issues he saw around the management centre were recorded in the form of an ideagraph. By the end of the session, it had been agreed that it would be valuable to investigate the perceptions of certain groups of people within the client's definition of the dominant scene. A series of interviews was thus carried out with a sample of individuals drawn to represent the view of the management centre from different locations in the organization (Figure 11.2 is actually an edited version of one of these). The results were interesting but (as so often with hindsight) not surprising. Generalizing grossly, it appeared that the 'higher' up the organization chart one moved, the more the management centre was seen as competing for resources and the more the abrasive personality of its director was seen as an issue. Moving in the opposite direction, the management centre was seen as remote and irrelevant to everyday concerns by staff at grassroots level, and a more open-minded, less hostile view was apparent. More detailed features also fell out of a comparison of ideagraphs across respondents, some highly suggestive of remedial measures. The perceptual audit was also valuable as a counterpoint to the client's own perception of other actors' viewpoints and in certain respects served to undermine his preconceptions and assumptions, thereby invalidating some intended courses of action. A fortuitous phone call from the director of the management centre to the client during one of the working sessions, and some agile verbal negotiations taking up actions which the work had suggested, brought about the sudden completion and fulfilment of the study little more than a fortnight after its inception.

The dialectic set up between perspectives in both this and the previous example is reminiscent of that encouraged in counter planning and used very productively in quite different ways in both Checkland's (1981b) and Mason and Mitroff's (1981) work. It is a challenge to belief and prejudice. The cases show how hypermaps were explored by a consultant, and how by juxtaposing perceptions across the map and by examining others in more detail, valuable decision-aiding support was provided.

In the next illustration, the notion of a genuine perceptual exchange – that is, an opportunity for people to learn about each others' views of a situation – enters for the first time, since the processes concerned involve the use of the hypermap framework to learn about others and their perceptions at first hand.

The first example concerns a short process designed to help a voluntary group to generate pay-offs which had some meaning to those involved. The group (of which the author was a member) had been working together for some time. There was scepticism as to how well members of the group understood each others' motivations for continued involvement in the group. The process was therefore based around the question, 'Why am I here?' with respect to group meetings.

As an orientating and 'loosening up' exercise, individuals first completed a private repertory grid analysis with group members as elements. The group then divided into subgroups of three persons each and carried out the following tasks:

1 each person set down alone his/her own response to the key question above;
2 each person set down his/her perception of the other two subgroup members' feelings about the question;
3 each person presented his/her own response (from step (1)) to the others in the subgroup;
4 subgroup discussions were held in the light of the interchange to see what actions were thereby suggested.

The subgroups then recombined to exchange and follow up the action outcomes generated. As well as helping to dispel some underlying mis-perceptions which had hampered certain personal relationships within the group, the process also legitimized some common doubts and uncertain-ties about the group's identity and highlighted some critical differences which had a bearing upon attendance at meetings. The majority of the actions proposed have now taken place. The process had provided a 'safe' forum for a degree of self-revelation to occur and had strengthened group solidarity. In hypermap terms, there had been a counterposing of personal perceptions between singular actors in the group situation, and in so far as these exchanges were honestly conducted, they served to cement group relationships and to further common purposes.

A rather different example of the use of hypermap ideas in team consultancy practice can be given. Here the approach was used by a number of independent project teams both to reflect upon the identity and stances of others significantly involved in their work and also to assist internal team processes. The former was achieved by each team working together, first to negotiate a common cast list and then by assessing, for each actor identified, the aims, beliefs, and preferences which were felt to underlie their thinking. The cast list negotiation in itself was revealing and gave all team members a broader appreciation of the consultancy situation in which they were engaged. There was even more discussion when it came to portraying others' perspectives. Some of the less acceptable viewpoints were expressed in the groups. For exam-ple, in one case the cynical way in which the team felt it was being exploited by a client for political ends was elucidated and so gave support to attempts to reorient the project as a result. The outcome in every case was a more realistic appreciation of what might be achieved in the work and some warning of aspects of each study which could potentially lead into difficulties.

In the final example of perceptual exchange, a more protracted process was involved and higher-order perceptions were invoked. The purpose this time was to attack the problem owned by an academic research group of how best to relate to others having an interest in the same subject area. Initial use was made of subgroups in a nominal group process to explore the major problem themes. This process developed some shared commitment to an issue and appreciation of each others' perspectives, from which a cast list was then negotiated. Individuals next worked separately to develop a picture of the group as seen from the perspective of an actor from this list who had special significance for them personally and feed back these perceptions in a further plenary session which took the form of an art gallery presentation, that is, a set of pen portraits of these actors on flip charts. Subsequent discussion revealed differences in perception within the group which proved to be of value in influencing the group's stance with respect to 'outsiders'. For individuals it also forced reflection upon some taken-for-granted relationships and gave a formal opportunity to voice hitherto unstated (and sensitive) beliefs about others.

In each of these last three examples where a group rather than an individual client was involved, the hypermap concept stimulated the purposeful exploration of a set of perceptions that might otherwise not have been made explicit. In doing so, mutual understanding within the groups was aided and issues that had not formed part of the legitimate currency of discussion were exposed, with consequent benefits for future development. Equally important, the choices open to the client group were more clearly exposed, so that subsequent analysis and eventual commitment to a package of actions was facilitated.

Crosslinking for Development

The hypermap concept originated as what Bennett (1985) refers to as an integration of decision-aiding formalisms, being conceived both as a generalization of hypergame analysis and also as a hierarchical matrix for cognitive mapping. Although it shares many common features with practical approaches using a coupling of the parent methodologies it has some distinctive features. These result from the hypermap emphasis on 'getting under the skin' of others, rather than of looking at them from 'outside' as agents in a game of the client's own construction. The associated approach goes some way to encouraging individuals to understand the experience of others whom they encounter in apparently problematic situations.

12

Gaming, Competitor Analysis and Strategic Management

CHRIS HUXHAM AND COLIN EDEN

An important element of strategic management in a commercial organization is a concern for the interaction between competitors. In some sectors, an ability to anticipate the dynamics between competitors is vital to survival.

These statements would appear to be truisms, yet little attention has been paid to this aspect in most of the literature on strategic planning. Such approaches to considering competition as do exist, tend to be rather inward looking. Porter (1985), for example, argues that the achievement of *'competitive advantage'* is dependent upon such factors as being able to produce a differentiated product, having wide and co-ordinated geographical competitive scope, and so on, and describes a 'good competitor' in terms of such attributes as 'understands the rules' and 'has realistic assumptions'. Such factors are undoubtedly crucial to competitive success, and by explicitly drawing attention to them, Porter has made great strides forward in our ability to discuss competitive strategy in organizations.

This sort of approach, however, does not pay attention to the *dynamics* of inter-company competition which may stop an organization achieving its advantage even though it is technically sound in other respects. Yet senior managers in highly competitive industries frequently focus on the actions of their competitors. What seems to be important to them is that they are putting their efforts into 'winners' and this is, to a large extent, determined by what others do. For example, it may be important to avoid putting resources into developing a new product if another organization is developing something similar, only better or more quickly. It is important not to decide to standardize on a particular model if a number of your major competitors agree, in coalition, to standardize on a different version; and so on. In addition, they are often also concerned about the actions of other parties. For example, they are often concerned to keep ahead of relevant new government legislation, to keep abreast of government support for, or subsidies to, their competitors in different countries, to predict the likely moves of their customers, and so on.

On the face of it, these concerns – focusing as they do on interactions between actors with various options – would seem to suggest that game-theoretic forms of analysis would have much to offer in the analysis of competitive interactions. However, we have found that, within the context of the use of SODA for strategic management (Eden and Huxham, 1988; Eden et al., 1990), *formal* game theory/analysis of options/hyper-game analysis has not been very helpful. Nevertheless the framework for thinking about competitors provided by gaming concepts has been helpful. In the next section of this chapter we shall try to outline, very briefly, some of the reasons for this.

Games within a SODA Context

Some of the ideas behind SODA as a group decision support system are discussed elsewhere in this volume (and in detail in Eden, 1989). For the purposes of this chapter, it is enough to say that SODA consists of a series of workshops in which participants discuss matters of strategic importance to them. It thus follows the style of 'strategic issues management'. Discussion at the workshops is relatively free, but the process is managed by a facilitator who, by documenting the discussion in the form of a 'cognitive map' (Eden et al., 1983), is able to draw participants' attention to aspects of argumentation which appear to be central, in need of elaboration or which suggest strategic options that might be evaluated.

Discussions at such workshops frequently revolve around past and possible future actions of competitors. We have therefore been continually on the lookout for situations that might be amenable to game-based analyses, in order to see whether a formal analysis of this type would provide worthwhile insights in the competitor analysis context. We were interested to see whether argumentation documented in map form from the free-flowing discussion could form the initial basis of such an analysis. If so, we would set up a workshop specifically to explore the situation further using the game framework. We have, however, been unable to find a suitable situation. It is not easy to explain fully why this is so, but a major problem seems to lie with a difficulty in defining an issue which can be worked on. Some reasons for this are given, in poorly articulated form, below (these are based on experience with a number of specific organizations and may not be generalizable):

– In many industries, it is difficult to assess the effect of competition because different companies produce products which have slightly different purposes. For example, it is not clear how sales of potatoes (or pasta or rice or scones) affect sales of bread, how sales of cars (or tractors or vans or elephants) affect sales of jeeps, how sales of desk-top computers (or office equipment or software) affect sales of mainframes, how sales of holidays abroad (or activity holidays or pop concerts) affect home tourism, and so on. Thus each company interacts with a wide range of types of competitor, but is only in partial competition with most of the individual competitors. Indeed the principle of seeking a high level of product differentiation from competing products will deliberately create such circumstances. Thus any one company in such an industry needs to keep abreast of movements in a variety of different areas. In trying to isolate an issue for analysis, we are therefore continually thwarted by the fact that every issue touches on a large number of other issues and a large number of competitors, and no one issue or competitor seems to be obviously of more importance than any other.

- When we force ourselves to focus on one issue (albeit roughly defined), the interconnectedness usually leads to a list of actors that is too long for practical analysis. Furthermore, the actors obviously have uneven amounts of influence, some being powerful while others, though quite healthy, have little effect on the market. Yet it tends not to be possible to ignore many of the actors for the purposes of analysis, partly because coalitions can turn weak actors into powerful ones and partly because weak actors in one aspect of the issue may be quite powerful in another.
- We have found it impossible to produce a coherent set of options for each actor from a free-flowing discussion documented as a map. The options expressed, or suggested by implication, during discussion usually relate to different aspects or levels of the issue and are hence only indirectly related to one another.
- Finally, the complexity of most market places makes it difficult to imagine what the consequences of any actions might be, so outcomes are very difficult to predict.

That competitive situations are messy is not surprising. We, and others, have stressed the importance of the interconnectedness of issues in the past by developing the concepts of 'interconnected decision areas' (Friend and Hickling, 1987) or interrelated clusters of concepts (Eden, 1989), 'preliminary problem structuring' (Huxham and Bennett, 1985), 'linked decision areas' and 'strategy and tactics' and so on (Giesen, 1981). Nevertheless, all such models have assumed that it is possible to define an issue of central importance; an assumption which seems difficult to live up to in the context of planning.

Despite these difficulties, we have managed, on several occasions, to get at least the semblance of an 'analysis of options' (Radford, 1981) together. However, these have tended to be about rather narrowly defined aspects of the competitive situation. Rather than let the analytical form drive the process, we have therefore been unwilling to pursue these with the client groups concerned. Our reluctance stems from a desire to use the small amount of time that senior members of organizations are willing to put aside for planning-type activities in the most effective way, and also from a concern to encourage clients to broaden their understanding of the competitive situation rather than focusing in detail on one small aspect.

In rejecting formal game-based approaches in this way, we are left with the niggling feeling that we have not really given them a fair trial. Perhaps we should negotiate a competitive game theory entrée with a client group and see whether an analysis can be sustained! Be that as it may, it is our view that game-based approaches are likely to have much greater value if used in an informal sense for we do believe that the framework they offer for modelling the world provides a useful means of structuring thinking and discussion. In the next section we will discuss this alternative approach to their use.

Game-theoretic Approaches and Role Play

We have argued elsewhere that the hypergame framework may be seen as a 'theory of the world' – that is it describes the way in which a part of the world works (Bennett and Huxham, 1982). The same argument applies to other game-based approaches. The previous discussion in this chapter would suggest that these are not particularly 'accurate' representations of some parts of the world. Nevertheless, we would argue that they do capture, in some sense, the essence of conflict, and therefore competitive, situations. To justify this statement empirically would take years of uninteresting research! However, analysis of *post hoc* and live case studies using the framework suggested by the theory has shown that at least some situations can be reasonably modelled in this way (Bennett and Dando, 1979, 1982; Bennett et al., 1980, 1981).

Taking, then, as given, that the game-type framework is a reasonable representation of the world, we have suggested in the past that even though one might not wish, or be able to, carry out a formal game-theoretic or hypergame analysis, key elements of the approaches might be used as a framework for individual thinking about, or questioning clients about, a particular situation. Thus, from game theory, we are led to ask about *who is involved in a particular situation, what they can do, what are their aims* and hence *their preferences* for various outcomes. The hypergame framework leads us to question also whether those involved might have a different understanding of the 'game' to ourselves or from each other. Other adjuncts to the theory lead us to ask about the effect of other situations that they are involved in, and so on. In the context of competitor analysis, we have gone one stage further than this and devised a process, based on role play, which not only asks clients key questions, but also helps to elicit answers from them (Eden, 1986). The process is very similar, in many respects, to that used by Radford (1984).

This process is based upon a workshop and may take from 2–3 hours

Figure 12.1   *A symbolic representation of competitor role play*

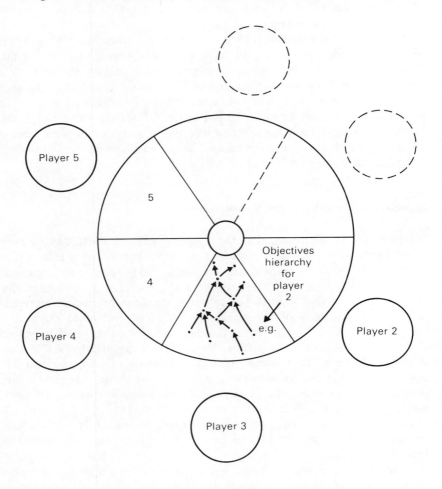

to 2–3 days. There are two basic forms of the workshop, but both can be *conceptualized* as a game as follows:

Players, representing the competitors, sit around a table (see Figure 12.1). In front of each of them is a 'goal hierarchy' for the competitor which is intended to guide the action of the player in the game. The goal hierarchy is derived from the statements members of the organization have made about competitors in their general discussions about strategy. The game starts by one player (usually the one representing the organization in which the game is being played) taking a strategic action. The next step is for any of the others to decide which competitor, if any, would notice, let alone act with respect to, what has happened in the market place. If a player believes that his competitor would notice the events, he then uses the goal hierarchy of the competitor to make a judgement about what action the competitor would take and when. The game unfolds in this way, until stability is reached.

Figure 12.2 *Example to illustrate a competitor objectives hierarchy*

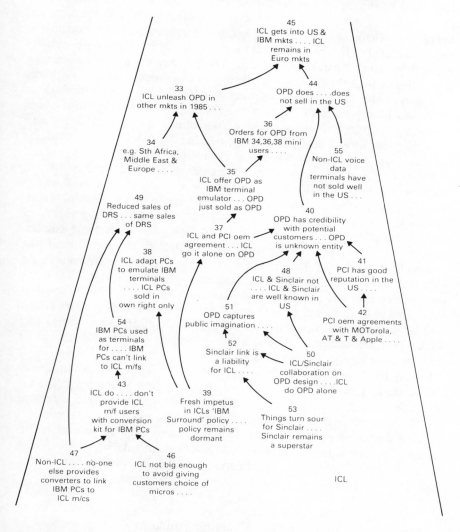

Source: For illustrative purposes data taken from 'ICL one per desk leads fight for US and IBM markets'. *Computing*, 18 July 1985: 19

In practice, the goal hierarchies will have been produced by 'slicing' out the chunk of argumentation relevant to each competitor from maps produced at earlier SODA workshops (see Figure 12.2). Because they have come out of general, rather than competitor-oriented, discussion, many of these models will be sparse and in need of elaboration.

In its simplest form, the game is set up in one room with the goal hierarchies, enlarged to flip chart size, on the walls. Participants are asked to think out the responses of all competitors jointly, thus sharing their understanding of competitor actions. As the game unfolds, participants begin to alter or elaborate the goal hierarchies and participants' deeper knowledge about the competitors is gradually surfaced and the models refined. The 'game' usually stops well before game-type stability is reached either because participants realize they do not know enough about their competitors to enable them to make guesses about their likely strategic action, or because they decide to rethink their own options in the light of early plays of the 'game' so that a rerun starting from a new position is required. In either case participants usually come away with a heightened awareness of their knowledge (or lack of it) of their competitors. This type of workshop typically takes half a day.

The 'game' can be played at much greater depth over a period of two or three days. In this mode, more people are usually involved and a small group (three or four people) is designated to 'role think' each competitor. Each group is allocated its own room and is given plenty of time to think its way into the role of its competitor. In these circumstances each role play room contains additional material about the personality profiles of key actors in each competitor organization. As with the hierarchical data, the personality data is drawn from the knowledge within the organization based on meetings with competitor executives at exhibitions, presentations, and other industry meetings. The data is presented using cognitive maps of each of the key actors, and these maps are continuously modified as the 'game' unfolds and more subconscious knowledge is surfaced.

During more extended workshops a game is replayed with continuously refined strategies for the proponent until the initial strategy 'forces' competitors to create market dynamics that support the overall direction of the proponent. In other words a form of 'stability' is reached.

These forms of competitive gaming have been used in several multinational organizations with the full involvement of directors of the company and selected senior managers. Those involved have regarded the workshops as highly successful for a variety of reasons:

- A heightened awareness of competitors, which in two instances led to fuller studies of competitor positioning following the guidelines set out by Porter. In one of these instances the managing director reported having developed an understanding of a lecture given by Porter, to the extent that he felt able to make some practical use of the ideas that he had heard at the lecture! In the other company a senior executive was given a commission to undertake a major re-evaluation of the way in which the product divisions '*managed* their competition'.
- A greater confidence in major strategic direction was developed following an extended *series* of competitor role play workshops.
- In one organization a senior manager carefully monitored the

sequence of competitor actions over the six-month period following a new product launch. The launch followed three separate and repeated one-day workshops involving, in all, fifty-two members of the organization from a director and his senior divisional managers, to a group of key product managers, and a third group of the 'boundary-spanning' people who would be continuously in contact with customers. The monitoring suggested that *every* outcome that occurred during those crucial six months of launch had been anticipated by the role plays and, more significantly, the contingency plans developed by the company as a result of the role play were judged to be correct. The company now holds regular competitor games, some run by one of the authors and some run internally.

Competitor Role Play in a Gaming Framework?

In introducing the role play processes just described, we suggested both that the approach had a basis in game theory and that it was similar to an approach described by Radford. To conclude this chapter, we will reconsider both assertions.

Firstly, then, we ask whether the approach can justifiably be considered to represent a form of game theory and, if so, what benefits this gives it. Whether or not it may be regarded as such depends on what is seen as crucial about game theory. Many argue that the formal analysis is what gives game theory its power because it is this that gives insights into unexpected outcomes. While formal analysis should not be underrated when it can be applied, it is the perspective on the world that game-based approaches give that importantly forces one to look outward into the dynamics of what other actors are doing or might do. Without such a framework, it is easy to slip into the mould of being inward-looking, treating everything that happens in the 'environment' as essentially uncontrollable forces of nature.

Of course, the process described only uses the game-based ideas to form the general framework within which thinking and discussion take place. The level of detail that is gone to is much greater than a game-type analysis could handle. That such detail is seen as important to the client groups suggests that game-based approaches on their own are not sophisticated enough. The use of maps to capture the wisdom of the participants about their competitors and about the market place is thus an important aspect of the process. In a sense, the process may be seen as an 'active' version of the more formal analysis combining maps and hypergames carried out by Huxham and Bennett (1985). The two components, maps and games, can thus be seen to complement each other, the game framework providing insight by directing the thinking process in a particular direction and the maps assisting creativity by allowing participants to 'dump' their own ideas and beliefs, assess those of others, and explore ramifications.

How close is this process to that described by Radford? There are some obvious differences. Radford's process is not specifically aimed at the analysis of competition, but at any situation where actors are interacting with conflicting aims. His process also does not make use of maps, so the discussions involved in building up knowledge about the role within each team are presumably less formally managed. In addition, the situations to which the method described here has been applied are not suitable for formal analysis. It is probable that this is also true for Radford's situations.

There are also some very clear similarities: the overall process of building up a picture of the role, followed by a 'move' by one of the participants is the basis of both. Both methods claim the same sorts of benefit; Radford (1984), for example claims that, 'managers actually taking part . . . had a sense of having been there before' and that they have 'a unique advantage in that possible reactions of other participants have been studied for some time in advance'. These statements are similar to those made in the previous section of this chapter.

PART IV
COMPUTER SUPPORTED GROUP DECISION-MAKING

Introduction

COLIN EDEN

Part IV considers two computer-based approaches to group decision support. They are both decision support *systems* in the sense that they are designed around a group process where the computer is there to support the facilitator, the analysis of content, and to help working with the group in 'real time'. *SODA* and *decision conferencing* have been designed around the idea of supporting a group and therefore have grown out of theories of group behaviour. Nevertheless each method comes from different views about the analysis of situations. Phillips sits within the college of relatively 'hard-nosed' decision analysts. He works with the notion that choice is related to the study of multiple criteria for judging the success of outcomes and the subjective probabilities of their attainment. Eden (who originally developed SODA) and Ackermann treat their decision-maker as a 'sense-maker' who will gradually move to a position of feeling comfortable about action without necessarily being able to fully articulate the rationality of the decision. Whilst Eden and Ackermann have experimented with bringing together SODA and decision conferencing at the level of tool (COPE combined with HiView: Ackermann, 1988) Eden believes that they are essentially incompatible. The metrication that follows from subjective probability assumptions is contrary to the personal construct theory perspective which drives SODA. This is one example of possible difficulties in the mixing of techniques without careful reference to the possibly different theoretical frameworks that underpin the techniques.

The purpose of this part of the book is to demonstrate that while computer support is not an essential characteristic of group decision support, there are facilitated methods of providing support which are substantially aided by the power of computers. The history of computers in organizations tends to act as a potential deterrent to extensive development and use of computer decision support to groups of senior managers. It is thus not surprising that SODA and decision conferencing each use software that has been specially developed and does not represent the computerization of tasks well known to managers (such as word processing or spreadsheets). To this extent the software used to aid group decision support tends to be complex and consequently difficult to learn. In addition, because it is only a small part of a complete GDS *system*, its success as software depends upon the overall skills portfolio of the facilitators. Indeed, each of these methods explicitly makes use of two facilitators in a way that clearly expresses the intention to combine process analysis and content analysis skills.

The models employed in most computer-based group decision support systems still maintain the form of those found at lower organizational levels: decision trees, multi-attribute utility models, and forms of cost-benefit algorithms. Crossing the boundary to the evaluation of whole systems makes such models obsolete. Vari and Vescenyi (1984), for example, have reported how decision-makers at the very highest organizational levels are unwilling to accept that they have no control over the states of nature in a decision tree, events the probabilities of which the decision analysis model implies can only be assessed but not controlled. Similarly, the role of utility and cost analyses is significantly undermined when their values no longer are fixed quantities to be estimated but rather are viewed as entirely tractable over a time span of 20 to 100 years. In fact, information in the usual sense has little extrinsic worth for supra-corporate decision-making, since the types of uncertainty that plague decisions at lower organizational levels carry hardly any meaning here. What is required are prospective theories about the way the world is likely to be, not how it was, except in so far as decision-makers draw on their understandings of the past to create a vision of the future. The requirement is for decision support which properly reflects Spender's theory that senior managers are 'knowledge creators as well as knowledge users' (1989).

There are indications that the use of computers for any future improvement in decision-making by very senior managers may incorporate a class of certainty-geared models that serve to clarify thinking about the dynamic interdependencies of complex systems. Such models might include maps of cognitive systems (see, for example, Axelrod, 1976; Eden et al., 1983) or socioeconomic systems. Cognitive maps and system dynamics models (Morecroft, 1984) are not only similar in that the causal relationships between variables typically are 'hard-wired' (rather than probabilistic) but also because they are typically 'information-free', that is, built on impression, belief, judgement, wisdom, and intuition rather than on formally gathered data. Representing the world through the construction of a 'processual toy' which can become a learning instrument seems to be a promising development (de Geus, 1988). '*In a sense, such models have exhausted empiricism and placed no bounds on rationality*' (attributed to Rohrbaugh at the Toronto conference on which this book is based).

The two chapters that follow represent two approaches to the use of computers in the provision of group decision support. Both approaches deliberately set out to provide help to decision-makers at the highest level and to do so with a focus on the management of group process and content. They have been used extensively with these strata of decision-makers and depend upon a high level of skill in facilitation as well as the availability of a technique and tool for the 'real time' analysis of content. Nevertheless they are signals of an infant that will yet grow into a powerful combination of computer power and social process. Unlike many of the developments of computer-aided group decision support in the US, the proponents of all the approaches discussed in this book argue that it is not their aim to replace the facilitator but rather to use computers to add to his or her skills and power.

13

The Role of Computers in Group Decision Support

FRAN ACKERMANN

The use of the computer in aiding the manager to cope with the ever-increasing complexity of problems presented to him or her has resulted in an interest in decision support systems and following that, group decision support systems (GDSS). The idea has grown from the escalating pressures on managers or other decision-makers to solve the 'messy' and complex problems in the most effective manner available and the presumption that computer technology has a role to play. As most of these individuals spend a considerable amount of their time in decision-making situations dealing with conflicting views, different areas of expertise, and huge quantities of data a more efficient system of managing this complexity should provide them with the power to gain a greater understanding and clearer picture of the problem and therefore lead to a better solution.

What is a Computer Supported GDSS?

George Huber in his paper 'Issues in the Design of Group Decision Support Systems' (1984) describes GDSS as 'a set of software, hardware, and language components and procedures that support a group of people engaged in a decision-related meeting'. This description correlates closely with the research and consultancy the author is, and has been, undertaking and this chapter is built upon these experiences. The experiences have been generated through work in the field of strategic management and shorter-term work on messy problems, with several large international companies (Shell International, British Telecom, ICL, and Reed Business Publishing). In all of these instances special purpose GDSS *software* has been used in the context of computer *hardware* including slave screen/large screen VDU projection facilities and a methodology of *procedures* for the facilitation of effective teamwork.

GDSS is not a new area of research. Huber (1984) argues that academic and public organizations (for example SUNY – Albany, Southern Methodist University, EXECOM Systems Corporation, Georgia Institute of Technology and CACI Inc., Cleveland State University) have been developing or implementing such systems for several years while others are developing well established techniques (Nominal Group Technique: Delbecq et al., 1975, and Delphi Technique: Dalkey, 1969) to incorporate the principles of GDSS into their methodologies. When comparing the different systems, however, it is interesting to note that there is little similarity between them, as each designer has defined his particular arena and built his system to suit that circumstance. Surprisingly, there is little written information about systems already developed and even less published material on the results of established systems which are currently being used with clients.

One such system, which has been described in detail, is the experimental meeting room called Colab designed by Xerox PARC (Palo Alto Research Center) 'to study computer support of collaboration problem solving in face-to-face meetings' (Stefik et al., 1987). This environment with its workstations networked together, 'chalkboards' and specially developed software allows participants (mostly systems analysts) to take part in a brainstorming session and then organize and evaluate the emerging ideas. Whether this is a *decision* support system is a moot point; discussion with the designer confirms that the system is mostly used to help a group structure a report or paper. Another specially designed *room* for decision management is the ICL POD (Austin, 1986) which includes computers, projection facilities, and a photocopying whiteboard and it was through being able to work with group *decision* support in this latter environment that some of the author's own ideas of GDSS emerged.

Most writers will argue that one key objective of the computer in decision support is to improve the efficiency of the use of managers' time. For example Keen (1980) states in his paper on decision support systems that 'it supports rather than replaces their [managers'] judgement. The overall aim is to improve the effectiveness of their decision making.' This description corresponds closely with the ideas of others (Huber, 1984; De Sanctis and Gallupe, 1986; Sarin and Greif, 1985) who believe that GDSS should increase the effectiveness of the group by holding on to the data and allowing members of the group to access it concurrently. It is helpful to view 'the computer's role not as a surrogate expert but as an intermediary – a sophisticated medium of communication' (Winograd and Flores, 1986). In this way the computer is able to carry out analysis, including the use of complicated heuristics to present the data in a series of different ways allowing each possible solution or option to be seen with all its ramifications and weighed against the other options being discussed.

GDSSs have grown up from managers using various decision support systems such as decision trees, risk analysis, repertory grids and such methodologies as nominal group technique to allow groups of managers to use the same facilities interactively. The computers act as useful databases containing large amounts of information and presenting it in forms which are both useful and relevant to the group. The system allows the group members to discuss the various options available to them, helps generate possible solutions and evaluate which of these potential solutions would be most appropriate. The use of tele-conferencing and video conferencing has been used to remove the constraint of distance and maximize the groups' effectiveness allowing companies with offices throughout the globe to have their members participate in corporate strategies during crisis handling in real time (Sarin and Greif, 1985).

Benefits from Computer Based GDSS

'A GDSS aims to improve the process of group decision making by removing common communication barriers, providing techniques for structuring decision analysis, and systematically directing the pattern, timing or content of discussion' (De Sanctis and Gallupe, 1985). Using the methodology developed by Eden and Ackermann (1989), a series of interviews are carried out with members of a preselected group. The data collected through these interviews or through brainstorming exercises is collated by the interviewees into a model. This allows people to view their ideas without being able to associate any particular idea with any member of the group, thus eliciting a more balanced appraisal of the data.

By allowing group members to view the data on a large central screen displaying some of the aspects of the issue currently being discussed, 'less forceful' personalities are able to contribute their ideas alongside those who would naturally dominate the air time, and the more junior members feel less overwhelmed by the social skills of their superiors. The ability to view the data on a screen, thus having time to think without the necessity for immediate action, permits a more rational perspective to be taken of conflicting argument and therefore allows the group member to modify his beliefs without loss of face. This aspect is important when aiming for group consensus as the anonymity of ideas presented and the increase of time available for reflection reduces the risk of participants feeling unable to back down from previously expressed views.

A greater cross-section of ideas ensues from working with those members 'at the coal face'. These members present views hitherto unknown to those further up the organizational tree and they in turn are shown the overall strategy as devised by those at the top of the organization. Thus a greater understanding of the organization develops. 'Social interaction in decision-making groups is characterised by such variety, complexity and apparent disorder that it seems to defy neat analysis. The key difficulty seems to be choosing an appropriate aspect of the group's behaviour' (Kerr, 1982). Detecting this aspect is important, as each group of decision-makers is different and contingency of action is therefore essential. To recognize these differences, a facilitator with a good working knowledge of the methodology can increase the possibility of the group achieving its fullest potential. The facilitator becomes an important part of the group's interaction amongst itself and the role of GDSS becomes a powerful *element* in the skill and resource base of the facilitator. This view of GDSS as a *part* of the overall role of a facilitator is in contrast to those who see GDSS as the 'facilitator' and expect participants to manage the technology and the process.

The Role of the Facilitator

Facilitators play a crucial part in the organization of GDSS as they allow the participants to concentrate on the issues at hand rather than struggle to use the technology themselves. Computer literacy and familiarity with a keyboard is seldom found in most of today's senior executives and this must be taken into account. Requiring the executive to use the computer may well jeopardize the event, as slow data manipulation and increasing frustration will result in disinterest and lack of support. Even computer-literate users need time to become familiar with the system in order to benefit fully. The support software is powerful because of its complex and contingent instruction base (this is the case not only for COPE but also for Hiview: Phillips, 1989a). Powerful software to deal with messy problems will invariably be complex (Ashby's Law of Requisite Variety) and thus demands a high level of knowledge about how to use the software in response to the needs of the group.

As each group decision process is vastly different the software needs to be as flexible as possible allowing for changes in direction, so the facilitator must be aware of all the possible abilities of the software to help the group most effectively. The facilitator also releases the group from needing to elect a leader who would experience difficulty in remaining both a member of the team and recording and directing the discussion. Milter and Rohrbaugh (1985) have stated that 'available time is fragmented as the group must simultaneously maintain and co-ordinate itself, master hardware and software operation, deal with the technical issues of decision modelling and of course resolve the controversial issues of the organizational problem'. A facilitator can reduce the pressure and enable executives to concentrate solely on the problem. Another consequence of having one member of the team directing the meeting is that members of the group may feel the leader is spending more time on issues relevant to him or her and not viewing the picture from the 'objective' viewpoint of an outsider.

Organization of Agendas

Agendas are also an important consideration in the structuring of decision support, as a believably logical and thorough route through the issues is vital. After creating a model from data collected in interviews, a good way to begin a session using SODA as a method of GDSS is to do a quick cycle around the accumulated data to refresh the members' memories of what they said and to let them view other members' points of view *in the context of their own views*. However, it is often difficult to keep to this as the ideas are debated and explored and the discussion usually moves off at a tangent. Hence a facilitator who is fully aware of the time management problem can gently suggest that the group moves on to the next issue when either time threatens to become a problem or the issue being discussed is generating a destructive and degenerative debate. This facilitation allows the group members time to think about the issue in a more rational manner, increasing the chance of consensus further. The creative powers of the group may also be enhanced as the facilitator can boost member participation by drawing in those members who are naturally quiet and in a way that is more encouraging than simply providing the non-participant with technology-based interview facilities (Gallupe, 1985).

Requirements of a GDSS

A GDSS environment includes both hardware and software, and a typical GDSS room could include a series of terminals or workstations linked together through some form of networking, a large main screen visible to all and controlled by the facilitator, large sheets of paper and/or a photocopying whiteboard to record the options as they emerge and a three-colour video projector or large monitor. It is hoped in the future that some groups, when familiar with the system, will become able to view the same model either on a large screen or on their own terminal simultaneously and link their contributions directly into the model using a keyboard. They will then be able to manipulate the data through the use of a keyboard or a mouse. This, however, could have important consequences on the social processes of the group, as members would be concentrating exclusively on the model through their terminal and would therefore no longer interact with one another verbally or non-verbally. Currently the information gained, either through previous discussions/interviews or preceding input from the session, can be seen and added to by all the participants. At any time the facilitator is able to show specific areas of the model created from the input on the large screen, enabling all the participants to concentrate on or review that particular aspect. This continuous inputting of data relieves the participants of the necessity of keeping notes and allows them to concentrate on the problem.

SODA as a GDSS

Development of a software program called COPE has been under way for some time. The program was written to help consultants deal with 'messy' and complex problems and to enable them to manage their data in an effective manner. The program stores all the ideas (concepts) into a central database (Eden and Ackermann, 1989) and then allows the user to view certain areas of the model in a variety of ways. It allows the user to explore the data, not in a two-dimensional form as would occur if it was viewed in a document format, but to see it in an n-dimensional form, which enables a better understanding of how concepts are linked to each other and how each concept interrelates with others.

Analysis of the SODA GDSS Model

A complex 'fourth generation' language is resident within the software, allowing the user to carry out various analyses using one of the programs already available or to write a program of his or her own choice to carry out a particular form of analysis. COPE also allows the user to map ideas, taking concepts from an n-dimensional space and, through a series of heuristics, placing them in a two-dimensional form. There is the facility to map the concepts either hierarchically or concentrically. This capability is very useful when feeding back information to clients or simply for understanding how certain issues are related. In a GDSS environment these maps provide a written format of the discussion for participants to refer to at a later date and can be produced 'on the hoof' within the GDSS workshop.

There is often considerable uncertainty about what issues are involved and how to represent them. By using the software, the group is able to see how each member views the situation in relation to their own views and can therefore gain a clearer understanding of the problem being tackled. Providing tools to change direction quickly and present a different aspect or application and having the experience and ability to act immediately enables the facilitator to manage the issue of contingency.

Generating and Modelling the Data

When starting to work on a problem area interviews with a limited number of people identified as involved in the problem area are carried out. The interviews usually last about an hour, during which the ideas and issues produced are turned into a 'cognitive map' (Eden et al., 1983). These rough maps are then keyed into the computer during the break between interviews so that the issues emerging can be tentatively explored in the following interviews. The model composed of all the gathered information is then analyzed and tidied, merging identical concepts and removing any extraneous links generated from compiling the different maps. An agenda is then created to cover all the key areas in the following GDSS workshop.

It is during follow-up workshops that a GDSS-type environment is used. Group members work on the information collected, deliberate on the emerging goal system/issues/options, and aim to move towards consensus and commitment and finally to an action package. In most cases a hotel conference room is hired which is dictated by detailed specifications (Eden and Ackermann, 1989). The equipment generally used is two computers (usually two portable Toshiba T3100) linked together, a three-colour video projector or monitor and large high-resolution screen and plenty of flip-chart paper stuck up on the walls.

Managing the GDSS Workshop

The workshop is run by two facilitators. One facilitator drives the software while the other leads the clients through the agenda explaining how the day will proceed and then, following the agenda, records the ensuing discussion on the flip charts. The facilitator driving the computers projects the data on to the main screen while constantly inputting and editing the new information being generated by the participants. The facilitator is able to conduct new analyses of the changing database, and guide the 'process' facilitator by appropriately updating the main screen. To allow this to occur without interrupting the main screen the second computer acts as a 'slave' allowing him to input, edit and search for cross-relating concepts. It is through this ability to search for equivalent ideas that a more effective use of participants' time is gained.

This updating in real time gives the group a greater feeling of ownership. Thus they are more likely to take an interest in working on the issues and feel more committed to actions agreed especially as they are seeing the issues they themselves have made only minutes before. 'The group aims to utilize the resources brought to the meeting by each individual and to generate a high level of motivation among the membership to solve the problem and implement the group's decision' (De Sanctis and Gallupe, 1986). Having the current issue projected on the main screen means members can listen to other people's ideas knowing that there will be time to introduce their own views and that this knowledge allows them to listen better.

The increased sense of ownership means they will be more committed to carrying any ensuing actions through. 'The solution is not a theoretical model but a practical strategy ready for implementation' (Quinn et al., 1985). This is especially important in 'situations where groups must, in fact, reach a decision, and where the intention is that the decision be implemented following the collaborative experience of the group meeting' (De Sanctis and Gallupe, 1985). This, however, is harder to achieve in a large meeting as consensus becomes harder to achieve (Hoffman, 1979) and cliques emerge within the group.

The Strategic Use of Colour

The use of colour has become a powerful medium of portraying the different elements of the problem. Being able to distinguish between an option, assumption or goal can be achieved easily as colours are attributed to them and if necessary a chart explaining the colours can be drawn up for easy reference until the participants become familiar with the process. Although the method had previously designated different types of concept (for example goals, strategic issues, options and assumptions) the ability to colour them, although simple, has proved immensely valuable especially as few other decision support systems incorporate colour. Being able to designate particular types of concept also aids the group member, who can understand that a goal is a top-order concept. To achieve it, he or she must look at the strategic issues underneath it and then the options under them. As each of these is colour-coded this becomes easy to spot and the process becomes more efficient and effective. The hierarchical structure also enables participants to question any of the links which support the arguments and if finding them to be untrue, the link can be deleted, possibly also deleting a now irrelevant section of the model.

Future Directions

One area currently being researched is using the methodology with written material, rather than interviews, as the form of primary input. The model generated from the selected documents will then incorporate all the issues concerning the issue at hand. Distilling information from a number of experts with conflicting or corresponding views means that careful coding is essential. Along with reading the documents, frequent visits to the client's company were necessary to clarify areas found to be confusing or lacking information. When feeding the model back to the client in the GDSS environment there was little of the ownership normally apparent when working with data from interviews and therefore less understanding and commitment to the model.

Moving to a situation where several computers are networked together so that decision-makers can concurrently access the model with guidance from a facilitator is one obvious route to be developed. But difficulties are anticipated, one example of which is the procedure arising when changes are made to the model. Two members altering one concept would result in the computer either changing the concept twice by accessing one member's alteration after the other's or refusing to edit either. Having a method for informing one user that another is already accessing a particular area of the model by either displaying a window or message on screen seems the most viable solution at present. This problem of accessing the data simultaneously was also encountered by Xerox PARC (Stefik et al., 1987), who engineered a locking device on any area being worked on. Another possible benefit from networking is that it would give participants the ability to view alternative areas of the model thus allowing them to follow chains of thought individually and explore the data. But as this could result in less social interaction between the group, as all their concentration would be directed towards the computer, it could have serious repercussions.

It is important to produce some form of documentation at the end of a session reviewing all the issues and options discussed and highlighting those agreed upon, to give the client a sense of achievement as well as a list to refer to at a later date. One of the key areas needing development is the production of a useful document containing this information during the workshop, and one avenue is to utilize the second machine more. This would allow the facilitator to project from one machine while being able to work on the second, creating documents as well as the usual editing, inputting and changing, and then swap over at appropriate times. To achieve this a network system between the two machines must be established as both machines would constantly need to update the model.

Availability of a GDSS environment is of key interest to the user and creating an environment that is permanently installed at the user's or customer's site (Huber, 1984) is one possibility. Another more powerful approach is to develop a method of working that is portable, but this can prove bulky and expensive. By hiring a three-colour video projector or monitor and using Toshiba T3100s and flip-chart paper the equipment can be moved to any suitable location. This relieves clients from spending a considerable amount establishing the GDSS room but allows them some flexibility as to where the meeting is held. Being away from the office is certainly an advantage; however the location must be feasible for those attending or greater complications will arise.

Conclusion

A GDSS-type environment of the type described has now been used with clients on real problems for three years, and during this period the technique has been altered and improved. The approach has been used for forming and implementing a corporate strategy in one company through a series of monthly workshops with directors. These directors have during this time become accustomed to the equipment and environment and find it very effective. A peripheral benefit is that it also ensures that by going through the model a new director can learn about the company and how its strategy was achieved.

The need for facilitators is still an interesting issue, with clients first experiencing the methodology needing most help. Enabling the decision-maker to become familiar with the process is a time-consuming task and, as mentioned before, a facilitator will spend a considerable amount of time recording the data as it is generated and being unable to contribute his or her own ideas. SODA usually requires two facilitators, but other methods use more, for example automated decision conferencing (Quinn et al., 1985) requires three – one more to take notes. As people become more computer literate and find using mice, keyboards or alternative input devices more natural the facilitator's role will be reduced. The group may gradually be able to maintain itself independently although there will always be the dilemma of becoming too involved in the process and overlooking the content.

GDSS has developed considerably since such programs as Thinktank, Framework and Freestyle (O'Conner, 1984) were launched. These programs were solely 'thought organizers' and little manipulation of the data was possible. Technology is rapidly improving all the time, resulting in greater speed in retrieval of data, better graphics and improved networking, increasing the potential of GDSS considerably. It is an area of work which can only benefit the decision-maker.

14

Decision Analysis for Group Decision Support

LAWRENCE D. PHILLIPS

In the United States, high-tech rooms are in operation to facilitate the work of groups. In many of these rooms participants sit around a U-shaped table at positions equipped with networked microcomputers that are recessed into the table. At the front of the room, a large projection screen displays the output of any one computer, or of aggregated information. Subgroups or individuals can move to small syndicate rooms, each equipped with microcomputers that are networked to the ones at the table, and a variety of software is available to help participants in their collective work.

Different approaches are evident on the other side of the Atlantic. Examples of two of these approaches which have similar aims, but which have been implemented differently, exist at the University of Strathclyde (see Eden, in chapter 15) and at the London School of Economics and at International Computers Limited. In the latter two rooms group members sit around a circular table in an octagonal room (called the 'POD' – Austin, 1986) the walls of which provide conventional and self-copying whiteboards, and two screens for displaying 35mm slides, overhead transparencies, drawings and printed material, videotapes and the output from computers. Save for a single infra-red hand-controller, which enables the user to turn the displays on and off, and to adjust the levels of room and board lighting, computers or other IT devices are less evident.

Differences in Group Decision Support

These two types of room reveal different approaches to group decision support. The Xerox (Stefik et al., 1987) and Arizona (Applegate et al., 1987) rooms are *workbench environments* which support a collection of software tools, whereas the LSE POD and Strathclyde group decision support room provide a *problem solving environment* that gives easy access to a variety of media, including computers. Although both types of room are said to support groups working on complex, ill-structured problems, they do so in very different ways. In the workbench environment, individuals interact mainly via computer models. In the UK, computers and other media support the participants who interact directly with each other. One is computer-based, the other group-centred.

Obviously the designers of these rooms differ in what they believe to be effective decision support for groups. Both perspectives were represented at a recent international working meeting on the future of group decision support systems. Given these differences in orientation of UK and US participants, it was surprising that agreement was reached on a definition of this type of group decision support system (GDSS):

The application of information technology to support the work of groups.

However, it is possible that disagreement arises in the notion of work, and how that work is best supported. Note also the difference between this IT-driven definition and that expressed in other chapters in this book.

The Nature of Work

Elliott Jaques (1976) defined human work as 'the exercise of discretion within prescribed limits'. The first part of the definition relates to the psychological component of work, 'the exercise of discretion', while the second part points to the organizational context that imposes limits on the scope of that discretion. The limits widen as one progresses up the organizational hierarchy, but at all levels discretion is exercised in deciding an appropriate balance between the pace and quality of work.

But what, precisely, is meant by 'the exercise of discretion'? Decision theory (Lindley, 1986) provides one answer. If decisions are to be coherent, that is internally consistent, then it is necessary to take account of two features that characterize all decisions: uncertainty and preference.

When facing a complex, ill-structured problem, we might be uncertain about many things: what is the problem, how should we proceed to solve it, what options should be considered, how likely are relevant future events and possible consequences? Data might help to answer these questions, and that is why management information systems (MIS) and intelligent knowledge-based systems (IKBS) are built into some decision support systems.

But uncertainty is only half the equation. We must also consider our preferences: subjective values associated with consequences, time and risk preferences, and tradeoffs between objectives. In the quest for an objective basis for decisions, many organizations attempt to 'objectify' these factors, often by referring to some external standard, without realizing that choosing a standard is in itself a judgement. But in the end, valuing a $5m loss as more serious than a $5m profit is good, or deciding to use a 12 per cent discount rate in a discounted cash flow calculation, or choosing a project that is sure to yield $1m over a project that has a 50–50 chance of $2m or nothing, or deciding to sacrifice short-term profit in order to establish market share, is a *matter of preference and judgement.*

In summary, 'exercising discretion' means that a person is considering uncertainty, forming preferences, making judgements and taking decisions. With this understanding of the nature of human work, consider an expanded definition of an IT-based definition of a GDSS:

> The use of information technology to help groups of people consider uncertainty, form preferences, make judgements and take decisions within prescribed limits.

Now the difference in approach between US and UK GDSS approaches may become more obvious. The US computer-based rooms were designed under the assumption that exchange of information is the main work of a group. De Sanctis and Dickson (1987) argue that 'the most fundamental activity of group decision making is interpersonal communication, and the primary purpose of a GDSS is to improve group communication activities'. But it could be argued that while interpersonal communication is indeed important, it is a means to an end, that groups often engage in work which has as its aim the creation of a consensus view and a commitment to action. Communication is the means by which individuals explore uncertainty, form preferences, make judgements and, finally, take decisions.

For these functions to occur in groups, more is required than computers. Individuals present information in the form of papers, slides, viewgraphs or other visual aids. The meeting room should be inviting even to individuals who are computer-illiterate, or who shun technology. As Eden and Hickling point out later in this book, the environment should be conducive to problem-solving, and make it easy for the leader or facilitator to use technology, including computers, when appropriate. This is the perspective taken by designers of problem-centred facilities.

GDSS through Decision Theory

The perspective offered on GDSS by decision theory leads to a problem-centred, action orientation, while decision analysis, the applied technology that was developed from decision theory (Howard, 1966; Raiffa, 1968; French, 1986), guides the process of problem-solving. There are several important roles for decision analysis.

First, decision analysis provides a language that participants can share. Wooler (1987) has shown that senior executives lack a common language for discussing strategic issues. Even within the same company, there is usually no shared understanding of terms like mission, vision, goal, objective, strategy, option, scenario, and risk. Decision theory provides a *language that makes it possible to fix the meaning of these terms* in a way that contributes to the subsequent development of a model.

Second, decision theory provides a *grammar for manipulating meaning* in ways that are not easy with words alone. For example, it would not be an exaggeration to say that all problems, in both public and private sectors, involve multiple objectives. Finding solutions requires that tradeoffs between objectives be considered. Tradeoffs can be accomplished within the context of a multi-attribute utility or value model. Lacking such a model, members of a group often find it difficult to establish priorities, for that usually requires a comparison of apples with oranges. The difficulty of making these comparisons is a major stumbling block for most groups, and enabling comparison is one of the most important contributions that decision analysis can make.

Third, decision theory provides a *structure to thinking*. The form of the model developed to tackle the problem at hand shows how the parts of the problem interrelate. The model is the expression of the language, and it shows how the grammar should be used. The model form most often associated with decision analysis is a decision tree. It provides a way of representing a problem in which there are a few options, uncertainty about the future, and where possible consequences differ in several ways – that is, they are multi-attributed. But managers find the decision tree representation too passive; it does not do justice to their ability to deal effectively with unexpected events as they arise. More frequently used are two model forms that seem to accommodate most of the concerns expressed by senior managers: evaluation and resource allocation.

Evaluation problems are characterized by a few options (strategies, projects, choices, systems, etc.) and many objectives or attributes. The goal is to find an overall ordering of the options, and this is achieved by scaling the options on the individual attributes, assigning relative weights to the attributes and then taking a weighted average of the individual scale. Multi-attribute utility (or value) modelling (von Winterfeldt and Edwards, 1986, chapter 8) is the approach favoured by many decision analysts.

Resource allocation problems present a large number of options (possible ways of dividing the pie) and only a few objectives. The goal is to find the best way of allocating a fixed resource (usually people, material, or money) and this is done by creating, for each budget category, a small multi-attribute model in which options at different resource levels are evaluated against the objectives, then assessing weights across the categories and objectives, and combining all models into one efficient curve that shows the best overall allocation for any given level of resource.

Resource allocation models play a crucial role in resolving a pervasive problem of organizational life: the commons dilemma. Even though several managers are using their available resource optimally, their boss can see that this use does not form a collective optimum. One solution is to centralize decision-making, but that may result in unrealistic decisions which are unresponsive to local conditions, and managers may lose incentive as they are stripped of responsibility. Decentralization restores motivation and allows realistic decisions to be made, but brings ineffective use of resources. The solution to the commons dilemma requires tradeoffs to be made between the managers, and this may be achieved through group participation in resource allocation modelling. Although some managers may lose resource, the resulting loss of benefits may be more than made up by gains in those areas to which the freed resource is allocated (Phillips, 1982).

Much of a senior manager's work is concerned with evaluating options and allocating resources in light of conflicting objectives and uncertainty about the future (which can be accommodated by incorporating alternative scenarios in a hierarchical multi-attribute model, or as a risk attribute). Thus, multi-attribute evaluation and resource allocation models are frequently used. To these two classes of model a third should be added: bargaining and negotiation. Barclay and Peterson (1976) have had considerable experience in using decision analysis as an effective tool in negotiating agreements.

Other model forms capture problems that are dominated by uncertainty rather than multiple objectives. Event trees, fault trees, and influence diagrams are good ways of modelling uncertainty about a target event by 'extending the conversation' to include related events, with assessed conditional probabilities representing the degrees of belief associated with the events. Bayesian models capture the influence of data on uncertainty, while hierarchical Bayesian models (Schum, 1987) have the added advantage of dealing with both the inferential uncertainty inherent in data and the errors of measurement or unreliability of the data. Finally, in credence decomposition models (Brown, 1971) a target variable is written as a function of other variables, whose probability distributions are individually assessed and then combined using the functional relationship to determine the probability distribution for the target variable.

The seven model forms discussed here can be placed along a continuum of problem types, from problems in which uncertainty dominates, to those where multiple objectives are paramount:

Problem dominated by

UNCERTAINTY		MULTIPLE OBJECTIVES
EXTEND conversation – event tree – fault tree – influence diagram	CHOOSE action – payoff matrix – decision tree	EVALUATE options – simple and hierarchical multi-attribute models
REVISE opinion – Bayesian models of simple and hierarchical inference		ALLOCATE resources – multi-attribute commons dilemma problem
SEPARATE into components – credence decomposition		NEGOTIATE – multi-attribute bargaining model

These seven model forms are sufficiently rich to cover a wide variety of problems faced by organizations and individuals.

Beyond Decision Theory

However, decision theory is not enough. A good GDSS must provide a balance between content, process, and structure. Eden (see chapter 5) postulates a multiplier effect between content and process: in an effective system, as content develops, it should alter the process by which the group works, but process often affects content. Both have to be managed effectively, and to do this requires knowledge of group processes. It is helpful to know how the inevitable anxieties that arise when individuals work in groups can affect the group, how groups impose roles on individuals who may then find themselves acting on behalf of the group, how different assumptions may operate covertly to influence the group's behaviour, how deflections from the task at hand can be managed with effective facilitation. Research on group processes has identified conditions and situations that increase the ability of groups to solve problems effectively (Low and Bridger, 1979), and it is knowledge of small group functioning that is used by a facilitator to help a group to achieve its goals.

Decision Conferencing

Now we turn to the question of how decision analysis can be used with groups of people. One approach, invented in the late 1970s by Cameron Peterson, is decision conferencing, which in its current state draws on experience and research from the three areas discussed earlier – information technology, decision analysis, and group processes.

Decision conferencing is an intensive two-day problem-solving session attended by a group of people who are concerned about some complex issue facing an organization. The group is aided by at least two people from outside the organization, a facilitator and a decision analyst, who are experienced in working with groups. The facilitator helps the participants to structure their discussion, think creatively and imaginatively about the problem, identify the issues, model the problem and interpret the results. The analyst attends to the computer modelling and helps the facilitator.

The purposes of a decision conference are to generate a shared understanding of a problem and commitment to action. This is achieved by creating a computer-based model which incorporates the differing perspectives of the participants in the group, then examining the implications of the model, changing it and trying out different assumptions. As actions are shown to be insensitive to differences of opinion, as new, more robust options are developed, and as higher-level perspectives emerge, participants develop a common understanding that facilitates agreement about what to do next.

Although every decision conference is different, most are characterized by several stages that can be distinguished. Before the conference begins, the facilitator meets with the client to establish the nature of the problem and whether a decision conference is appropriate. If so, objectives are set, problem owners are identified, preparation required of participants is determined, and the key points of a calling note are agreed.

At the start of the conference, after an initial introduction by the facilitator, the group is asked to discuss the issues and concerns that are to be the subject of the conference. An attempt is made to formulate the nature of the problem. Does the group wish to reconsider strategy, or is a fundamental change of direction required? Perhaps budget items or projects need to be prioritized. Evaluating alternative plans, ventures, systems, bids or projects may be required, especially if objectives conflict. During this phase the facilitator has to decide whether exploration in depth or breadth will best help the work of the group.

Once the nature of the problem has been formulated, the facilitator chooses a generic structural form for representing the problem (usually one of the seven types discussed earlier), and the group begins to provide the content that is used in constructing the model. This is usually a simple, though not simplistic, representation of the group's thinking about the problem. The model is drawn by the facilitator on the whiteboards in the room, and at the same time the analyst inputs the model to the computer. Both data and subjective judgements are added to the model, and the computer output is projected on to a screen so all participants can see the results.

These initial results are rarely accepted by the group. Modifications are suggested by participants, and different judgements are tested. Many sensitivity analyses are carried out; gradually, intuitions change and sharpen as the model goes through successive stages. Eventually this process of change stabilizes, the model has served its purpose, and the group turns to summarizing the key issues and conclusions. An action plan is created so that when participants return to work the next day, they can begin to implement the solution.

Decision Conference Rules

Experience with decision conferencing has shown that following these three rules contributes to the success of the session:

1   The decision maker and all major problem owners must be present. If organizational constraints prevent this, then participants are chosen to represent the differing perspectives on the problem. The modelling process helps to create a new perspective out of the separate views.

If any key perspective is not represented, the recommendations of the group may be rejected by an influential individual who feels that the group did not consider certain crucial factors.

2   No papers or printed material may be consulted during the problem formulation stage. Printed materials often detract from the real problem.

3   The problem must be a live one. Using decision conferencing to justify decisions already taken doesn't work because hindsight biases prevent the development of an agreed model, and for problems that are not yet 'on the boil', judgements are too ill-formed to give meaningful results.

Benefits of Decision Conferencing

Organizations using decision conferencing report that the service helps them to arrive at better and more acceptable solutions than they can achieve using their usual procedures, and agreement is reached much more quickly. In large part, this is because there is no attempt during the model construction to obtain agreement about every aspect of the model. Instead, a rough model is constructed quickly so that it can be explored to discover those areas where disagreements matter to the results. For substantial portions of the model, the range of disagreement will have no effect on the overall result, so group work can focus on those few issues that matter.

Many decision conferences have broken through stalemates created previously by lack of consensus, by the complexity of the problem, by vagueness and conflict of goals, and by failure to think creatively and freshly about the problem. We find that the model helps participants to create new, more robust options, and to generate more satisfactory perspectives on a problem.

The model lends structure to thinking and allows all perspectives on a problem to be represented and discussed. This helps to take the heat out of arguments that seem to arise from differences of opinion. Thus, the process facilitates communication among participants, providing a 'way to talk differently', as one person put it, and it surfaces assumptions that are often different from one person to the next. Overall, decision conferencing develops a sense of common purpose.

Requisite Modelling

Models created in the above manner are 'requisite' (Phillips, 1984): they are sufficient in form and content to solve the problem at hand or, more generally, to resolve the issues of concern. Requisite models represent the shared social reality created by the group. Any one individual would have a more detailed understanding of his or her part of the problem, so the model is a simplified representation of each individual's perspective on the problem. Yet by combining many perspectives in one model, new meta-perspectives emerge.

The model is generative in that an existing situation is described in such a way that new insights emerge, and it is possible to see how the situation can be transformed into a new social reality (Gergen, 1982). Requisite decision models always involve human activity systems, so while they may be descriptive of a currently perceived social reality, and always suggest how that reality may be transformed (because alternative options are considered), they are rarely predictive of what people will actually do. *The model is only a guide to action, not a normative prescription*, and it is at best conditionally prescriptive.

In addition, the model differs from purely descriptive models in that it participates in the reality it is supposed to model. As the results of the modelling become available to participants, they *compare these results to their holistic judgements*. It is the inevitable discrepancies that arise, especially early in the modelling process, that drive the dialectic. By exploring these discrepancies, understanding deepens and changes, and new perspectives are reflected back as changes to the model. Thus, the model-building process is interactive and iterative, the social reality that is shared by the group changing as the model is revised. Eventually, participants are satisfied with the model and unable to derive any further insights from it. At that point, major conclusions and issues are summarized in the decision conference and an action plan is drawn up. The model has served its purpose, and the group returns to its usual way of communicating without the model.

Conclusions

The effectiveness of decision conferencing as a form of GDSS seems to be the result of the combination of several factors, no one of which is unique. First, a suitable environment is required. The POD is a high-tech version, but low-tech surroundings can be created even in country hotels with suitable use of whiteboards or flip-charts and a projection screen, a comfortable arrangement of seating, and a convenient supply of refreshments. Second, information technology at the service of the group is needed to combine the parts of the model and to facilitate instant replay of results. Third, decision analysis helps to provide structure to thinking, a language for expressing concerns of the group, and a way of combining differing perspectives. Fourth, attention to group process ensures that the group remains task oriented, and that anxieties do not seriously disrupt group work. Overall, a balance is maintained between content, process, and structure, helping to ensure that the work of the group is facilitated in effective ways.

PART V
THE ENVIRONMENT FOR SUPPORTING GROUPS

Introduction

COLIN EDEN

This book started by considering the context of group decision support, and moved on by introducing new developments in enabling a group to clarify issues related to the interactions between actors in the situation and options that face the group. The last section concentrated on developments in computer-supported methods of group support. Each of these elements of the book has discussed the intellectual properties of providing support to groups. The discussions have presumed that the group can be got together (a non-trivial issue involving developing the roles of process champion, cheerleader, as well as sponsor – Bryson and Roering, 1987), can work effectively and without hindrance from the physical setting, and can be provisioned with more than adequate physiological support. These latter conditions are regarded by most prac-tising facilitators as crucial to the success of group decision support and as much a part of the GDS *system* as the need for process and content management. And yet they are rarely spoken about, they are treated as if they were trivial, commonsense, or obvious. Part V tries to introduce the issue of the design of the group decision support environment as a serious topic worthy of proper discussion and research.

Earlier in this book attention was paid to the issue of designing and managing process with respect to content. The chapters by Ackermann and Phillips discussed methods that pay particular attention to facilitat-ing process and content management. Both methods usually employ two consultants where one concentrates on attending to the dynamics of social exchange and the other attends to real time recording and analysis of what is being said, *using a computer* for the purpose. The roles are not completely distinct but rather, are intertwined. The content facilitator is guiding the process, and the process facilitator is guiding analysis. It is interesting that the proponents and originators of these methods are committed to understanding group processes on the one hand but on the other are also committed to developing a role for the computer in GDS. It is probably no accident that approaches that use computer assistance are forced to attend to the physical environment. The imposition of computer hardware on the activity means that a workshop must be set up in advance and that the physical layout of the room must be adjusted to accommodate the hardware. This forces the facilitator to think about the way the setting influences the success of the workshop. It also ensures that 'theories-in-use' get explored and developed. The requirement for two facilitators means that there will be competing views about the design of the room, so forcing reflection on, and testing of, the intuitive theories.

It is also probably significant that proponents of those approaches which have been most extensively employed within a 'hard-nosed' consultancy setting (each of strategic choice, decision conferencing, and SODA having been applied to dozens of different clients) are always most keen to discuss the more 'trivial' aspects of their practice. They do so because they believe the physical setting, nature and timing of refreshments, use of work space, and the everyday tools (such as 'newsprint' pens) influence the probability of success.

The next three chapters discuss some of these 'trivialities' in an attempt to suggest formally that they be taken seriously. Eden starts this section by trying to elucidate a conceptual framework within which discussion can be set. He builds on experience of running workshops in high-tech environments as well as considerable experience of designing hotel settings for GDSS work.

This is followed by a personal commentary from Huxham (this is the only personal statement within the book and reflects her frustrations in dealing with environmental matters within her own work situation as a university MBA director). It considers the reticence of managers and team members to take the issue of room design seriously.

These views are amplified by Allen Hickling who sets out the practical requirements of effective design of the physical environment for working with groups. Hickling addresses the problem from the standpoint of someone with a vast amount of experience of using strategic choice in practice, but also with a background and training as an architect. His chapter is immediately practical and suggests the way in which different rooms and furniture layout are required for each of a number of different purposes.

Eden and Hickling have worked in several hundred designed environments including purpose-built conference facilities, high-technology rooms such as the ICL POD, and 'make-do' hotel meeting rooms. Because they have an overriding belief in the importance of physical settings they have deliberately set out to experiment informally with different designs. Eden has been forced to pay attention to setting because the use of computer support means having to set up rooms well in advance of the meeting. Deciding where to position the computer, content facilitator, and a large computer display means paying attention to other characteristics of the room, and having the time to do something about them. Hickling has a personal commitment to design and environment through his background as an architect. In both cases their own interest has indirectly rubbed off on their client groups who will remark on the appropriateness and efficacy of the designs. When clients are introduced to new ways of working with their environment they quickly become attuned to the significance of such factors in the success of facilitated group work.

If this part of the book does nothing else other than raise the topic to the level of legitimate intellectual debate amongst decision support consultants, designers, and commentators then it will have succeeded.

15
Managing the Environment as a Means to Managing Complexity

COLIN EDEN

Much of the professional ability of a management consultant rests on a skill in managing complexity. An ability to absorb large amounts of qualitative and quantitative data and yet reject 'noise' is traditionally regarded as a key skill. Alongside this absorption skill lie the more difficult analytical skills for identifying the 'nub of the issue' and spotting realistic organizational interventions. It is the last of these that we shall be addressing in this chapter.

Many authors have referred to the extent to which spotting organizational interventions is dependent upon political 'nous' (Mangham, 1986; Margerison, 1988) and the management of the process of consensus building. This chapter will argue that the management of process is made *unnecessarily complex* because too little specific and formal attention is paid to the role of environment and architecture when working with teams. Although there is an 'everyday world-taken-for-granted' (Young, 1977) body of knowledge that good consultants use to help them manage these elements of process (for example, many consultants pay attention to the size of room, relative seating position of participants, the position from which the facilitator will operate) little of this knowledge has been explicated.

A central component of the work that the author has undertaken with small teams is the use of computer technology as a way of building qualitative models in *real time* and visible to all members of the team (Eden, 1986a). As a result the facilitators have gone beyond their own 'world-taken-for-granted' theories and attempted to establish some design parameters when working with teams using 'high-tech' facilities. The requirement is, to some extent, in contrast to that of other 'soft' methodologies for group decision support (Friend and Hickling, 1987) where computer technology is not central, and is more in line with the needs of decision conferencing (Phillips, 1989a).

In chapter 13 Ackermann discusses the specific nature of SODA as a group decision support *system*, an important part of which is a large screen that can portray the colour output from a computer VDU. Using a large visualization of a model is not solely an outcome of the use of computers. For several years there has been a commitment to focusing the attention of team members away from one another as social beings and towards an interactive model being continuously constructed and modified in front of the participants (Sims and Eden, 1984; Eden and Huxham, 1988). Modelling 'on-the-hoof' and in public view has been a central tenet in the aim for attaining model ownership, and so although SODA involves more backroom preparation than is the case with strategic choice (for example) when it comes to bringing the team together it is the power of *interactive modelling* that is foremost.

The Demands of Interactive Modelling

The experience of the author points to some conflicting aspects that result from the needs of interactive modelling. Interactive modelling is dependent upon the ability of the decision support facility to record, in real time, the views expressed by participants; the participants must be aware of the record being made so that they are able to verify and take ownership of the model as it grows and changes. This probably means that the model must be in full view and the process of making changes must also be seen. Computer graphics and appropriate software (such as HiView and COPE)[1] seem an obvious way of doing this. Entries can be made from a keyboard remote from the screen and displayed for confirmation, and the data can be fitted into the model immediately and seen in the full context of the model. The common alternative of using flip charts demands exceptional writing skills on the part of the facilitator, and the data must be recorded within the constraints of a two-dimensional surface. Using flip charts provides no opportunity to reorganize previous material to reflect the addition of new material.

However, another important part of building ownership comes from giving a group a *sense of history* during a workshop. This can be achieved by building up an array of flip charts so that charts produced early in the meeting can be referred to later in the meeting. In addition, the human brain remembers pictures and shapes as much as content. Reference back to previous *pictures* reaffirms ownership because the shape is remembered. Thus the benefits of rebuilding the structure of the model in real time can work against ownership; it is the equivalent of writing notes by hand, and feeling comfortable with them, and then 'suffering' the computer software imposing its own order on the notes.

Similar issues persist when a 'photocopy whiteboard' is used.[2] There are important advantages in using this type of technology – a client group can be given photocopies of the equivalent of two flip chart sheets during the workshop. It is the equivalent of a standard whiteboard and can therefore give the facilitator an opportunity to modify material by cleanly rubbing out unwanted material. On the other hand, the history of previously recorded material takes longer to recall because it must be wound back one 'page' at a time and holds only a limited amount of pages.

The benefit deriving from the relative efficiency of recording and reorganizing material that can result from computer decision support systems can, however, make a client team feel as though little progress is being made. There can be something very reassuring about seeing piles of flip chart paper covered with past material, whereas the feeling of progress from using 'efficient' systems depends upon an intellectual rather than concrete experience that order is being achieved and complexity managed.

Many of these conflicts could be resolved as the low-level (rather than computer) technology changes. We can reasonably expect that multiple screens will become possible without using weighty and large three-tube/colour high-resolution projectors currently available. The development of more sophisticated software 'windowing' systems is already changing the way in which a group may access the history of meetings.

Refreshing Mental Ability

'Out of the Office'

'We do not act as a result of consideration, but as a way of being' (Winograd and Flores, 1986: 146). Providing participants in group decision-making events with a 'way of being' is encouraged by managing the environment and includes using technology, software, and architecture to refresh a person's mental ability continuously. The principle of 'away-days' is well established as a way of helping senior managers think in an uncluttered way about new ventures, be reflective about old ventures, and design strategy. Such away-days are generally thought to be more effective if they take place 'in the country' – which is usually taken to imply a rural setting and an 'old' country house. However, surprisingly, it is rare for this consideration to extend to the design of the internal setting.

The principles underlying a move 'to the country' are: removal from telephones/desks/subordinates and other trappings of fire-fighting management; the ability to take a break in the proceedings so that participants can get a 'breath of *fresh* air'; the physical surroundings are different from everyday settings through the use of a special purpose room, be it a simulated boardroom or sitting room; the group can be kept together, and separate from others, during breaks for eating. There is no reason to suppose that these principles should be discounted in GDSS environments. However some of the incrementalism in 'refreshing' abilities might be developed into a more continuous refreshment, and some of the physical environment might be more specially designed. Nevertheless there is a danger that these 'taken-for-granted' principles are overwhelmed by the technological surge for modernity.

The pros and cons of flip charts versus large screen projection facilities were discussed earlier. In the strive for the more extensive use of computer software there is a possibility for forgetting that the use of currently available large-screen colour projectors leads to darkened rooms. In the POD[3] and other examples of high-tech GDSS rooms this outcome is hidden from significance because the rooms are overtaken with sophisticated lighting patterns. Notably this was also the case in the Churchill War Room used during the Second World War where, within the constraints of the lighting systems of the day, attempts were made to use lighting to focus attention on some data and not on others. The general level of light was nevertheless higher than that allowable when computer-linked projectors are used.

Eden has in excess of seventy experiences of using projection facilities, for interactive modelling, in a large variety of hotel conference rooms, the conference rooms of multinational companies, and in special-purpose rooms such as the POD. These experiences lead to unhappiness about the impact of darkened rooms on the dynamics of problem-solving. Let alone the obvious problems of eye strain and the difficulty of combating sleepiness after lunch, there are other worries about the impact a darkened room has on the nature of social interaction. Whilst providing a structured and contentful focus of attention is a significant aim of GDSS, to do so at the cost of social awareness can have disastrous consequences. If we take seriously the extent to which social activity, with all its non-verbal trappings, is a 'symbolic interaction' (Blumer, 1969), then it is dependent upon the total performance of individuals for the full meaning of the communication to be efficiently transmitted. Thus although the aim of GDSS-enshrined problem-solving is to focus attention on content rather than process and so reduce interpersonal dynamics, if the consequence is withdrawing the opportunity for a 'complete' *interaction*, then it could significantly fail in its aim for more effective (but possibly more apparently efficient) use of managers' time. We suspect that the relatively overpowering nature of a bright visual image and dark surround shifts the balance too far in favour of focus on the model. Controlled spotlighting can to some extent overcome this difficulty: this occurs with the POD where the spotlights can draw attention to the social arena of the round table without casting light on the screen itself. Spotlighting used in this way is undoubtedly dramatic and therefore noticeable, which may or may not be an advantage.

Alongside the role of darkened rooms and artificial lighting we need to explore the role that daylight plays in such settings. Our experience has led us to take every opportunity to open curtains, draw blinds – *let in light*. When we do so there is vocal appreciation of the extent to which this acts as mental refreshment. Nevertheless it is significant that although there is a lack of daylight in the POD at all times, the businesslike environment that is created and the well appreciated gains to be made from the group decision support system that we operate ('real-time SODA') means that most management teams want to come back and use the facility again, unless provided with a 'low-tech' alternative such as a pleasant hotel or conference centre.

Relieving Boredom – the Role of Computer Graphics

The first part of this chapter has concentrated on some of the ramifications of the use of high-tech GDSS technology on mental tiredness. This section will argue that good GDSS computer hardware and software has a role to play in relieving the natural process of cycles of boredom in any meeting. This role must be seen within the context of model ownership as the key element of maintaining excitement and interest.

For several years COPE operated in monochrome, indeed HiView still does. It had developed out of mainframe/teletype DSS software for use by consultants and so the display had never been regarded as particularly important. As COPE was increasingly used with clients as a GDSS it was realized that colour displays could serve two purposes: firstly, helping manage the complexity of the content by colour-coded classification, where concepts were coded white for goals, purple for 'strategic issue' labels, blue for potential options, and green for agreed actions, with yellow for arguments linking other concepts; but secondly, as more *decorative and entertaining* displays.

Aside from the impact of colour coding on the ability of the group to work more effectively with complexity and richness it became clear that more decorative displays are important in maintaining higher levels of interest in the problem-solving process as a whole. The ability of the software to operate in 'real time' and take in new material so that the display *changes* more frequently to reveal current material not only affects ownership but also reduces boredom levels. There is a significant difference between presentations of preprepared material and material that is being built 'on the hoof'. If the software can be driven to reflect overtly the contingencies of *the group process as it unfolds* then it is clear that interest is more likely to be retained. In addition the ability to change the display through small increments of progress allows for a *continuity* of interest.

The quality of interactive graphics in DSS software such as Stella (Richmond, 1987) is profoundly changing expectations. However the current high cost of high-resolution colour projection equipment is a constraint to both portability and 'everyday' use. The advent of less costly facilities for projecting colour output via standard overhead projectors (for example a colour version of the Kodak Datashow) could change the possibilities for the wider use of high-tech GDSS facilities.

The Social Dynamics of GDSS

It is a remarkable fact that association with at least a dozen very large organizations reveals a dearth of variety in the design and architecture of conference rooms. For example, a tour of British Telecom, Shell International offices in London, and ICL will reveal rectangular conference rooms containing rectangular tables with at best a flip chart easel and an overhead projector. Undoubtedly such rooms are derivative of the boardroom layout.

As intimated in the first section of this book, the effectiveness of GDSS demands consideration of the *design* of social interaction and thus consideration of the environmental trappings to support consensus seeking and creative problem-solving. In this section of this chapter, some of the simple, but important, non-technological aspects of such an environment will be discussed.

Probably the first issue to address is the role of a table in a GDSS room. Most high-tech GDSS rooms have taken for granted the need for a table as the housing for VDUs and keyboards: they are generally round or horseshoe shaped rather than rectangular. A table of any sort has a significant impact and potentially damaging effect on the social dynamics of problem-solving meetings lasting over one hour. A table places participants in fixed positions relative to one another. Given that interaction occurs predominantly between persons sitting opposite one another (Steinzor, 1950) because the non-verbal responses to events are always in view, then it is inevitable that dynamics of the meeting are partly governed by seating position. This outcome can clearly be used as a design parameter. However it is possible that creative thinking and consensus building is more likely if interactions are less rigid and more fluid.

If a table is required, then a round table will allow one-to-three, rather than one-to-one, dominant interactions and the ability to see all participants. Most of us have experienced the difference between the social dynamics of sitting at a rectangular rather than a round dining table. And yet, as stated earlier, few conference rooms are equipped with round tables, and few so-called 'conference centres' are able to supply round tables.

GDSS architects such as Metapraxis (Preedy and Biddlestone, 1985) have, in contrast to the above arguments, deliberately set out to provide back-projected displays in the boardroom of a company so that the architecture (including seating and table) of the boardroom is not changed. They have sensibly concluded that if they are to get GDSS facilities into the real power base of companies then they must not change the symbolic character of the decision-making chamber. This approach is particularly interesting in the light of the bold architecture embodied in Stafford Beer's GDSS room designed for President Allende during his abruptly terminated leadership of Chile.

When possible it seems appropriate to generate more fluidity by denying the role of a table altogether. The aim is to create the most fluid setting possible by allowing the fullest possible opportunity for participants to change their position relative to one another. Thus coffee tables may be used but at the periphery of the room, so that the position of seating can be changed as easily as possible. Chairs are comfortable and on easily running castors so that participants are encouraged to refer to content displayed as a part of the support system (be it flip charts, whiteboard display, or large-screen VDU output) by remaining seated and 'gliding purposefully' across the room on their chair. Once having reached the position to point to a display they are not encouraged to regain their old position. In this way participants are continuously changing their position relative to others. Unfortunately the use of conference centre facilities demands the import of three-colour projectors which currently sit in the middle of the room at coffee table height and detract from potential fluidity of participant positioning. At present the use of purpose-built facilities with projectors neatly hidden at ceiling height (for example the POD) as an alternative to conference centres does not allow for the removal of the central table.

Our experiences with hotel facilities is very discouraging in these respects and tends to reinforce the expectation that effective problem-solving settings are 'boardrooms'. Eden (1985) reported elsewhere on the disaster potential from assuming hotels will understand the needs of GDSS facilitators. Experiences during the last two years confirms the need for wariness – few hotels can provide large amounts of wall space for flip charts, many do not permit the use of temporary adhesives such as Blu-tak to hold flip charts on the wall, few hotels can provide comfortable chairs with castors (on several occasions a furniture van in tow has been the only solution!). It is possible that environmental characteristics are taken too seriously. It is clear that other clients of hotels and conference centres do not take these matters seriously. And yet both experience and the thinking set out here suggest otherwise. In a design for a non-portable GDSS facility great care will be taken to provide no table, computer workstations on castors, and comfortable chairs on castors.

Directions

This chapter is dominated by tentative knowledge gained from several years' experience of working in high-tech GDSS environments – from the carefully designed POD to 'lash-ups' in hotel conference rooms based on the use of portable equipment. The discussion is not based on careful research but rather the threading together of the implications of the goals of GDSS, with current technology, with theories and research in the field of small group behaviour. What is needed is for practitioners to come together more often to share their 'taken-for-granted' theories of designing high-tech or low-tech group decision support for real clients paying real fees and demanding significant outcomes. Most academic GDSS consultants are able to operate in the context of 'action research' where clients know that the 'consultants' are academics involved with a research unit. However it is undertaken for clients who want to address real problems and pay the university full commercial rates. This chapter is designed to prompt more discussion about the elements of successful GDSS work that are often regarded as trivial.

Notes

1. HiView is software developed at the London School of Economics Decision Analysis Unit for helping teams with resource allocation problems. COPE is software developed by the authors for work on strategic management and developing creative solutions to messy problems (Eden, 1989a).

2. A photocopy whiteboard is the equivalent of a traditional 'dry whiteboard' which is written on using 'dry-wipe' coloured pens. It provides approximately 5ft × 4ft of writing area. However, the writing surface is flexible and so can be wound on to reveal up to five further screens. Each screen can be instantly copied to produce any number of A4-size photocopies.

3. The POD is a high-tech conferencing room designed by International Computers Ltd in the UK (Austin, 1986). It is octagonal in shape and contains a round table. Computer output can be projected on to one of the walls using a three-colour high-resolution projector. The same projector can be used to project from a variety of other sources such as TV, a closed-circuit camera looking down on the table, or video-recorders. Other facilities include wall flip charts, an automatic whiteboard, 35mm slide projector, and whiteboards.

16

On Trivialities in Process

CHRIS HUXHAM

This chapter is concerned with *trivialities*. The intention is to convince you that the trivialities to which I refer are important (and hence non-trivial!) aspects of the decision-aiding approaches referred to in this book. In particular I hope to demonstrate that these trivialities represent an important aspect of complexity that has hitherto been unrepresented as a serious topic for discussion. Indeed it is possible that many budding decision management consultants feel inadequate because they have a less than complete understanding of these complexities but do have a complete understanding of the methods they wish to employ.

Let us examine what I mean by the term *triviality* in this context. Aspects which come into this category tend to be concerned with the processual side of the approaches rather than with their modelling methods. They also tend to be matters of a somewhat detailed (rather than general) nature. Some examples might be:

- in connection with the use of flip charts, the need to have a readily available, fully working set of good quality *water-based* pens, the need for good *handwriting* skills, the need for *paper hanging and paper management* skills, the need for wall space, and so on;
- in connection with the use of whiteboards, the skill of managing the limited available writing space and of knowing when to rub out;
- in connection with the use of computers, the technology required for *good projection*;
- the use of colour and *artistry*, whatever modelling medium is used;
- the *physical surroundings* in which a workshop or meeting takes place;
- the clothing and general *appearance of the consultant* and of the client team;
- the punctuality and general *state of organization* and reliability of the client team;
- the *time between workshops* or meetings and the general schedule for the project.

These examples have two things in common which earn them the label of triviality. Firstly, they are generally perceived to have little or no intellectual content, being either skills oriented or purely practical. Secondly, they tend to be regarded by many as either unimportant issues ('book any room you can find for that meeting . . .') or as self-evident ('of course you have to have pens available to use flip charts . . .').

These two attributes – which we may regard as the defining attributes of a *triviality* – are almost certainly the main reasons why these subjects have been largely ignored in the literature on the approaches. However, recent publications by Friend and Hickling (1987) and Eden (1985) have begun to tackle the issues. Supposed lack of intellectual content has been seen as disbarring them from an academic audience and more seriously from the management or practising consultant audience. Yet observation, both of the approaches in use, and of normal managerial practices (i.e. outside the decision support environment), would suggest that the issues are neither unimportant nor (in practice) self-evident.

A major concern of many of the authors in this book, including the current one, is the difficulty of transferring decision-aiding approaches from the researcher-consultants who have developed them to other consultants or to practising managers (Huxham, 1987), a process which, to date, has happened slowly and often by the apprenticeship method (i.e. the approaches have been taken up primarily by people who have worked closely with those who developed them and by past clients of the approach). If, as hypothesized earlier, trivialities are, in fact, non-trivial aspects of the approaches, their lack of documentation must surely be an element in the slow rate of transfer. It is therefore worthwhile spending some time examining this hypothesis.

Reflecting on Room Layout: Personal Experiences with Groups and Furnishings

Let me begin this section by wearing my lecturing hat. In this context I frequently run seminars in which students are expected to discuss ill-defined issues concerned with the process of management science projects. Clearly, a classroom set up in the traditional way is inappropriate, and I frequently request students to rearrange the tables into a more amenable formation. Infallibly, this request is received with groans. This is, perhaps, not surprising at the first session of a series if the students are already settled, but I am perpetually amazed that the groans persist at subsequent seminars. It is almost unheard of for students to take the initiative to do the reorganization before I arrive. With some groups, to reduce predicted hostility, I have resorted to arriving early at the seminar and moving the chairs and tables myself!

The effect is not restricted to young, unworldly-wise students; practising managers attending part-time or short courses often also fail to appreciate the benefits that can be added to a discussion by being comfortably able to see other participants without having to resort to contortions. I do perceive, however, that awareness of the issue in older, more experienced course members is greater than in 'raw graduates'. If this observation holds weight, it would suggest that there is a learning process involved in the recognition of the benefits.

One advantage that I have when acting as a lecturer, however, is that course members generally grant me the 'power' to 'force' them to pay attention to seating layout. This however, does not normally apply in my role as manager. For in this context I usually feel less able to influence the environment since I am rarely the most senior member of the team and quite frequently am not previously well acquainted with all the team members.

If writers on management behaviour are to be believed, then most managers spend a very high proportion of their working days in verbal interaction (Mintzberg, 1975; Kotter, 1982). This is certainly true of my own behaviour, since a great deal of my time is spent in meetings of groups of two to about ten (and occasionally twenty or more) people. These meetings are mostly concerned with planning in one form or another, at a range of levels from the purely technical, through tactical to strategic. In keeping with Eden's experience, the notion of 'away-days' in the country (or at least at a separate location within the organization) is made use of by some of my colleagues, but room design is virtually never considered as a relevant issue. Some of my colleagues are not even concerned that the room should be pleasant in appearance and comfortable; occasional attempts by me to brighten things up by booking a room in a different, better-furnished building have been met with incredulity! Though the strength of reaction varies, depending on who is present, I tend to meet with the same apathy from colleagues as from students if I suggest that we should alter the room layout before we start. Some of those whom I know well enough to have raised the issue with a number of times, seem to regard my infatuation with furniture removal as something of a joke. If I am the first to arrive at a meeting, I sometimes resort to the same ploy as with students, and sneakily rearrange the tables before the others arrive. On other occasions, we simply hold the meetings sitting in odd formations – for example (1) at right angles down two sides of a set of tables arranged in an oblong; (2) at great distances from each other around the room; (3) down opposite sides of giant long thin rectangular tables so that the people at the ends have no hope of becoming involved in the discussion, or (4) even by haphazardly arranged desks that we cannot get our legs under.

If the experiences related in the last few paragraphs could not be generalized outside of the organizations in which they obtained, they would not be worthy of note. Yet meetings or workshops which take place in customer or client organizations all tend to have the same characteristics. Even personnel managers, who you might think ought to know something about these matters, have been known to arrange meetings in rooms with the seating so spread out that eye contact is difficult.

Organizations vary in the degree to which they are prepared to spend money on furnishings. I have visited many that are very plush and others that are spartan. I have only encountered one meeting room (other than the POD referred to in other chapters) which had a round table in it (all the others being arranged in the traditional rectangular fashion, as Eden suggests). Unfortunately, the benefits that might have been gained from the use of this table were marred firstly by the size of the room (only just large enough to house the table, let alone the chairs), secondly by the dingy lighting (one small window in one corner of the room) and finally, and most spectacularly, by the decor (the chairs, carpets and curtains were all in a startling shade of very bright green).

The point of relating these events – which I would imagine most readers would find unsurprising – is to give weight to the point that many people do not seem to regard room layout as relevant, let alone important, to the process of effective discussion and planning. Nevertheless – and this is again anecdotal – meetings in which people are able to feel comfortable, perhaps take their shoes off, curl up on the seat, wander around the room, and so on, are, in my experience (as Eden claims) the most effective. Achieving this kind of atmosphere is not solely dependent on room layout, since personalities and norms of those involved are also important. The research group described in Huxham et al. (1988), for example, can manage to achieve this atmosphere in almost any setting. However, with most combinations of personalities and organizational norms, room layout is likely to be a very important factor. Yet unless the most senior member of a team recognizes this, it is most unlikely to be taken into consideration, let alone acted upon.

The Physical Setting and the Technological Setting

In the previous section I focused on the lack of awareness by managers of the effect that room design may have on meeting effectiveness in a normal organizational setting. However, in the context of decision support, issues surrounding the physical environment cannot be separated from other process-related issues. Thus the precise desirable characteristics of a room will be dependent on the particular decision-aiding approach taken, as exemplified by the different perspectives taken on the issue in each of the two preceeding chapters. In particular, Eden has emphasized the link between the technological and physical environments and has shown how the choice of technology type and the use made of it within the physical setting effectively means resolving a number of dichotomies. Specifically, he suggests a need to resolve:

- the degree to which it is desirable for participants' attention to be focused on the model being created rather than on each other;
- the degree to which keeping a historical account of the workshop (or

series of workshops) visible should be compromised to make way for the progression of new ideas, and vice versa;
- the degree to which the freedom to change and update the model should be compromised in order to keep the form of the model (i.e. its visual *shape*) unchanged, and vice versa.

He suggests that computer technology will, in general, facilitate a focus on the model but that the model will be continually changing as it is progressed and updated. Flip chart technology, on the other hand, provides a wider focus of attention, and tends to promote a sense of history.

We can take these ideas further and note that the type of technology is also likely to affect the ability of members of the client group to participate directly in model building. For while Eden has implicitly suggested that all modelling is carried out by the consultant, Friend and Hickling (1987) argue that the client should be encouraged to 'write on the walls themselves'.

The benefit from direct client involvement should be an increased sense of ownership of the model and of the process, and hence of any proposals that emerge from it, so commitment to act should be more likely to result. However, this could be counterbalanced by the forfeiting of some elements of consultant control of the process. Taken to extremes, it might, for example, result in members of the client team having very uneven amounts of influence on the way the model is developed and hence a more uneven feeling of ownership towards it than would otherwise be the case. Client participation may also be at the expense of making best use of the consultant's expertise in model building.

In principle, any level of client participation is possible, but in practice it would normally be more difficult to involve clients in computer-based modelling since that would require detailed knowledge not only of the model type but also of the details of the software that drives it. Flip charts or whiteboards clearly reduce this problem, though it can be speculated that artistic, handwritten, non-reproducible, consultant-produced graphics may inhibit clients from wishing to change the model, particularly by using their own, unpractised handwriting skills.

The technology type may also affect the degree to which the consultant needs to intervene in client discussion in order to build a model himself. Some kinds of modelling (for example the building of a map in SODA – at least in its initial stages) require little intervention, while in others (such as those used in decision conferencing, game-based approaches and, to some extent, strategic choice) the consultant takes quite an active role in directing discussion. A major factor in this need for direction is the extent to which the model requires answers to *specific* questions. Thus SODA and decision conferencing, which are both computer-based, have quite different requirements in this respect. Nevertheless, since computers can process data much faster than is possible with flip charts, there will be less need to intervene purely for the purpose of keeping ahead of discussion, thus giving the consultant working with a computer a greater freedom to choose his or her intervention level.

In summary, we may conclude that the philosophical stance a decision support consultant chooses to adopt cannot be separated from the kind of technology he or she chooses to use. While issues, such as those mentioned earlier, surrounding the technological context may *prima facie* be regarded as less trivial than those of the physical context, it is clear that the two things are not wholly separable. One cannot, for example, design a process that balances the focus on other participants and on the model unless both the technology is adequate for the type of model building desired and the physical arrangements facilitate viewing of both the model and the other people. Likewise, a process designed to encourage clients to participate directly in model building on flip charts is unlikely to work if the seating arrangements are not conducive to movement. The philosophies which underpin the approaches referred to in this book are therefore bound up *with what is practically possible and with what practical arrangements are chosen* from both a technological and a physical viewpoint. If the philosophies are non-trivial, the technological and physical settings must be non-trivial.

Conclusions

At the beginning of this chapter I defined a triviality as an aspect of the processual side of decision-aiding approaches which is often regarded as both non-intellectual and either self-evident or unimportant. In the last two sections I have aimed to show that the issues concerned with one apparent triviality – room layout – are interwoven with the philosophical, and hence the intellectual, basis of the approaches. I have also tried to argue convincingly that the issues are neither self-evident to many people, nor unimportant to effective team problem-solving or planning.

Similar arguments could be made for the other 'trivialities' listed in the introduction. For example, I personally know of no one (other than some of the authors of this book) who carries, as a matter of course, a set of good-quality, water-based pens. The use of flip charts on a stand is in fairly common usage, but it is rare to see anyone display them around the walls; the number of people with whom I work (again, authors in this book excluded) who have the paper management skills to do this effectively is negligible. It would be possible to quote examples of this type concerning each of the trivialities listed earlier to show how poorly equipped people generally are with skills of this type.

Yet in order to carry out effective decision support, a consultant must be able to manage the relevant trivialities – they are fundamental to the approaches. Furthermore, it is these aspects of the approaches which, because of their very simplicity, are likely to be of most use to managers directly, outside of the decision support environment. It is not necessary, for example, to use sophisticated models to gain benefit from improved room design, or from the use of basic flip chart technology, or from an informal environment generated by casual, rather than formal, dress, and so on.

That these 'trivial' skills are not easily learnt – even by those who recognize their importance – is not surprising. Action researchers have developed their own skills and understanding of the issues over many years, so it would be curious if others could pick them up very quickly. But if consultants and managers are to take advantage of the other ideas in this book, they will need to come to terms with these also. We should be grateful to Eden and Hickling for beginning the process of knowledge transfer.

Some years ago Eden and Sims (1979) followed Argyris and Schon (1974) by arguing that operational researchers should pay attention to being more reflective about their professional practice. This chapter is an attempt to go beyond the more sophisticated aspects of professional practice and explore 'theories-in-use' in the design and management of complexity associated with what we have hitherto regarded as 'triviality'.

17

'Decision Spaces': A Scenario about Designing Appropriate Rooms for Group Decision Management

ALLEN HICKLING

A Chance Encounter

The facilitator is all upset, having just been through yet another difficult interactive working session in a totally inappropriate room (as most of them are). On leaving he meets an old friend and ex-colleague whom he has not seen for a long time.

He remembers that she is an architect-designer and, frustrated by the seemingly inevitability of having to work in such unhelpful spaces, he decides to invite her for a drink. Perhaps he will at last get a chance to let off steam to someone who might begin to understand his problem. And this is what he wants to say.

– The rooms are always difficult to use – often too small, or at least too narrow – sometimes fancy shapes – occasionally with changes of level such as tiers or a podium – and with columns which intrude.
– Hardly ever is there easy access to adequate 'alternative' space – interior or exterior – useful when the group takes a break – or has occasion to split itself.
– Walls are often minimal – there are many large windows – even inside walls are often made of framed glass – doors, columns, and lights get in the way – what walls there are frequently have plush finishes – or have some strongly sculptured decoration.
– Subdividing partitions tend to be like unstable vertical ploughed fields – which do little to reduce the transmission of noise – impossible to work on.
– Frequently the furnishing is in the form of a large, heavy conference table (with chairs to match) – in extreme cases fixed to the floor – in worse situations even the chairs are fixed.
– The lighting is usually focused on the central table – leaving the walls dark.
– Fixed-position technical support such as projectors (overhead and

- 35mm), fancy rail systems or hanging flip chart sheets and so on – in worse cases a lectern with microphones attached – all get in the way of the process.
- Hardly ever is there a ready supply of coffee and refreshments – the process being interrupted at prescribed (usually unhelpful) intervals – usually designed for the convenience of the supplier rather than the consumers.

Group Decision Management

The architect-designer has not seen her friend the facilitator for some time, and is not quite sure what he is talking about. She asks for a quick run-down on his approach. The facilitator produces some sketches from a recent handbook he has written (Figure 17.1), and without going into details he outlines his style of work.

- The role is one of process consultant to various interdisciplinary, inter-organizational, inter-professional, inter-cultural groups faced with difficult decisions.
- The aim is to help people to work effectively together – which means managing the complexity, uncertainty, and conflict without which there would be no difficulty.
- The work is with groups of up to thirty people – writing on large sheets of paper on the wall to keep track of progress – the group sometimes divided into subgroups.
- It is usually helpful to take the tables away – or to stack them around the perimeter of the room – and, with groups of up to twelve or fifteen participants, to arrange the chairs in variations on a semi-circle facing the best bit of wall available (Figure 17.1, layouts 1a and 1b).
- When it is sensible to subdivide the group, for example to get frequent quick interaction between as many participants as possible, it can be helpful to use a few tables arranged in a fan (Figure 17.1, layout 2a), which can be varied to include a semi-circle if there are to be longer sessions in plenary as well.
- With even larger numbers – say twenty-five or more – a wide variety of layouts can be used – often with special rules to control the number of people actually interacting at any one time – and generally with provision for more frequent breaks, thus allowing input from those less involved.
- Only when there are substantial documents to be discussed is it sensible to bring the tables back – and then they tend to be placed in a semi-circle (Figure 17.1, layout 4) – the conventional meeting format not being excluded, but rarely used.
- But in all cases, assembly of a jointly prepared instant record of events (sometimes called the 'group memory') written up on the wall – which

Figure 17.1 *Alternative furniture layouts*

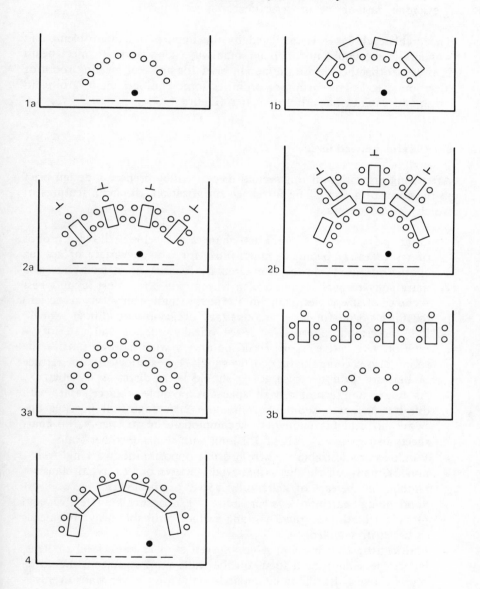

Source: Hickling and de Jong, 1986

grows and evolves in response to the mutual learning process – is an essential part of the process.

The architect-designer is intrigued by the implicit design problem, and wonders if she could not help in some way. They agree to meet again in order to together devise the design brief for an ideal meeting room or 'decision space'. The facilitator promises some photographs of groups in session to explain his problem better (Figure 17.2).

On Careful Reflection

After long discussion at this second meeting, they prepare a design brief in the form of a sort of performance specification, the main features of which are as follows.

– Clear space, free of columns and changes of level is needed for groups of six to thirty people – must allow for a wide variety of seating configurations – mostly semi-circular, focused on a wall, but also more conventional – square plan format will serve most layouts best – choice of size varies from 5m × 5m for small groups (say six to ten) to 10m × 10m for larger groups (say twenty-five to thirty).
– Easy access to 'alternative' space (ideally interior and exterior) – interior 'alternative' space could be a very wide hallway outside the room (also accommodating coffee supply?) – exterior could be terrace or balcony (in either case access should be as direct as possible).
– As much uninterrupted wall space as possible – large, flat, with durable surface – should be minimum 2.5m high – if possible one 'working' wall big enough to accommodate up to twenty flip chart sheets in two rows – about 7m long with doors in other walls.
– Windows are desirable – where possible opposite the 'working' wall – none actually on the 'working' wall – views out to avoid claustrophobia, but beware of glare – high-level or rooflights.
– Subdividing partition system must be acoustically effective and provide a hard, flat, rigid working surface, probably heavy but needs to be easily handled.
– Artificial lighting must provide an even all-over basic level of light, but at the same time a focus on the walls – arrangements should be very flexible (with dimming capability?) – must cover walls evenly – floods not spots.

During the process of developing this quite elaborate and detailed set of physical requirements, the architect-designer is putting them quickly into graphic form (Figure 17.3). The discussion then moves on to less concrete considerations.

Figure 17.2 *Photographs of groups in action*

Sources: Hickling and de Jong, 1986; Friend and Hickling, 1987 and Allen Hickling

Figure 17.3 *Notes on a prototypical decision space*

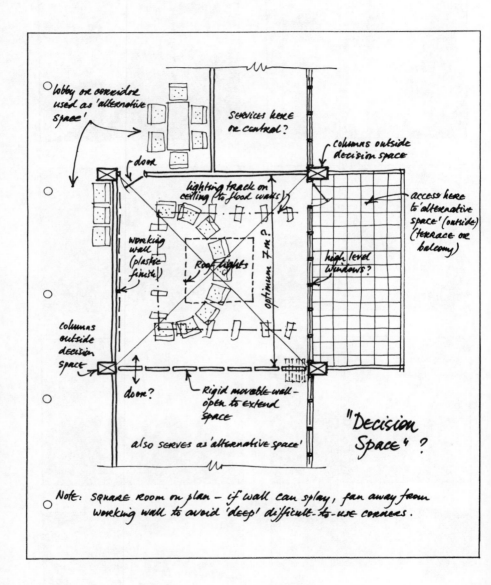

- Furniture should be reasonably comfortable (but not too much so) – easy to move around (lightweight) – suitable for a wide variety of arrangements – modular system of tables (could be 0.75m × 0.75m or 0.75m × 1.5m) – no 'speciality' shapes, but with specially designed resilient edges to avoid damage when they are moved frequently – seating for four or six per table.
- Wide variety of technical support (for example projectors of various types, and perhaps computer aid) to be provided without obstruction of the process – multiple options for access to power supply – no fixed technical apparatus.
- Easy access to a continuous supply of refreshments, and to toilets and other services – communications, data, copying and stationery supplies, secretarial, etc.

The architect-designer explains that she needs a lot more time to reflect on the brief before she can come up with a proper design. They agree to meet again in two weeks time.

The Architect-designer Reports Back

The architect-designer returns to her studio to study the brief. After initial preliminary sketches she prepares a report, together with design drawings, for the prototype of a building specifically designed to support a wide range of interactive decision-making processes (Figure 17.4).

She notices in passing that the design process she is using bears a strong resemblance to the cyclic decision-making process which her facilitator friend has been advocating. She decides to raise this in discussion.

In presenting her ideas, her commentary is as follows:

- The design is focused on the idea of a multi-functional 'forum', which can be used for lectures, demonstrations, exhibitions, receptions, meetings, and conferences, as well as interactive group decision-making sessions.
- The 'forum' is expressed externally by the high-peaked pyramid roof form which serves as a light well, leaving the walls of the main decision space free of windows – and thus available for use.
- At the hub is the square plan-form developed for the decision space in the design brief, although the corners have been cut off to create a sort of octagon – thus avoiding the problem of difficult-to-use 'deep' corners.
- The main decision space has been turned through 45° in order to create four triangular subsidiary spaces, which can be used separately as smaller decision spaces or be combined in various ways to provide a hierarchy of alternative decision spaces.

Figure 17.4   *Sketch designs for a decision centre*

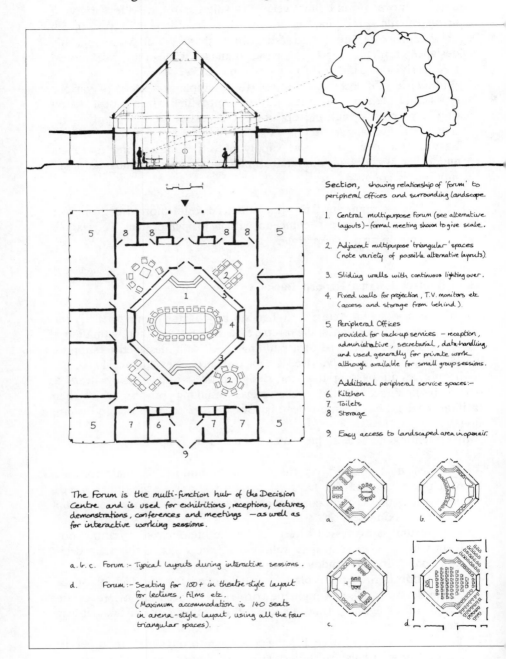

Section, showing relationship of 'forum' to
peripheral offices and surrounding landscape.

1. Central multipurpose Forum (see alternative
   layouts) - formal meeting shown to give scale.

2. Adjacent multipurpose 'triangular' spaces
   (note variety of possible alternative layouts).

3. Sliding walls with continuous lighting over.

4. Fixed walls for projection, T.V. monitors etc.
   (access and storage from behind).

5. Peripheral Offices
   provided for back-up services — reception,
   administrative, secretarial, data-handling,
   and used generally for private work
   although available for small group sessions.

   Additional peripheral service spaces:-
6. Kitchen
7. Toilets
8. Storage

9. Easy access to landscaped area in open air.

The Forum is the multi-function hub of the Decision
Centre and is used for exhibitions, receptions, lectures,
demonstrations, conferences and meetings — as well as
for interactive working sessions.

a.b.c. Forum :- Typical layouts during interactive sessions.

d.   Forum :- Seating for 100+ in theatre-style layout
                 for lectures, films etc.
                 (Maximum accommodation is 140 seats
                 in arena-style layout, using all the four
                 triangular spaces).

Source: Based on the International Ecotechnology Research Centre at Cranfield Institute
of Technology. Architects: Chamberlin Powell Bon and Woods, London, UK

- The necessary back-up services (administrative, secretarial, reception, data-handling, kitchen, toilets, and storage) have been provided at the periphery and, with only minor increases in size, could support one or two individual 'forum'-like spaces if required.

The Story Continues

The facilitator is well pleased with these results.

In fact it reminds him about the discussions he had some time ago about the possibility of a 'National Decision Centre'. The idea was to provide a decision-making environment which had none of the disadvantages of so many of the currently available venues. He wonders if this could not be the beginning of something completely new.

The architect-designer says that, if she is going to take on such a project, this current design could be no more than a starting point. They would have to spend a lot more time working the requirements of such a national centre into a new design brief.

But that is the beginning of another story.

PART VI
KEY THEMES AND FUTURE DIRECTIONS

18

Of Tools, Methods, and Methodology

ROLFE TOMLINSON

The variety of approaches to the resolution of problems in small groups which are discussed and described in this book have many origins and appear to be distinctly different. Nevertheless, they also have some appearance of possessing a common ethos and of using some common tools. The purpose of this chapter is to explore how far that commonality really goes and the degree to which the commonality is induced or discouraged by the use of the computer. We shall ask whether those who have developed one approach can make direct use of the tools and models developed by others. How far can the approaches be taught? If they can, must pupils learn only one approach or should they study them all – perhaps making their own selection for use in particular circumstances?

These are not trivial questions. The number of problems that need to be solved in organizations is several orders of magnitude greater than the number of specialist facilitators available, or likely to be available. Most of these problems must be solved in-house, either by the managers themselves or by in-house groups of professional problem solvers (by OR groups and management services staff). Is there, then, something from those approaches that managers or OR professionals should learn? If the answer to that is negative, then how do we categorize those problems which call for facilitation and, more particularly, define which kind of problem is appropriate for which facilitation approach?

It is important to realize that the approaches represented in this book bring together experience, knowledge, and understanding from many disciplines, many of which are often thought to be mutually incompatible. There are elements of hard science, social science and systems science, of psychology and psychiatry. Since most of the practitioners employing the methods reported are demonstrably successful in their work, we may justifiably claim that this work is a corpus of highly effective and intellectually respectable interdisciplinary applied research. It is, however, still not clear whether the corpus consists of material connected primarily by the mutual interest of working with small groups to achieve a common objective or whether there is a deeper unity.

Much of the work has arisen from practitioners whose background is in operational research, starting from the basic belief that *the* way to the solution of problems and acquisition of knowledge was through rigorous problem definition, collection of relevant and reliable data, hypothesis formulation, model building, and verification. Most OR workers cling to these principles as part of their intellectual foundations but increasingly have found that descriptions of their work based on those elements do not adequately match practice, a practice which for the most part is becoming increasingly successful. The search for better descriptions, which goes hand-in-hand with improved practice, has gone in many directions, but two are most important. The first, drawing on the scientific tradition, places emphasis on the dynamics, complexity, and uncertainty of organizational and economic reality. It moves away from didactic statements, such as that the purpose of an investigation is to obtain the optimum solution to a specified problem, to more general statements, such as that the purpose is to improve management performance or to remove symptoms of unease. The second direction, drawing more on the social sciences, recognizes the central importance of the interpersonal elements of organizational life, and concentrates attention on the way that decisions are actually built and consensus obtained. Those following the first route have tended to draw on *systems* ideas as their prime intellectual strength, using their experience and general reading in the social sciences to round off their approach (Checkland, 1981b). Those following the second have tended to draw their intellectual strength either from psychology or social science (Eden, 1989; Phillips, 1989a). There has been some contra-movement of specialists from these 'softer' social science disciplines, but in general the barriers between the 'hard' and 'soft' sciences seem to be lower when moving from hard to soft, than vice versa.

Those who have made the transition most successfully have, in the course of building their expertise, developed tools, models, methods and methodologies. Any understanding of what they have achieved must start with a recognition of these separate elements in the resolution of problems. The main part of this chapter will be devoted to a discussion of how these elements compare and contrast between the different facilitation approaches discussed in this book. However, since this is an area in which each of the four words tends to have many varieties of interpretation, we must first of all define them as interpreted in the present context.

A *tool* is a means by which a facilitator helps to achieve his immediate task whether that is to impart or extract knowledge, achieve interaction, force judgement and so on. Tools discussed in this book are many, including design of the POD, arrangement of seating, use of whiteboards and flip charts and, of course, the use and viability of computer aids. Huxham ironically suggests that consultants think of these as the 'trivial' elements of facilitation. Nevertheless, the use of the correct tool for the job (and the development of better tools) is essential for success.

A *model* is a means of describing some part of the organizational situation that is of concern to the participants of the study. All useful models are particular to an individual situation, but most models belong to an identifiable class. Some classes of models discussed in the symposium are: system models, cognitive mapping, root definitions, hypermaps, games, simulation, flow diagrams, and utility models. These are all 'standard' models, in the sense of being well known and described in the literature, if not in everyday use. It is important to realize that a given type of model can be used to describe very different things – for example conceptual ideas and physical flows – and for the very different purposes of understanding and evaluation. It is also important to recognize that modelling is an activity common to most (if not all) facilitators, and is certainly not confined to quantitative analysis, but is more common to those helping clients with choice.

A *method*, which is at a higher level of generality, is a general approach to a problem. Thus, the scientific method is commonly formulated in terms of the sequence 'problem – definition – data collection – hypothesis – verification'. CATWOE, a mnemonic for Customers, Actors, Transformation, Weltenschauung, Owners and Environmental constraint, at the heart of the Checkland methodology, may be thought of as a method, as are SODA and strategic choice. Decision conferencing is also a method. There are methods for developing forecasts, for evaluating options, for developing strategies – to mention only a few.

Finally, a *methodology* encompasses the philosophical and theoretical beliefs that underpin and lead to the construction of methods. One of the key questions we have to consider is the validity of methods when they are separated from their methodology.

Of all these terms, methodology is perhaps the one that is most loosely used. At the International Institute of Applied Systems Analysis, methodology was a label given to the area in which mathematicians and economists developed mathematical models. The implication was that the researchers were seen as 'backroom' model builders, rather than applied researchers. In other circles, however, the word has the wider connotation used here.

Before starting to 'contrast and compare' it may be helpful to draw an analogy from the longer established but still comparatively young disciplines of management science and OR. In the early 1960s there were individuals, and indeed whole groups, identified with a single model or groups of models. Some companies exclusively used mathematical programming, some converted all problems into simulation studies, some showed incredible ingenuity in bringing queuing theory into everything and some tried to avoid using any mathematical models at all. Their methodology was to find elements in the problem situation that could be brought together as a problem which could be described by a model of that form. Now that the subject has matured, it is recognized that competent OR workers have to be aware of the full range of these models, and willing to use them as appropriate.

Moreover, they realize that the problem determines the tools and models that are appropriate and that standard models are hardly ever a full representation of reality. This does not mean that they will all tackle a problem in the same way, because their underlying methodologies are still different. Some believe that their underlying purpose is to optimize, others see themselves as evaluators, leaving all choice or decision to the client. Some see their distinguishing mark in the application of computers, some see their role as general problem-solvers with computer competence as an important adjunct skill. These differences are primarily *methodological*, and have led to differences in method (for example on the degree of interaction with the client) whilst the tools and models are now generally of common knowledge and acceptance. In this chapter we shall be exploring the implied hypothesis that small group facilitation is following the same development pattern and, if so, how far the development has gone. More specifically, the hypotheses that are to be tested are:

that the tools are virtually common;
that there is a common recognition of many of the models (with conflicting ideas on their range of validity);
that most practitioners stay firmly within a single methodology;
that there is little progress so far in relating methods or methodologies to particular classes of problem.

Even though it might be argued that this is a large set of hypotheses to base on what is still a relatively small group of 'experts', the penetration of these ideas into the wider community of craft investigators and management developers is such that the time is now ripe for its consideration.

Tools

We start with the *tools*. The authors represented in this book show remarkable little controversy over these. As with all tools, they have to be matched to the particular user and the particular purpose – everyone selects tools suitable to their own method. But within that constraint – which is applicable to tool users everywhere – there is little controversy and much consonance. It is also agreed that there is appalling ignorance among managers and investigators working with groups generally in regard to the tools that were available and their importance. It is wickedly wasteful, either for the quality of group decisions or for the speed in reaching a consensus, to ignore what we now know about the impact of the environment on group work – for example the need for a plentiful supply of surfaces for recording; the need to retain what has been discussed for reconsideration at a later stage; the effective use of computer aids; the importance of comfort and convenience in the working environment (see Part V). Well designed conference/seminar rooms hardly exist; partly, no doubt, because the stereotypes on which the designers work are wrong. In university business schools there are major battles, first with architects and then with estates staff, to gain acceptance of specifications for the way in which the teaching rooms should be laid out. The problems are not of conflicting theory, but of convention combined with lack of thought in relating design to purpose.

The use of computerized tools deserves special mention. It is sometimes forgotten how pervasive the computer is in organizational issues, particularly in problem resolution. We shall find it to be important when we look at all aspects of the process.

The essence of a computerized tool is that it needs to be thought of, and developed, in advance of its use. Some variation in use can be expected, as with an adjustable spanner, but if that is so the variation in use must also be carefully thought out beforehand. In this regard the presence or absence of tools can have a major impact on the models used (which need particular tools in their construction), and on method (a person who cannot use quantitative tools is incapable of adopting certain methods).

In decision conferencing a number of well defined computing tools are developed to deal with questions of uncertainty and multiple objectives. These tools are themselves not specific to any particular method, or even methodology, but in conjunction, offered together in a particular toolbox, they constitute a powerful incentive towards a particular methodology. Nevertheless, as we are able to identify that certain kinds of tool are regularly used, so we can refine these tools and make them more widely available.

However, computer tools are not all concerned with calculation. The tools of data storage, retrieval, and display are of the utmost importance and are still in the early stages of application. SODA, as a method, would be less powerful without the computerized tool which enables the facilitator to group and analyze clusters of concepts.

It is certainly true that all of the new tools that have been developed have arisen because of a need discovered within a particular method of approach. That being the case and simply because they are only tools, they have a potential which can be widely recognized as having an absolute validity beyond the particular method, or the methodology, which has encouraged the development.

All in all, we may take it that our first hypothesis that tools are virtually common stands up to experience. Not all tools are used by all practitioners: that was not the proposal. But there is a general awareness of the tools available and an understanding of their range of validity, as well as a surprising commonality of use.

Models

When it comes to *models*, much more divergence exists – ranging from questions of preference and range of belief to a concern that models developed within different methodologies might themselves be, in some sense, incompatible. Certainly, attempts to match models have, as Bennett discussed, given rise to severe difficulties in some cases. Here again, the analogy with traditional management science and OR may be helpful. The mixing of models in an OR investigation is certainly common. It is quite likely that flow diagrams and systems models will be used in the opening stages of the investigation, and that a number of quantitative models may be used in the course of the investigation, some feeding into each other. A stochastic simulation model may even contain within itself certain optimization elements, though not usually vice versa. When mixing models in this way it is important to ensure the coherence of the underlying assumptions, that the levels of detail required are compatible and, of course, that the models are relevant to the purpose of the investigation. *A model built for one purpose may make appropriate assumptions for that purpose, which may then become inappropriate when transferred to a new problem.* It is a fundamental rule in all modelling that someone using a model in other than a specifically designated situation should understand the assumptions made within the model as well as the principles underlying its construction – even if they do not understand the detailed working of the algorithm that leads to the output.

Even in the hands of experienced analysts models are surprisingly value laden. In 'The Electronic Oracle', Dana Meadows and John Robinson (1985) describe and contrast different world models, each of which not only embodies accepted economic relationships but, also and more importantly, is structured according to the designer's beliefs about the way that economic and social forces act. The results, unsurprisingly, tend to confirm the beliefs of those who built them. To try and combine the results of such models would be absurd. On the other hand much can be learned and gained, even within the same investigation, from the insights that each model provides and from the classical exercise of 'contrast and compare'.

All models need to be used with skill and understanding and there needs to be a recognition that they all embody within them some belief about the way that the world works. But, and this may not always be apparent, apparently similar models are often models of very different things. Arrows on a diagram can refer to flows, to influence, to causality, to time sequence, to accountability, to defined relationships. The elements can be physical, organizational, or conceptual.

Any realistic discussion of the place of models in group facilitation has to start from an understanding that models are for two quite different purposes. One set of models (process models) is used to describe the relationships within the decision-making group and the process by which a decision can be reached. The other set (product models) attempts to describe the world outside and present ways in which the relevant facets of this world can be brought together and related. Thus, Friend (in chapter 2) talks of models of accountability in decision-making groups (process models), and Phillips (in chapter 14) discusses model forms that seem to accommodate most of the concerns expressed by senior managers: evaluation and resource allocation (product models). These two types of model are not entirely separate. Product models must relate to the perceptions and goals of the decision-making group, and process models will be influenced by the product models to be used – both will be determined to some extent by the local circumstances. Nevertheless, the essential difference is clear. Differences relating to one class of model need not lead to non-acceptance of models used in the other class.

The models are all used to structure thinking, to collate and evaluate information rapidly, to suggest consonances and discrepancies, to explore – and even suggest – alternatives. The majority of models are common currency, in that most of the facilitators from different schools can discuss them with a degree of insight that indicates that they might be considered a common heritage. Although fears have been expressed that some models are incompatible with certain methodologies, no real examples of this incompatibility have been put forward. Models can be incompatible of course, making different assumptions, using different time scales, aggregating data in different ways, but the differences are all explicit in the model description, or at least they should be. Philosophical incompatibility may exist, but may not often be apparent.

As an aside at this point, we should refer to the more difficult question that arises from client understanding, and model ownership. It is a matter of principle (at least the principle of this author) which is not explored in this book, that a client should – at an appropriate level – have an understanding of all that goes on in the course of the investigation. In particular, if a model is to be used they should know what data are being used, what assumptions made and what the output means. If several models are being used which seem to make conflicting assumptions then the client will become confused or, more seriously, will withdraw attention and support. However, the problem is often not one of assumptions so much as language. Getting a client (or group of clients) involved in problem resolution often involves their becoming involved in learning a new language. Their facility in moving between languages (and a model is always language based) is a skill which the facilitator may have, but the client may find difficult. One of the arts of facilitation is to ensure continuity of language.

A full resolution of the issues raised here would need a more systematic review of models and model types. We have at least given some indication that the use of models from different methodologies does not lead to intrinsic incompatibility, but that there may be practical problems of comprehension. It is worth remarking, however, that a much wider range of model types is available to the general investigator (or facilitator) than are commonly employed or taught. These should be known and recognized more widely than they are.

Methods

We come now to the question of *method*, and here our problem of analysis becomes more difficult by an order of magnitude. Many of the authors in this book have developed their own methods of facilitation from scratch, based on a personal methodological approach to the subject. It is hardly surprising that they generally use that method most of the the time: it is both inherent to them and also part of their trademark. People seek their advice *because* of their method. A real understanding of the relative position of the different methods can probably only be understood from the second generation of facilitators and soft-problem solvers. Will they find it necessary to follow just one of the masters, or will they treat them as a library, drawing the appropriate one as seems desirable? There could be different reasons for following the former approach: belief that one approach was 'right' on the one hand, personal preference or simply choosing the most saleable product on the other. We are still far from resolving that issue.

The idea that choice of method is an option open to any individual seems to be acceptable to students. For two years the author has been teaching a post-experience MSc course to systems professionals based on one-week residential modules. One of the modules, entitled 'Craft of Investigation', is assessed by asking the students to prepare their own manual (design a method) on how to tackle fuzzy problems. The module itself takes substantial chunks of material from leading systems thinkers set within a format which asks students to relate these ideas to the building blocks of any investigation – problem definition, data, model building, solution formulation and implementation. The manuals they produce are usually based on one of the leading thinkers whose work is discussed in the module, but the proposals are not dismissive. They see that different methods are appropriate to different situations.

If you look at the practice of management science investigators, most of whom have of necessity developed their methods on an apprenticeship or on an experimental basis, you will find that most will have a preferred method of approach, but will vary this as occasion demands. The preferred method will depend on the situation they are most commonly confronted with, as well as their own personal style. There are confrontations, of course, which derive from the methodologies of the protagonists, but most practitioners see such confrontation as unreal and counterproductive. They would argue that some problems are hard, some soft, or that all problems contain elements of both, in which case one requires a mixture of methods.

The real difficulty is that, although one can practise and compare 'hard' methods at a desk in the absence of a critical customer, 'soft' methods cannot easily be acquired in the same way. They need either supervised study or learning on the job. This is a painful way of learning, risking the exposure of one's incompetence to a client. It would be quite natural if budding facilitators were less inclined to try and master more than one 'soft' method.

There has been a fair amount of exchange in the UK between the facilitators who have developed different methods. This has induced respect between the experts, and a certain amount of borrowing of ideas, but there is little evidence that the methods have become common. Certainly, there are many dialogues of the kind which have suggested parallel experiences, but none that said 'But, when I tried your method I got a different result.' It is too early to say that this is because methods are only applicable within the methodology within which they were developed. It may be due to the relative youth of what one might call 'scientific facilitation', combined with the relatively high price of entry into the 'multi-method' stakes. When sufficient people have paid that price, we may find that few of the methods are irrevocably tied to the methodology that begot them.

What part can the computer play in this? The computer is, of course, primarily linked to tools and the models. But in making certain tools accessible to a wider range of users, the computer will also have its impact on method. The question is 'How much impact?'. Decision conferencing as a method appears to be wholly dependent on the computer technology, since the skill level remains firmly with the facilitator, who remains the central key figure (and whose models are of little value without the computer). SODA holds out hopes of providing a computerized aid which will enable the staff investigator, if not the manager, to take over the facilitation role. The question of managers making intelligent use of computer support is fascinating, but it is still a question. On the whole managers are very perceptive in their understanding of what the computer can do. They know that it can tackle complex, definable questions very quickly. They see that there are major problems of interaction and communication, and are intensely suspicious that it can often introduce spurious certainty into situations where it is inappropriate. Computer models with many in-built assumptions are distrusted, whereas much more complex models of a known physical system are trusted. The person who develops computer aids in the art of facilitation walks a slippery tightrope.

Overall, then, we have to say that our hypothesis concerning method is, perhaps unavoidably, unproven. We do not yet know how far methods can be used by generalists, or how much we must rely on specialists. Only time can provide the evidence. At this stage, no practitioner can state that the methods used by another are 'wrong' in any general sense. They may however be 'wrong' in a particular context, which is another way of saying that all methods have their limited region of validity. It has thus become important to describe the methods and their appropriate contexts together. Only when this has been done shall we seriously understand the craft of small group facilitation.

Methodology

Finally, we come to the question of methodologies. There is no doubt that the differences in underlying theory are considerable and important. There are fundamentally different beliefs about the ways in which groups interact and decisions are made. Some of these beliefs (theories?) are contradictory, some only claim partial validity. We have to remember, with humility, the lesson of natural science that it is only possible to gain insight and make progress by making use of contrasting and apparently contradictory theories. Perhaps we should say that if we are to be successful problem-solvers, the richness and variety of our understanding (and thus of the methodologies we may use) must match the richness and variety of the problems we have to face. At this stage of our knowledge, one methodology will simply not suffice. Certainly we all have our own outlook on the world, which will affect our judgement on the matter; what we decide to do will reflect our own personal set of underlying theories and assumptions. For those who devise a methodology and their disciples, the underlying theory on which they have worked may be of overriding importance, making other methodologies and methods unsound. Most practitioners who wish to improve their personal skills will be forced to make their decisions pragmatically on the basis of method. They must examine the alternative approaches available and the assumptions underlying them. They will look at the facilities required, the data needed, and the kind of outcome to be expected. The final choice will depend on that analysis, on experience and personal beliefs. The real problem lies in acquiring, first, the information to make that choice and then the skill in putting it into practice. And we do not yet know how far the computer can aid that learning process.

Conclusion

To summarize, the development of methods for facilitating decision-making in small groups – in which aids for rational analysis combine with the insights of social theories of small group working – have made tremendous progress in the past ten years. Whereas, in the early stages, each researcher in the field tended to be an individual entrepreneur –

bound to the set of techniques they had developed, and seeing other approaches as flawed and unsatisfactory – the situation has now been reached where many common elements have been identified, and different approaches can be discussed and compared. A community of experts recognizing each other is starting to exist. Some tools are seen to be common and many models are widely known and discussed, although their widespread use is more limited. There is more difference in the methods adopted and major conflict in the underlying methodologies. But many of these conflicts derive from the context, and disappear when consideration is given to the problem situation and the kind of relief that is needed. It is the belief of the present writer that attempts should now be made to bring the work that has been done, with the tools, models, and methods developed, to the wider attention of all who are involved in the craft of investigation.

Appendix
A Brief Guide to the GDS Methods Referred to in this Book

COLIN EDEN

Strategic Options Development and Analysis (SODA)

Proponents and Developers

Originally developed by Colin Eden at the University of Bath, UK and subsequently by Colin Eden, Fran Ackermann, and Steve Cropper at the University of Strathclyde.

Orientation

Generally regarded as a 'soft' method. Founding principles are the need to provide a management team with a model which can act as a device to aid *negotiation*, working with individuality and subjectivity as the basis for problem definition and creativity. Tends to generate increasingly rich models rather than move towards abstraction or simplicity. Sees strategic management in terms of changing thinking and action rather than planning.

The method aims to develop high levels of ownership for the problem through the attention paid to problem definition and negotiation.

The method is built from theories and practice about small groups. Thus the method is aimed at groups of four to ten participants.

Technique

Focuses on the individual member of the group in the first instance through one-to-one interviews. Uses 'cognitive mapping' (as developed by Eden, Jones and Sims, 1983, at Bath) as the basis for capturing individual views of the issue. Cognitive mapping is based on the 'psychology of personal constructs' and aims to record the basis of how a person makes sense of the situation in terms of values/goals and explanations/theories of the world. The technique exists around a body of coding guidelines for modelling argument, and lives within an action-oriented view of problem formulation.

Group maps are constructed through the aggregation of cognitive maps. These group maps are used to facilitate negotiation about value/ goal systems, key strategic issues, and option portfolios. The map is used to manage the content of the problem but with attention to the affective, political, and process dynamics in the group.

Technology

Attention is paid to the design of the group support environment, which is influenced by the use of large monitor computer displays. The process is managed by two facilitators – one who attends primarily to content and one to process. The content facilitator uses sophisticated computer software to display and manage complexity of data and to record, in 'real time' the qualitative arguments arising from the group problem-solving process. The real time problem structuring is able to influence the group process by continual cross-linking of issues and ideas and by 'on-the-hoof' analysis.

Technology requirements are thus: two 'DOS'-based personal computers (one acting as a slave), special software (COPE), one (preferably two) large monitors, blank wall space, large sheets of paper, and water-based pens.

Use

Primarily private sector, but recently tackling major policy issues in the US and UK public sector. Strategy development and review with several private organizations over long periods. Proponents have been involved in over 300 strategic issue workshops for large organizations and community groups.

Group Time Demands

Typically a strategic workshop demands two 1.5-hour interviews from each participant and a 1–2 day GDS workshop. Facilitator time demands of approximately 8–10 man-days for a management team of ten people and a 2-day workshop. Some 'board of director' groups meet once a month for GDS workshops on major strategic issues, and once a quarter for a GDS workshop on strategy review.

Further Reading

Rosenhead (1989), Eden, Jones and Sims (1983), Eden (1989a), Eden and Huxham (1988).

Strategic Choice

Proponents and Developers

First developed in the 1960s by John Friend and Allen Hickling at the Institute of Operational Research and Tavistock Institute of Human Relations. Continually redeveloped by Friend through IOP Consulting, and by Hickling through Allen Hickling Associates. Historically linked to public sector planning methods.

Orientation

Focuses on uncertainty in strategic issues – uncertainty about values, uncertainty about related issues, and uncertainty about the environment. Aims to work with a group from the start rather than pre-work with individual participants. Gains ownership by active involvement in the process from all participants. Seeks to gain agreement about interconnected decision areas and options as they apply to each decision area. The method has developed with respect to the difficult task of working with multi-organizational groups, and therefore orients itself to issues across organizations, particularly in respect of 'representatives' rather than decision-makers.

The method and the facilitation can cope with large groups of up to twenty to thirty members.

Technique

High level of participation in problem structuring within a predefined template of types of uncertainty and options. Uses many paper-oriented 'idea management' techniques in combination with 'nominal group techniques'. Uses physical space, particularly wall space, as a massive flexible organizing and complexity managing device.

Moves on to formally identify and 'analyze interconnected decision areas' (AIDA) by eliciting mutually exclusive options within each area and evaluating 'feasible' combinations. Decision analysis is formal but uses 'fuzzy' evaluations with respect to multiple criteria.

Technology

Primarily attention is paid to managing group dynamics through consensus building. Extensive use of coloured pens, graphical representation, paper management techniques, and categories to manage complexity. Thus attention is paid to the physical setting for group work. Process management is facilitator dependent.

Computer support is currently being developed by IOP Consulting.

Use

Primarily public sector policy issues in Third World as well as developed world. Significant successes in helping groups develop policy on public planning and environmental issues. Gradually being used more extensively within private sector organizations.

Group Time Demands

Almost anything from several hours to several months.

Further Reading

Rosenhead (1989), Friend and Hickling (1987).

Decision Conferencing

Proponents and Developers

Originally Cam Peterson of Decision and Designs Inc., but extensively developed by Larry Phillips at Brunel University and subsequently at the London School of Economics. Also promoted by John Rohrbaugh at New York State University.

Orientation

The psychology of decision analysis through consideration of measures of utility and value, multiple criteria, and option evaluation.

Founded on the principle of negotiation across the group with the formal decision-theoretic model acting as the device to elicit debate. Group process is important and is largely founded on Tavistock Institute of Human Relations models of group dynamics.

Technique

Involves the construction of value hierarchies and the identification of, preferably, quantifiable estimates of success indicators against values. Involves the evaluation of the relative importance of objectives and the extent to which particular options/policies succeed in meeting lower-order objectives.

The 'decision conference' is carefully designed as a group process and generally lasts two or three days. The two, or sometimes three, facilitators expect the group behaviour to follow well established patterns over this time period.

Technology

Often uses high-tech decision support rooms to facilitate computer output projection and environment control. Specially designed decision analysis software (HiView and Equity running on IBM PC compatibles) is used to enable complicated calculations of the outcome of the subjective evaluations made by the group. The software also provides for an evaluation of the sensitivity of outcome to small changes in any of the ratings.

Use

Extensive use in the private and public sector in the UK and US. Particularly successful in helping senior executive teams decide on the strategic allocation of resources to products, operating companies, markets, etc.

Group Time Demands

Two-day 'decision conference'. Facilitators involved in careful design of conference based on about half a day pre-work with client to establish the universe of discussion. Also facilitators expect to use 1–2 days in follow-up report writing.

Further Reading

Phillips (chapter 14, this volume), Phillips (1989a).

Metagame/Hypergame Analysis

Proponents and Developers

Nigel Howard developed metagame analysis at MIT, and subsequently at the University of Waterloo and Aston University in the UK. Peter Bennett developed Hypergame Analysis in the late 1970s at the University of Sussex, with colleagues including Chris Huxham and Martin Giesen. Parallel work has gone on elsewhere, especially in Canada.

Orientation

Both approaches focus on issues of conflict and co-operation between 'actors' – defined at an individual or collective level. They provide analysis of situations in which there are several interested parties, each with particular aims and possible strategies. Technically, both developed from the mathematical 'theory of games', though placing less emphasis on quantification. Metagame analysis places greater stress on co-operation than did the original theory and, latterly, seeks also to analyze actors' emotions. Hypergame analysis adds the extra dimension that those involved in a situation may perceive it very differently.

Technique/Technology

Each approach provides various problem-structuring methods, in which a picture of issues, actors, strategies, outcomes, and aims can be built up interactively by a group. Analysis is usually done with, and on behalf of, one of the interested parties, concentrating on external conflicts rather than internal disagreements. (However the possibility of using hypergame analysis during mediation is being explored.) Structuring can then be followed by analysis in order to predict what the effects of difficult strategy choices are likely to be, and to identify stable resolutions of the situation. There are various software to support metagame analysis, of which Howard's CONAN is best known. Hypergame analysis is still usually done manually using flip charts, but software may be used in the future. Both approaches are normally carried out with a client 'task force' group of three to ten people.

Use

Public and private sectors, mostly where reasonably obvious conflicts have been identified.

Group Time Demands

Vary widely according to problems and mode of analyst involvement, but useful analysis can be undertaken in half a day.

Further Reading

Rosenhead (1989), Howard (1989), Bennett (1980).

Soft Systems Methodology (SSM)

Proponents and Developers

Developed over twenty years out of a research programme developing methodologies for tackling complex human problem situations. Peter Checkland of the Department of Systems at Lancaster University is the main developer of the methodology, which has been strongly influenced by Geoffrey Vickers.

Orientation

SSM attempts to foster learning and appreciation of the problem situation between a group of stakeholders. This is contrasted with other 'harder' methods which set out to solve a predefined problem. The complexity of many organizational/social problem situations defeats attempts at defining a problem: in many such situations the problem is 'what is the problem?'. SSM provides a framework for tackling such situations.

Technique

There are two main modes within SSM, real world activities and systems thinking about the real world. Initial work involves interviews and meetings to gain an understanding of the problem situation, which is represented by the use of so-called 'rich pictures'. Systems thinking using concepts of hierarchy, communication, control, and emergent properties are used to identify 'relevant systems' which may provide useful insights. These relevant systems are logically defined, by constructing 'root definitions', which are then used to generate 'conceptual models' of the selected systems. Different conceptual models representing different viewpoints are then used as the basis of a debate, which through an 'appreciative process' can lead to feasible and desirable change and then to action.

Technology

A major skill in SSM is in selecting 'relevant systems' which can be used to structure a useful debate. Apart from various low-technology devices such as flip charts, used in running meetings, SSM does not provide guidance, or any tools for running group debates.

Use

The research programme at Lancaster University has involved many 'soft systems' studies forming the basis of student projects, and also many consultancy projects through a university company called ISCOL. Projects have been successful in both the private and public sectors.

Group Time Demands

Individual interviews/meetings and group debates require an investment of time, how much time depends on the study.

Further Reading

Checkland (1981b), Wilson (1984).

References

Ackermann, F. (1988) 'Decision support on the run!' paper presented to the Young OR Conference, University of Warwick.

Ackermann, F. and Eden, C. (1989) 'Issues in the provision of GDSS: a US/UK comparison', paper presented to the OR Society National Conference, Southampton, (September).

Ackoff, R.L. (1974) *Redesigning the Future*. New York: Wiley.

Ackoff, R.L. (1978) *The Art of Problem Solving; Including Ackoff's Fables*. New York: Wiley.

Ansoff, H.I. (1965) *Corporate Strategy*. New York: McGraw-Hill.

Applegate, L.M., Chen, T.T., Konsynski, B.R. and Nunamaker, J.F. (1987) 'Knowledge management in organizational planning', *Journal of Management Information Systems*, 3: 20–38.

Argyris, C. and Schon, D.A. (1974) *Theories in Practice*. San Francisco: Jossey Bass.

Austin, N.C. (1986) 'A management support environment', *ICL Technical Journal*, International Computers Limited, Oxford.

Axelrod, R. (1976) *The Structure of Decision*. Princeton, NJ: Princeton University Press.

Banker, R.L. and Gupta, S.K. (1980) 'A process for hierarchical decision making with multiple objectives', *Omega* 8: 137–49.

Barclay, S. and Peterson, C.R. (1976) *Multi-attribute Utility Models for Negotiations*, Technical Report 76–1, Decisions and Designs, Inc., McLean, (March).

Bardach, E. (1977) *The Implementation Game: What Happens after a Bill Becomes a Law*. Cambridge, MA: MIT Press.

Baum, H.S. (1982) 'The advisor as invited intruder', *P.A. Review*, 42: 546–55.

Beckhard, R. (1969) *Organization Development: Strategies and Models*. Reading, MA: Addison Wesley.

Beer, S. (1972) *The Brain of the Firm*. London: Allen Lane.

Benjamin, C.M. and Powell, C.A. (eds) (1986) *Peace and Change*, special issue: 'Choice, strategy, bargaining and negotiation'.

Benjamin, C.M. and Powell, C.A. (eds) (1988) *Game Theory*. Special Issue of *Peace and Change*, 13: 65–94.

Bennett, P.G. (1980) 'Hypergames: developing a model of conflict', *Futures*, 12: 489–507.

Bennett, P.G. (1985) 'On linking approaches to decision-aiding: issues and prospects', *Journal of the Operational Research Society*, 36: 659–69.

Bennett, P.G. and Bussell, R.R. (1986) 'Conflict and strategic choice' in L. Wilkin and A. Sutton (eds), *The Management of Uncertainty*. Dordrecht: Martinus Nijhoff. pp. 275–82.

Bennett, P.G. and Cropper, S.A. (1986) 'Helping people choose: conflict and other perspectives', in V. Belton and R. O'Keefe (eds), *Recent Developments in O.R.*. Oxford: Pergamon/OR Society.

Bennett, P.G. and Cropper, S.A. (1987) 'Maps, games and things in between: modelling accounts of conflict', *European Journal of Operational Research*, 32: 33–46.

Bennett, P.G. and Cropper, S.A. (1989) 'Uncertainty and conflict: combining conflict analysis and strategic choice', *Journal of Behavioural Decision Making*.

Bennett, P.G. and Dando, M.R. (1979) 'Complex strategic analysis: a hypergame analysis of the fall of France', *Journal of the Operational Research Society*, 30: 23–32.

Bennett, P.G. and Dando, M.R. (1982) 'The arms race as a hypergame', *Futures*, 14: 293–306.

Bennett, P.G. and Huxham, C.S. (1982) 'Hypergames and what they do: a "soft OR" approach', *Journal of the Operational Research Society*, 33: 41–50.

Bennett, P.G., Dando, M.R. and Sharp, R.G. (1980) 'Using hypergames to model difficult social issues: an approach to the case of soccer hooliganism', *Journal of the Operational Research Society*, 31: 621–35.

Bennett, P.G., Huxham, C.S. and Dando, M.R. (1981) 'Shipping in crisis: a trial run for live application of the hypergame approach', *Omega*, 9: 579–94.

Bennett, P.G., Cropper, S.A. and Huxham, C.S. (1989) 'Modelling interactive decisions: the hypergame focus', in J. Rosenhead (ed.), *Rational Analysis for a Problematic World*. Chichester: Wiley.

Berne, E. (1964) *Games People Play*. New York: Grove Press.

Blumer, H. (1969) *Symbolic Interactionism*. Englewood Cliffs, NJ: Prentice-Hall.

Boothroyd, H. (1978) *Articulate Intervention*. London: Taylor and Francis.

Brams, S.J. and Wittman, D. (1981) 'Nonmyopic equilibria in 2X2 games', *Conflict Management and Peace Science*, 6: 39–62.

Braybrooke, D. (1974) *Traffic Congestion Goes Through the Issue Machine*. London: Routledge & Kegan Paul.

Braybooke, S. and Lindblom, C.E. (1965) *The Strategy of Decision*. New York: Free Press.

Brown, R. (1971) *Research and the Credibility of Estimates*. Homewood, IL: Richard D. Irwin.

Bryant, J.W. (1983) 'Hypermaps: a representation of perceptions in conflicts', *Omega*, 11: 575–86.

Bryant, J.W. (1989) *Problem Management*. London: Wiley.

Bryson, J. (1988) *Strategic Planning for Public and NonProfit Organizations*. San Francisco: Jossey-Bass.

Bryson, J. and Roering, W. (1987) 'Applying private sector strategic planning to the public sector', *Journal of the American Planning Association*, 53: 9–22.

Bunker, B.B. (1980) 'Developing a theory of practice for experiential learning', in C.P. Alderfer and C.L. Cooper (eds), *Advances in Experiential Social Processes*, Vol. 2, New York: Wiley. pp. 121–41.

Chamberlain, N.W. (1950) *Management in Motion*. Labor and Management Center, Yale University.

Checkland, P.B. (1981a) 'Towards a systems-based methodology for real world problem solving', in Open Systems Group (eds), *Systems Behaviour*, 3rd edn. London: Harper & Row.

Checkland, P.B. (1981b) *Systems Thinking, Systems Practice*. Chichester: Wiley.

Checkland, P. (1985) 'Achieving desirable and feasible change: an application of soft systems methodology', *Journal of the Operational Research Society*, 36(9): 821–32.

Ching, W. (1985) 'Non-trivial error in metagame analysis', paper delivered at the 1985 International Studies Association Conference, Washington, DC.

Ching, W., Powell, C.A. and Benjamin, C.H. (1987) 'Computer assisted interactive conflict analysis utilizing the CONAN 1.0/2.8 simulator', paper prepared for the 10th Annual Scientific Meeting of the International Society of Political Psychology, San Francisco (5–7 July) Panel on Formal and Psychological Aspects of Decision-Making.

Churchman, C.W. (1967) 'Wicked problems', *Management Science*, 4(4) Dec.: B 141, 142.

Churchman, C.W. (1971) *The Design of Inquiring Systems*. New York: Basic Books.

Cray, D., Mallory, G.R., Butler, R.J., Hickson, D.J. and Wilson, D.C. (1984) 'Sporadic, constricted and fluid processes: three types of strategic decision-making in organizations', Working Paper Series 84–07, Carleton University School of Business, Ottawa.

Cropper, S.A. (1984) *Ways of Working*. Brighton: OR Group, University of Sussex.

Dalkey, N. (1969) *The Delphi Method: an Experimental Study of Group Opinions*. Santa Monica, CA: Rand Corporation.

De Geus, A.P. (1988) 'Planning as learning', *Harvard Business Review*, March–April: 70–4.

Delbecq, A.L., Van de Ven, A.H. and Gustafson, D.H. (1975) *Group Techniques for Program Planning*. Glenview, Illinois: Scott Foresman.

De Neufville, R. and Stafford, J.H. (1971) *Systems Analysis for Engineers and Managers.* New York: McGraw-Hill.

Denning, B. (1984) 'Report on the Paris conference on making strategy work', *Society for Long Range Planning Newsletter*, Jan.

De Sanctis, G. and Dickson, G.W. (1987) 'GDSS software: a "shell" system in support of a program of research', *Proceedings of the Twentieth Annual Hawaii International Conference on System Sciences.* pp. 589–609.

De Sanctis, G. and Gallupe, R.B. (1985) 'Group decision support systems: a new frontier', *Database*, 16 (winter): 2–10.

De Sanctis, G. and Gallupe, R.B. (1986) 'A Foundation for the study of group decision support systems', *Management Science*, 33: 589–609.

Dyson, J.W. and Purkitt, H. (1986) *An Experimental Study of Cognitive Processes and Information in Political Problem Solving*, final report to the National Science Foundation, Florida State University and US Naval Academy.

Eden, C. (1985) 'Perish the thought', *Journal of the Operational Research Society*, 36(9): 809–20.

Eden, C. (1986a) 'Managing strategic ideas: the role of the computer', *ICL Technical Journal*, Nov: 173–83.

Eden, C. (1986b) 'Problem solving or problem finishing', in M.C. Jackson and P. Keys (eds), *New Directions in Management Science*. Aldershot, Hants: Gower.

Eden, C. (1989a) 'Strategic options development and analysis – SODA', in J. Rosenhead (ed.), *Rational Analysis for a Problematic World*. London: Wiley.

Eden, C. (1989b) 'OR as negotiation', in M. Jackson, P. Keys and S. Cropper, *Operational Research and the Social Sciences*, New York: Plenum.

Eden, C. and Ackermann, F. (1989) 'Strategic options development and analysis – using a computer to help with the management of strategic vision', in G.I. Doukidis, F. Land and G. Miller, *Knowledge-based Management Support Systems*. Chichester: Ellis Horwood.

Eden, C., Ackermann, F. and Timm, S. (1990) 'Strategic performance and the performance of strategy', presented to joint Strategic Planning Society and Operational Research Society meeting, 9 Feb, London.

Eden, C. and Huxham, C. (1988) 'Action-oriented strategic management', *Journal of the Operational Research Society*, 39: 889–99.

Eden, C. and Sims, D. (1979) 'On the nature of problems in consulting practice', *Omega*, 7: 119–27.

Eden, C., Jones, S. and Sims, D. (1979) *Thinking in Organizations*. London: Macmillan.

Eden, C., Jones, S. and Sims, D. (1983) *Messing about in Problems*. Oxford: Pergamon.

Etzioni, A. (1967) 'Mixed scanning: a "third" approach to decision making', *Public Administration Review*, 27: 385–92.

Foster, G. (1989) 'Mintzberg's strategic force', *Management Today*, April: 74–6.

Fraser, N.M. and Hipel, K.W. (1984) *Conflict Analysis: Models and Resolutions*. New York: North-Holland.

Fraser, N.M. and Hipel, K.W. (1986) 'Conflict analysis techniques in strategic choice', in L. Wilkin and A. Sutton (eds), *The Management of Uncertainty*. Dordrecht: Martinus Nijhoff. pp. 264–74.

Fraser, N.M., Benjamin, C.M. and Powell, C.A. (1985) 'Optimizing the decision process: structure and stability in complex conflict', *Proceedings of the Society for General Systems Research*.

Fraser, N.M., Powell, C.A. and Benjamin, C.M. (1987) 'New methods for applying game theory to international conflict', *International Studies Notes*, 13: 9–17.

French, S. (1986) *Decision Theory: An Introduction to the Mathematics of Rationality*. Chichester: Ellis Horwood.

Friend, J.K. and Hickling, A. (1987) *Planning under Pressure*. Oxford: Pergamon.

Friend, J.K. and Jessop, W.N. (1977) *Local Government and Strategic Choice*, 2nd edn. Oxford: Pergamon.

Friend, J.K., Power, J.M. and Yewlett, C.J.L. (1974) *Public Planning: the Inter-Corporate Dimension*. London: Tavistock.

Gallupe, R.B. (1985) 'The impact of task difficulty on the use of group decision system', Ph.D. dissertation, University of Minnesota.

Gergen, K.J. (1982) *Toward Transformation in Social Knowledge*. New York: Springer-Verlag.

Giesen, M.O. (1981) 'Toward an applied theory of complex decisions', D.Phil thesis, OR Group, University of Sussex.

Gouldner, A.W. (1959) 'Organizational analysis', in R. Merton, L. Broom and L.S. Cottrell, Jr. (eds), *Sociology Today: Problems and Prospects*. New York: Basic Books.

Hall, A.D. (1962) *A Methodology for Systems Engineering*. Princeton, NJ: Van Norstrand.

Harris, T.A. (1973) *I'm OK, You're OK*. London: Pan Books.

Hickling, A. (1985) *An (Inter) National Decision Centre? – Some Thoughts on What it Might Be Like*. An AH + A Occasional Paper. Long Itchington, Rugby: Allen Hickling and Associates.

Hickling, A. and de Jong, A. (1986) *STRAF Handreiking*. Allen Hickling and Arnold de Jong for the Ministry of Housing, Planning and Environment (Directorate for Waste Management and Clean Technology in the Directorate General for the Environment) in The Netherlands.

Hoffman, L.R. (1979) *The Group Problem-Solving Process*. New York: Praeger.

Howard, N. (1971) *Paradoxes of Rationality*. Cambridge, MA: MIT Press.

Howard, N. (1987) 'The present and future of metagame analysis', *European Journal of Operational Research*, 32: 1–25.

Howard, N. (1989) 'CONAN 3.0', Nigel Howard Systems, 10 Bloomfield Road, Birmingham B13 9BY, UK.

Howard, N. (1989) 'The manager as politician and general', in J. Rosenhead (ed.), *Rational Analysis for a Problematic World*. London: Wiley.

Howard, R. (1966) 'Decision analysis: applied decision theory', in D.B. Hertz and J. Melese (eds), *Proceedings of the Fourth International Conference on Operational Methods*. New York: Wiley-Interscience. pp. 59–71.

Huber, G.P. (1984) 'Issues in the design of group decision support systems', *MIS Quarterly*, 8(3): 195–204.

Huxham, C. (1987) *Description and Transferability of Decision-aiding Approaches*. Strathclyde: University of Strathclyde, Department of Management Science.

Huxham, C.S. and Bennett, P.G. (1985) 'Floating ideas: an experiment in enhancing hypergames with maps', *Omega*, 13: 331–47.

Huxham, C., Eden, C., Cropper, S. and Bryant, J. (1988) 'Facilitating facilitators: a story about group decision making', *OR Insight*, 1: 13–20.

Huxham, C.S., Cropper, S. and Bennett, P.G. (1989) 'Decision aiding demonstrated', *OR Insight*, 2: 15–21.

Jackson, M. (1986) 'New directions in management science', in M.C. Jackson and P. Keys (eds), *New Directions in Management Science*. Aldershot, Hants: Gower.

Jaques, E. (1976) *A General Theory of Bureaucracy*. London and Exeter, New Hampshire: Heinemann Educational Books.

Jaques, E. (1982) *Free Enterprise, Fair Employment*. London: Heinemann.

Jenkins, G.M. (1981) 'The systems approach', in *Systems Behaviour*, 3rd edn. London: Open Systems Group, Harper and Row.

Jones, G. (1989) 'Where angels fear to tread', *OR Insight*, 2: 8–10.

Jones, S. (1983) 'The policies of problems: intersubjectivity in defining powerful others', *Human Relations*, 37: 881–94.

Keen, P.G.W. (1980) 'Decision support systems: translating analytic techniques into useful tools', *Sloan Management Review*, 21(3): 33–44.

Kerr, N.L. (1982) 'Social transition schemes: model, method, and application', in H. Brandstatter, J. Davis and G. Stocker-Kreichgauer, *Group Decision Making*. New York: Academic Press. pp. 59–79.

Kotter, J. (1982) 'What effective general managers really do', *Harvard Business Review*, Nov.–Dec.: 156–67.

Lewin, A.Y. and Minton, J.W. (1986) 'Determining organizational effectiveness: another look, and an agenda for research', *Management Science*, 32: 514–38.

Lindblom, C.E. (1959) 'The science of muddling through', *Public Administration Review*, 19. pp. 79–88.

Lindblom, C.E. (1979) 'Still muddling, not yet through', *Public Administration Review*, 39: 154–73.

Lindley, D.V. (1986) *Making Decisions*. Chichester: Wiley.

Long, N. (1958) 'The local community as an ecology of games', *American Journal of Sociology*, 44: 251–61.

Low, K.B. and Bridger, H. (1979) 'Small group work in relation to management development', in B. Babington-Smith and B.A. Farrell (eds), *Learning in Small Groups: A Study of Five Methods*. Oxford: Pergamon.

Mangham, I.L. (1986) *Power and Performance in Organizations*. Oxford: Blackwell.

March, J.G. and Simon, H.A. (1958) *Organizations*. New York: Wiley.

Margerison, C.J. (1988) *Managerial Consulting Skills*. Aldershot, Hants: Gower.

Marschak, J. (1954) 'Towards an economic theory of organization and information', in R.M. Thrall, C.H. Coombs and R.L. Davis (eds), *Decision Processes*. New York: Wiley.

Mason, J. and Mitroff, I. (1981) *Challenging Strategic Planning Assumptions: Theory, Cases, and Techniques*. New York: Wiley.

Matthews, L.R. and Bennett, P.G. (1986) 'The art of course planning', *Journal of the Operational Research Society*, 37: 579–90.

Mayon-White, W.M. (ed.) (1986) *Planning and Managing Change*. London: Harper & Row.

Meadows, D.H. and Robinson, J.M. (1985) *The Electronic Oracle: Computer Models and Social Decisions*. Chichester: Wiley.

Milter, R.G. and Rohrbaugh, J. (1985) 'Microcomputers and strategic decision making', *Public Productivity Review*, 9: 175–89.

Mintzberg, H. (1975) 'The manager's role: folklore and fact', *Harvard Business Review*, July–Aug.: 49–61.

Mintzberg, H., Raisinghani, D. and Theoret, A. (1976) 'The structure of unstructured decision processes', *Administrative Science Quarterly*, 21: 246–75.

Morecroft, J.D.W. (1984) 'Strategy support models', *Strategic Management Journal*, 5: 215–29.

Mumford, E. (1983) *Designing Participatively*. Manchester, UK: Manchester Business School.

Murray, E.A., Jr., (1978) 'Strategic choice as a negotiated outcome', *Management Science*, 29: 960–72.

Nutt, P. (1984) 'Types of organizational decision processes', *Administrative Science Quarterly*, 29: 414–50.

O'Conner, R.J. (1984) 'Outline processors catch on', *Infoworld*, 2: 30–1.

Open University (1986) *Planning and Managing Change*. Milton Keynes: Open University Press.

Parsons, T. (1959) 'General theory in sociology', in R. Merton, L. Broom and L.S. Cottrell, Jr. (eds), *Sociology Today: Problems and Prospects*. New York: Basic Books.

Pettigrew, A.M. (1973) *The Politics of Organisational Decision-Making*. London: Tavistock.

Pfeiffer, J. (1981) *Power in Organizations*. Boston: Pitman.

Phillips, L.D. (1982) 'Requisite decision-modelling: a case study', *Journal of the Operational Research Society*, 33: 303–12.

Phillips, L.D. (1984) 'A theory of requisite decision models', *Acta Psychologica*, 56: 29–48.

Phillips, L.D. (1989a) 'People-centred group decision support', in G.I. Doukidis, F. Land and G. Miller, *Knowledge-based Management Support Systems*. Chichester: Ellis Horwood.

Phillips, L.D. (1989b) 'Decision analysis in the 1990s', in A. Shahani and R. Stainton, *Tutorial Papers in Operational Research 1989*. Birmingham: Operational Research Society.

Phillips, L.D. (in press) 'Requisite decision modelling for technological projects', in C. Viek and G. Cvetkovisch (eds), *Social Decision Methodology for Technological Projects*.

Popper, K.R. (1945) *The Open Society and Its Enemies*. London: Routledge & Sons.

Porter, M.E. (1985) *Competitive Advantage*. New York: Free Press.

Porter, M. (1987) 'The state of strategic planning', *The Economist*, 23 May: 21–8.

Powell, C.A., Dyson, J.W. and Purkitt, H. (1987) 'Opening the black box: cognitive processing and situational complexity in foreign policy decision-making', in J. Rosenau, C. Hermann and C. Kegley, *New Directions in Foreign Policy Analysis*. London: Allen & Unwin.

Preedy, D.K. and Biddlestone, R.G.A. (1985) 'OR and the boardroom of the 90s', *Journal of the Operational Research Society*, 36: 787–94.

Pritchard, W. (1986) 'What's new in organizational development', in Mayon-White (ed.), *Planning and Managing Change*. London: Harper & Row.

Quinn, J.B. (1980) *Strategies for Change: Logical Incrementalism*. Homewood, Illinois: Irwin.

Quinn, R.E. and Rohrbaugh, J. (1983) 'A spatial model of effectiveness criteria: towards a competing values approach to organizational analysis', *Management Science*, 29: 363–77.

Quinn, R.E., Rohrbaugh, J. and McGrath, R. (1985) 'Automated decision conferencing: how it works', *Personnel*, 62: 48–55.

Radford, K.J. (1975) *Managerial Decision Making*. Reston, VA: Reston Publishing.

Radford, K.J. (1977) *Complex Decision Problems*. Reston, VA: Reston Publishing.

Radford, K.J. (1978) 'Decision making in a turbulent environment', *Journal of the Operational Research Society*, 29: 677–82.

Radford, K.J. (1978a) *Information Systems for Strategic Decisions*. Reston, VA: Reston Publishing.

Radford, K.J. (1980) *Strategic Planning: an Analytical Approach*. Reston, VA: Reston Publishing.

Radford, K.J. (1981) *Modern Managerial Decision Making*. Reston, VA: Reston Publishing.

Radford, K.J. (1984) 'Simulating involvement in complex decision situations', *Omega*, 12: 125–30.

Radford, K.J. (1986) *Strategic and Tactical Decisions*. Toronto, Ontario: Holt McTavish.

Radford, K.J. (1988) 'Analysis of an international conflict: the US hostages in Iran', *Peace and Change*, 13: 132–44.

Radford, K.J. (1990) 'The strategic/tactical model for facilitating the resolution of complex decision situations (SANTA)', *Information and Decision Technologies*, special issue on conflict analysis.

Radford, K.J. and Fingerhut, B. (1980) 'Analysis of a complex decision situation – the Simpsons/Simpsons-Sears merger proposal', *Omega*, 8: 421–31.

Raiffa, H. (1968) *Decision Analysis: Introductory Lectures on Choices Under Uncertainty*. Reading, MA: Addison-Wesley.

Richmond, B. (1987) *The Strategic Management Forum: from Vision to Strategy to Operating Policies and Back Again*. Lime, New Hampshire: High Performance Systems.

Rickards, T. (1985) *Stimulating Innovation*. London: Frances Pinter.

Rickards, T. (1986) 'Making new things happen', in W. Mayon-White (ed.), *Planning and Managing Change*. London: Harper & Row.

Rosenhead, J. (1986) 'Custom and practice', *Journal of the Operational Research Society*, 37: 335–44.

Rosenhead, J. (1989) *Rational Analysis in a Problematic World*. London: Wiley.

Sarin, S. and Greif, I. (1985) 'Computer-based real-time conferencing systems', *Multimedia Communications*, Oct.: 33–45.

Schein, E.H. (1969) *Process Consultation: Its Role in Organizational Development.* Reading, MA: Addison-Wesley.

Schelling, T. (1960) *The Strategy of Conflict.* Cambridge, MA: Harvard University Press.

Schon, D.A. (1979) 'Generative metaphor: a perspective on problem-setting in social policy', in A. Ortony (ed.), *Metaphor and Thought.* Cambridge: Cambridge University Press.

Schon, D.A. (1983) *The Reflective Practitioner: How Professionals Think in Action.* London: Temple Smith.

Schum, D. (1987) *Evidence and Inference for the Intelligence Analyst.* Lanham, MD: University Press of America.

Simon, H.A. (1960) *The New Science of Management Decision.* New York: Harper & Row.

Simon, H.A. (1965) *Administrative Behavior*, Glencoe, IL: Free Press.

Simon, H.A. (1985) 'Human nature in politics: the dialogue of psychology with political science', *American Political Science Review*, 79: 293–304.

Sims, D. and Eden, C. (1984) 'Futures research – working with management teams', *Long Range Planning*, 17: 51–9.

Spender, J-C. (1989) *Industry Recipes.* Oxford: Basil Blackwell.

Spink, P. (1980) 'Organisational change and operational research – an initial basis for triangulation', summary of scientific meeting, 10 June 1980. Centre for Organisational and Operational Research, Tavistock Institute of Human Relations, London.

Stefik, M., Foster, G., Bobrow, D.G., Kahn, K., Lanning, S. and Suchman, L. (1987a) 'Beyond the chalkboard: computer support for collaboration and problem solving in meetings', *Communications of the ACM*, 30: 32–47.

Stefik, M., Foster, G., Bobrow, D.G., Kahn, K., Lanning, S. and Suchman, L. (1987b) 'Beyond the chalkboard: computer support for collaboration and problem solving in meetings', *Communications of the ACM*, 30(1): 32–47.

Steinzor, B. (1950) 'The spatial factor in face to face discussion groups', *Journal of Abnormal and Social Psychology*, 45: 552–5.

Strodtbeck, F.L. and Harmon, H.L. (1961) 'The social dimensions of a twelve man jury table', *Sociometry*, 24: 397–415.

Thompson, J.D. and Tuden, A. (1984) 'Strategies, structures, and processes of organizational decision', in D.A. Kolb, I.M. Rubin and J.M. McIntyre (eds), *Organizational Psychology*, 4th edn. Englewood Cliffs, NJ: Prentice-Hall.

Toulmin, S.E. (1958) *The Uses of Argument.* Cambridge: Cambridge University Press.

Vari, A. and Vescenyi, J. (1984) 'Selecting decision support methods in organisations', *Journal of Applied Systems Analysis*, 11: 23–36.

Vroom, H.H. and Jago, A.G. (1984) 'Decision making as a social process: normative and descriptive models of leader behavior', in D.A. Kolb, I.M. Rubin and J.M. McIntyre (eds), *Organizational Psychology*, 4th edn. Englewood Cliffs, NY: Prentice-Hall.

Warfield, J.N. (1974) *Societal Systems Planning, Policy and Complexity.* New York: Wiley.

Wilson, B. (1984) *Systems: Concepts, Methodologies and Applications.* London: Wiley.

Winograd, T. and Flores, F. (1986) *Understanding Computers and Cognition.* New Jersey: Ablex Publishing.

Winterfeldt, D. von and Edwards, W. (1986) *Decision Analysis and Behavioral Research.* Cambridge: Cambridge University Press.

Wooler, S. (1987) *Analysis of Decision Conferences: Interpretation of Decision Makers' Activities in Problem Identification, Problem Expressing and Problem Structuring.* Technical Report 87-2, London: Decision Analysis Unit, London School of Economics and Political Science.

Young, K. (1977) 'Values in the policy process', *Policy and Politics*, 5: 1–22.

Zagare, F.C. (1985) 'The pathology of unilateral deterrence', in M.D. Ward and U. Luterbacher (eds), *Dynamic Models of International Conflict.* Boulder, CO: Lynne Rienner.

Index